A BIBLICAL THEOLOGY OF EXILE

OVERTURES TO BIBLICAL THEOLOGY

A BIBLICAL THEOLOGY
OF EXILE

Daniel L. Smith-Christopher

FORTRESS PRESS
MINNEAPOLIS

Library of Congress Cataloging-in-Publication Data

Smith-Christopher, Daniel L.
    A biblical theology of exile / Daniel L. Smith-Christopher.
        p. cm. — (Overtures to biblical theology)
    Includes bibliographical references and index.
    ISBN 0-8006-3224-9 (pbk. : alk. paper)
        1. Jews—History—Babylonian captivity, 598–515 B.C.—Biblical teaching.
2. Bible. O.T.—Criticism, interpretation, etc. 3. Jewish diaspora—History.
I. Title. II. Series.

BS1199.B3 S55 2002
230'.041—dc21

                                      2002070014

Manufactured in the U.S.A.
06   05   04   03   02   1   2   3   4   5   6   7   8   9   10

CONTENTS

EDITOR'S FOREWORD

D ANIEL SMITH-CHRISTOPHER HAS WRITTEN A BOOK TO WHICH CLOSE attention must be paid. He has read biblical texts well and has made compelling connections to contemporary church practice that invite a rethinking and a repositioning of church in U.S. society. In his earlier book, *The Religion of the Landless: The Social Context of the Babylonian Exile* (Meyer Stone, 1989), Smith-Christopher had begun to explore the decisive reality of exile in the Old Testament and to probe the resources available in that crisis for theological interpretation and for missional church practice.

Since then, several things have happened that make the present book an important advance in his work and an imperative read. First, Old Testament scholarship has advanced to see that the Old Testament itself, in its canonical form, arises from and responds to the crisis of exile; as a consequence attention is no longer focused on the "early traditions" but is now on the *reuse* of what purport to be "early traditions" in the later post-exilic period. Second, the disestablishment of the Christian church in Western (and now specifically U.S.) society is now invariably visible to any discerning observer, so that the questions raised in the literature of the exile cannot be avoided in serious church interpretation of the Bible. Third, Smith-Christopher's own work has matured from his first offer of a published dissertation to a sophisticated proposal that will evoke the engaged attention of both scholars in the field and church practitioners.

Smith-Christopher has addressed the difficult question of the historical status of the exile, building upon his recent, more technical scholarship. There is now a powerful skeptical opinion among some scholars, especially in Britain, concerning the deep characterization of exile reported in the Old Testament text. That opinion suggests that exile is largely an ideological construct designed to advance the influence and legitimacy of one segment of emerging Judaism. Against that view, Smith-Christopher exhibits his powerful capacity as an historian and offers a persuasive critical case that the testimony of the text itself is to be taken seriously as an authentic witness to an historical crisis that becomes, in the text, a profound theological pivot point.

Smith-Christopher's judgments about historicity are matched by close attention to the biblical texts, something the skeptics sometimes do not do. I have found his study of Lamentations and Ezekiel especially illuminating, but his work traverses a great rage of textual traditions, including Leviticus, Proverbs, the narrative of Daniel, as well as the historical narratives of Ezra and Nehemiah. He takes full advantage of the fact that the Persian period was one of enormously generative literary, liturgical, and theological reflection. Thus the book is compellingly "sense making" of the texts and contexts of Judaism of the Persian period in a way that the older reductionist understandings of emerging Judaism were not able to accomplish.

Smith-Christopher's historical and textual work is readily informed by textual and social parallels both ancient and contemporary. Thus, for example, he evidences that Ezekiel's seemingly "bizarre" behavior and utterance can be better understood in terms of characteristic responses in the traumatic ways of displaced refugees and victims of disaster; this comparative study includes as well a propensity to view Israel's suffering fate in terms of its own guilt. From the thirteenth century he comments on the ways in which the Mongol emperors employed Chinese Confucian scholars in the affairs of state, a suggestive parallel to the ways in which Jews were recruited into the service of the Persian Empire. While the theological claims Israel makes in their text concerning this imperial engagement are peculiar to Israel, a recurring sociology of oppression indicates that the response of faith through social practice is readily understood through parallel situations.

Not to be missed in this powerful exposition is Smith-Christopher's own rootage in a "Peace Church" tradition and his own zeal about the continuing vocation of such communities in society. Thus, for example, his playful identification of Ezra as an "Amish elder" permits an interaction between ancient text and current practice in a way that illuminates both. The book voices no special pleading for "sectarian" perspective, but it does suggest that the "hard men" of Niebuhrian "critical realism" can have no monopoly on biblical faith and may not easily maintain their hegemonic interpretation in the future as they have been able to do in the past. Smith-Christopher nicely notices that in the Old Testament, the people of God are finally left in neither a romantic tribal nor an established monarchical setting, but in fact are left, as the Old Testament ends, in an imperial situation of displacement and vulnerability. It is this latter context that became a durable condition that was generative and healthy for the people of God, albeit not "convenient" in a political, economic sense.

Something like the fingerprints of James C. Scott are all over this manuscript. Scott has considered the ways in which "hidden transcripts" become "weapons of the weak," that is, means whereby the powerless sustain themselves by stealth in the face of great and unresponsive social power. The book concludes with an articulation of "diasporic practicality" that evidences the rich range of texts to be not merely "statements," but "strategies" that actually do something for the community, its purposes and its identity. Perhaps the ultimate act of resistance toward the state is to "laugh at the state" and so to create emotional and social space for an emancipated alternative. Such a "laugh" of resistance and alternative hovers around the texts to which this book attends. Smith-Christopher shows how to make a responsible interpretive move from old text to new context, a move that dares to work outside conventional "mainline" assumptions.

In rather dramatic ways this volume is an indication and embodiment of the great changes in Old Testament studies that have been the subject of the series. The transfer of attention to the later period that Smith-Christopher so ably occupies was not on the horizon when the series was initiated. The decisive employment of sociological theory and interpretive strategy was not yet fully legitimated, as historical criticism had then only barely begun to lose its commanding position in the field. It is obvious that from now on, moreover, all of our interpretive work in the United States will be done in the wake of the events of September 11, 2001, and that fact coheres appropriately with the current assumption about exilic displacement. Smith-Christopher explicates a practice of faith not even entertained a quarter century ago, but now required and happily shown to be credible.

There are many to thank as this Overtures series surpasses twenty-five years, among them George W. Coats, John R. Donahue, Norman C. Habel, Norman Hjelm, John Hollar, and Marshall D. Johnson. It was particularly John Hollar who brought energy to the series as he did to his many tasks of leadership among us. All of those named are of an older generation. Smith-Christopher, along with many recent authors in the series, is by contrast of a younger generation and brings to our common work awarenesses, passions, and sensibilities that reach well beyond what we had taken as "overtures" decades ago. The "overtures" reflected in the series have by now largely become accepted consensus positions in much of scholarship; such is the happy dynamism of our scholarship, a dynamism that this book serves well.

Walter Brueggemann
October 17, 2001

ABBREVIATIONS

AB	Anchor Bible
ABD	*Anchor Bible Dictionary*, ed. D. N. Freedman. 6 vols. 1992.
ABRL	Anchor Bible Reference Library
ANET	*Ancient Near Eastern Texts Relating to the Old Testament*, ed. J. B. Pritchard. 3d ed. 1969.
ARA	*Annual Review of Anthropology*
BA	*Biblical Archaeologist*
BAR	*Biblical Archaeology Review*
BETL	Bibliotheca ephemeridum theologicarum lovaniensium
Bib	*Biblica*
BibOr	Biblica et orientalia
BZAW	Beihefte zur Zeitschrift für die alttestamentliche Wissenschaft
CBQ	*Catholic Biblical Quarterly*
CBQMS	Catholic Biblical Quarterly Monograph Series
FOTL	Forms of the Old Testament Literature
FRLANT	Forschungen zur Religion und Literatur des Alten und Neuen Testaments
FS	*Festschrift*
HSM	Harvard Semitic Monographs
ICC	International Critical Commentary
ISBE	*International Standard Bible Encyclopedia*, ed. G. W. Bromiley et al. Rev. ed. 4 vols. 1979–89.
ITC	International Theological Commentary
JAOS	*Journal of the American Oriental Society*
JBL	*Journal of Biblical Literature*
JNES	*Journal of Near Eastern Studies*
JSOT	*Journal for the Study of the Old Testament*
JSOTSup	Journal for the Study of the Old Testament: Supplement Series
JSPSup	Journal for the Study of the Pseudepigrapha: Supplement Series

JTS	*Journal of Theological Studies*
KAT	Kommentar zum Alten Testament
NCBC	New Century Bible Commentary
NIB	*New Interpreter's Bible*, ed. Leander Keck et al. 12 vols. 1994–.
NICOT	New International Commentary on the Old Testament
OBO	Orbis biblicus et orientalis
OBT	Overtures to Biblical Theology
OLA	Orientalia lovaniensia analecta
OTL	Old Testament Library
PTSD	Post-Traumatic Stress Disorder
SBL	Society of Biblical Literature
SBLDS	SBL Dissertation Series
SBLMS	SBL Monograph Series
SBLSymS	SBL Symposium Series
SBT	Studies in Biblical Theology
Transeu	*Transeuphretène*
VT	*Vetus Testamentum*
VTSup	Supplements to Vetus Testamentum
WBC	Word Biblical Commentary

PREFACE

THEMES OF "EXILE" HAVE BEEN OF INTEREST TO ME SINCE I COMPLETED my dissertation on the Babylonian exile under the patient guidance of Professors John Barton and Bryan Wilson at Oxford University. I was particularly grateful, therefore, to Walter Brueggemann when he suggested in 1999 that I consider writing a new work on the biblical exile with a more directly theological orientation, as a volume in the Overtures to Biblical Theology series. I was honored to be asked to join this series, and I am deeply humbled by the company I now keep.

It is important to note that some of the material I have used in this work has appeared in the context of other writings. While none of the chapters reproduces exactly any of my previous work, chapter two is a greatly revised and expanded version of "Reassessing the Historical and Sociological Impact of the Babylonian Exile (597/587–539 BCE)," in *Exile: Old Testament, Jewish and Christian Conceptions*, edited by James M. Scott (Leiden: Brill, 1997) 7–36. Similarly, elements of chapter three appeared in a different form as "Ezekiel on Fanon's Couch: A Postcolonialist Dialogue with David Halperin's *Seeking Ezekiel*," in *Peace and Justice Shall Embrace*, ed. Ted Grimsrud and Loren Johns (Telford: Pandora, 1999) 108–44, a *Festschrift* for Millard Lind. Finally, elements of chapter six were drawn from chapter six, pages 139 to 152, in my first work on the exile, *The Religion of the Landless*, albeit in a new context.

I would like to thank Walter Brueggemann for his kind invitation, my editors at Fortress Press, K. C. Hanson and Beth Wright, and copyeditor Gary Lee for their attention to this work despite my delays in making reasonable deadlines. I am grateful to my friend Professor William Schniedewind at UCLA who very kindly does not ever mention how much cleverer he is than I and what a better job he could have done with many of these subjects. He kindly read through the manuscript and suggested places where I would be particularly liable to reasoned criticism. That weaknesses in my arguments remain is due to my stubbornness and not to his having missed them.

I am especially mindful of the significance of thinking about biblical theology in the Peace Church tradition as I prepare to take up my new teaching assignment at Bluffton College, Ohio, beginning in the fall of 2003. I offer this work as a gift to my Mennonite teachers and friends, who have given me more than I could ever repay and who will all recognize their influence on my thinking. I ask their patience with my oversights.

Finishing a book is always a strain on a young family, and I appreciate my wife and children putting up with the worries and stresses of trying to finish a manuscript when I should have spent more time at Little League practice and Brownie meetings. My colleagues who have helped me with this project will all understand, therefore, when I dedicate this work to my wife, Zsa Zsa, my son, Jordan, and my daughter, Sydney.

1.

BIBLICAL THEOLOGY:
On Matters of Methodology

I WAS RECENTLY ASKED TO PARTICIPATE IN A SEMINAR SPONSORED BY THE Jewish Studies Department at UCLA on "The Ten Commandments." The organizers had asked two speakers, in this case one Christian and one Jewish, to deal with each of the commandments, and I was asked to speak on the commandment against "False Witness" (usually considered the ninth commandment). I began my contribution with the traditional approach, citing the differences between the form of the commandment in Exodus and the form in Deuteronomy, and whether the difference between the versions was really significant. But I knew that the organizers had hoped that I would not simply offer a bit of historical-critical analysis. The idea was to think about what these commandments say to "us" in the modern world. The idea, in short, was to do what at least some scholars want to call "biblical theology."

As I thought about "bearing false witness," it began to occur to me that I was being asked to participate in an enterprise—namely, biblical theology—that since the mid-1990s has often been declared difficult or impossible, and an enterprise that has been somewhat officially declared "in crisis" since 1970. In other words, does the study of the Bible have implications for modern people seeking wisdom for modern Christian faith and practice?

The reasons for pessimism on this question are legion and continue to change. I write this theology of exile in the wake of major shifts in biblical studies in the last twenty years, especially surrounding the term *postmodernism*. What has this to do with writing biblical theology, much less offering a paper on the ninth commandment? Quite simply, the postmodernist emphasis on context and the contingency of all knowledge renders the ninth commandment somewhat problematic: the question is whether we can ever "bear" a *true* witness! Or at the very least a witness that is "objective" and represents "only the facts." As I argue in the work that follows, I believe it is possible to do a biblical theology in this modern era. But I try to be mindful of the many ways that doing biblical theology has become difficult. What I write in the chapters that follow is not intentionally a "false witness." But it is certainly written from both a theological and sociological context, which I hope to clarify in this opening chapter.

Biblical theology unavoidably involves a tension between faith and history. This is hardly news. In their helpful text, *The Flowering of Biblical Theology*, the editors spend a great deal of time discussing the interesting exchange between Walther Eichrodt and Otto Eissfeldt on the matter of biblical analysis and theology in earlier twentieth-century German theological debate.[1] In responding to Eissfeldt's insistence that the historical and theological must be kept separate, Eichrodt sounded strangely modern (in anticipating a good deal of postmodernist controversy) when he insisted that "the discussion about historical scholarship in general teaches us that there just is no history of Israelite religion independent of all subjective presuppositions."[2]

What is new, however, is that *both* faith *and* history are now seen as endeavors that involve an inexact matter of perspective and bias—an accusation that a previous generation of biblical scholars directed almost exclusively to enterprises that involved explicating faith-related issues. Those scholars writing under the influence of some postmodernist tendencies now question (in postmodernist lingo, they "interrogate") history writing itself as a discipline that is too comfortable with what it aspires to achieve (e.g., just the "facts"). It has been my impression that many contributors to the field of biblical theology often thought of themselves as engaging, at least partly, in the discipline of historiography, but that a certain discomfort with "contemporary applications" of biblical analysis led to many scholars treating biblical theology itself as an exclusively "historical" enterprise. In this narrower definition, what biblical theologians are supposed to do is draw conclusions about what the ancient Israelite writers of the Bible experienced, what they "believed," and how they lived, particularly in relation to their religious ideas or practices. While some of these biblical theologians may have had an unstated assumption that their

---

1. Otto Eissfeldt, "The History of Israelite-Jewish Religion and Old Testament Theology," in *The Flowering of Biblical Theology*, ed. B. Ollenburger et al. (Winona Lake, Ind.: Eisenbrauns, 1992) 20–29; followed by Walther Eichrodt's reply, "Does Old Testament Theology Still Have Independent Significance within Old Testament Scholarship?" in *Flowering*, 30–39.

2. Eichrodt, "Does Old Testament Theology," 36.

analysis had modern religious implications, their books in biblical theology usually stopped short of developing these modern interests. Many of the previous contributions to the Overtures to Biblical Theology series exemplify this approach—to describe what ancient Israelites "thought," and thus the best way to understand what they wrote. Theology, in this case, meant *their* theology and not directly our own.

One could go further, however, and note that many recent critics of biblical theology suspect that any combination of the terms *Bible* and *theology* inevitably involves the attempt to draw out a coherence of religious ideas that requires a move beyond the evidence of the textual and archaeological data, and thus "filling in" the gaps with contemporary religious notions.[3] Note, for example, that Mark Brett clearly feels a need to spend a good part of the entire final chapter of his recent (and fascinating) study of Genesis by devoting that section to defending himself against charges of bias, ulterior motives, and unconscious or even conscious theological agendas.[4] This, despite the fact that postmodernist theorists in the last fifteen to twenty years have raised serious objections to anyone who exhibits too much confidence about writing "history" that is not, at the same time, a measure of contemporary concerns, assumptions, and agendas. This is because all knowledge is "contingent" upon one's own context, identity, and setting, and a claim to writing an "objective history" is a myth—occasionally even a dangerous myth.

Such arguments, however much I tend to sympathize with them, are a two-edged sword. While one can argue that postmodernist insights can arm a hostile critic finally to dismiss "biblical theology" with an interest in contemporary practice as inevitably dubious when compared to historical analysis of artifactual and textual evidence, the defenders of this kind of biblical theology can just as easily return fire by noting that at least the ecclesiologically interested biblical theologians are more forthcoming about their bias and interests, and thus do not pretend to be writing a chimerical "scientifically objective" historiography.[5] The reasoning can become hopelessly circular as the combatants argue over whose arguments are more subjective (your unconscious assumptions vs. my methodologically reasoned presuppositions . . . and so it goes).

There is not likely to be a resolution of these metamethodological issues any time soon, and a number of possible procedures suggest

3. See James Barr, *History and Ideology in the Old Testament: Biblical Studies at the End of a Millennium* (Oxford: Oxford Univ. Press, 2000) 123–24; and his larger work, *The Concept of Biblical Theology: An Old Testament Perspective* (Minneapolis: Fortress Press, 1999).

4. Mark Brett, *Genesis: Procreation and the Politics of Identity* (London: Routledge, 2000) 137–46.

5. Barr, *History and Ideology,* 163–78.

themselves in the meantime. One can reject the annoyingly relativist insistence of postmodernist arguments about the ultimate contingency of all knowledge, and most especially "historical" knowledge that is based, after all, on interpretations of either text or artifact, and proceed (pretend?) to write ostensibly objective historical accounts of ancient Israel.[6] Of course, it seems hardly coincidental that the quality of such recent "critical" or "scientific" writings is often thought to be measured by how fragmented, hesitant, and incomplete the resulting published work appears, as well as the requirement that the writer frequently rehearse standardized phrases like "we simply cannot say more," "beyond this would be mere conjecture," and the like.

Similarly, one can avoid grand theories like the plague and focus on detailed analyses of particular themes and texts, carefully avoiding any observations or suggestions that would reveal the slightest hint of an ulterior motive, ideological commitment, or, even more serious, a religious inclination that may stand behind one's interest in such themes or texts. By no means dare to penetrate "complexity" by suggesting a theology that might attempt to connect the dots.

I am certainly not innovative, however, in suggesting that there may be other alternatives. My somewhat cynical tone with regard to the previously mentioned strategies, then, would only be an appropriate tone to take with authoritarian claims of *exclusive* legitimacy on the part of hypercritical approaches to historiography using biblical, archaeological, and epigraphical materials. But a further option is to accept much of the force of postmodernist criticism and thus be cautious of any attempt to avoid contingency, and thus proceed with one's study using a variety of tools common to critical analysis, but also try to be as forthright as possible with regard to the motivations, contexts, and interests that are inevitably part of one's attempt to write a biblical theology that is also intended to be of interest to Christians seeking to know how the Bible might guide their modern lives of faith and practice. It is probably not a surprise, given my opening comments, that I choose to write a biblical theology that will not only use many of the critically accepted tools of historical and textual analysis of the Bible, but also be forthright about the contemporary concerns, assumptions, and interests that inform my selection of texts and tools.

Part of the task of paying critical attention to my assumptions, as I have tried to practice in the past (similar to what others have referred to

6. Barr's recent ironic complaint that biblical scholars "used to speak" about proposals and insights "commonly called 'results'" seems to fall into such a category. See Barr, *History and Ideology,* 24.

as "social scientific criticism," "sociological exegesis," etc.), is my attempt to "teach my assumptions" and thus to be more aware of the variety of human behavioral responses to events that are similar (however generally so) to the events related in the selected biblical texts. Therefore, in my dissertation, which resulted in *Religion of the Landless* (1989), I read a good deal of the available literature about displaced populations (at least that which was available in the mid-1980s).[7] In my work on the mixed-marriage issues of Ezra-Nehemiah, I also read a considerable amount of material on contemporary analysis of mixed marriage across a number of cultural settings. Finally, in my work on the book of Daniel, I found direct interaction with Christians from minority cultural backgrounds (Aboriginal Australian, First Nation Canadian, and Native American), as well as surveying older postcolonialist literature including the classics of Fanon and Memmi, to be strikingly suggestive for my analysis of that book.[8]

Here, then, I continue to work with this somewhat inexact method of reading contemporary analysis while I study historical texts. Reading anthropological and sociological literature, at the very least, forces us to question our assumptions about group behavior in ancient Israelite settings: Do people *really* behave as I have suggested? Can I give examples or comparisons?[9]

In the work that follows, I have tried to follow a fairly obvious outline. In this first chapter, I survey some of the theoretical issues on the theological study of "exile" and clarify the presumptions that have gone into this work. In the second chapter, I provide a summary of the historical events of the Babylonian exile (at least as much as we can say, given the

---

7. It is significant to report that this area of inquiry, now appropriately labeled a "field of study," has exploded since then with entire journals dedicated to "Forced Migration" and "Refugee Studies"—a sad commentary on the fact that the human data for these studies has multiplied exponentially worldwide. While I worked on my dissertation at Oxford, the program in Refugee Studies was only just beginning, and I was not aware of it at the time. Now Oxford has become one of the most important centers for the study of refugees, and the source of the important journal *Refugee Studies*.

8. I have always reacted the same way to the inevitable and frequent response to this method, namely: "You are only trying to read into the Bible your modern notions." But as my critics are inevitably fellow moderns, it seems to me that their ideas are equally and inevitably modern notions—but without the benefit of intentionally enriching one's "modern" judgment with a variety of possible theories based on reading many sociological and anthropological cases. Until my critics can establish that their "nonsociological" theories of interpretation are based on direct experience of the sixth century, perhaps through some time machine, I remain largely unmoved by this particular argument.

9. See Daniel Smith-Christopher, "Hebrew Satyagraha: The Politics of Biblical Fasting in the Post-Exilic Period (Sixth to Second Century B.C.E.)," *Food and Foodways: An Interdisciplinary Journal* 5 (1993) 269–92.

lack of evidence), and the subsequent Persian conquests. Rather than attempting to be comprehensive about the events of the exile and Persian rule, however, I have focused on those elements of the exilic experience and subsequent Persian period that I consider particularly relevant to the study of biblical texts related to the exile. In the remaining chapters, then, I select a number of themes and related texts that collectively serve to fill out our understanding of ancient Israelite responses to the exile and Persian rule, with the expressed goal of arguing that many of these ancient responses may be suggestive for modern Christians.

In other words, the central assumption of this work, and the ideas that I hope will contribute the most to further work on this period and these texts, is that the specific Babylonian exile must be appreciated as both a historical human disaster *and* a disaster that gave rise to a variety of social and religious responses with significant social and religious consequences. Perhaps more hazardous, however, is my further contention that these varied social and religious responses can be arranged into a coherent picture of a social/theological response to the transhistorical conditions of diaspora, and that this has great contemporary theological significance for modern Christian movements.

In this work I am not exclusively focused on the exilic events of the ancient Judeans. I argue that ancient Israelite responses to exile and diaspora, as reflected in the biblical texts, can provide the building blocks for rethinking the role of the Hebrew Bible in informing the modern Christian theological enterprise. Stated in another way, I hope to establish that attention to the realities of the exilic crisis can lead to important conclusions about the impressive creativity and reformulations of tradition that can be seen in biblical texts. As this is a somewhat grand claim, I would like to dwell on this theological task at more length in this introduction.

The Emergence of Diasporic Theology

My religious convictions with regard to this study are a significant part of my interest in the subject. As I have intimated, my interest in the exile stems from my interest in how the Bible can inform the contemporary realities of Christian faith and practice. To be specific, I agree with recent suggestions, especially by John Howard Yoder, Walter Brueggemann, and Stanley Hauerwas, that an "exilic theology" promises to be the most provocative, creative, and helpful set of ideas that modern Christians can derive from the ancient Hebrews' religious reflections on their experiences. If my interests in how the Bible may inform contemporary Christian faith and practice occasionally suggest to readers that I am guilty of looking for a theological coherence in biblical texts, including texts where the evidence is thought to be scant, I have but one response: mea culpa. But I would go further, mainly because I no longer have much interest in, or patience with, attempting to hide the theological agenda that partially motivates my interest in the subject of the Babylonian exile and the Hebrew textual and religious responses.

John Howard Yoder, before his untimely death in 1997, was in the process of drawing together a lifetime's work of articulating a critical Christian theological stance that involved building on the resources of his own Anabaptist theological heritage, a project inaugurated most widely into the public domain by his 1972 work, *The Politics of Jesus*.[10] The particular themes that seemed to Yoder to be the most productive for this project late in his career were the themes of exile and diaspora existence. Perhaps most important for my present purpose is his essay with the revealing title, "Prologue and Prototype: Galuth as Calling," which was itself a major advance on his much older programmatic essay, "Exodus and Exile."[11] Yoder's unfinished project, the articulation of an "exilic theology," was at least partially inspired by his association with the late Professor Rabbi Steven Schwarzschild, whose influence can occasionally be noted in, for example, Yoder's references to the European Jewish playwright Stephen Zweig (a Schwarzschild family friend, after whom Schwarzschild himself was named). An outspoken pacifist, socialist, and non-Zionist, and an enthusiastic advocate of Yiddishkeit,[12] Schwarzschild's complex philosophical writings[13] only occasionally revealed his diasporic interests, but his personal influence on both Yoder and myself can be measured by our mutual appreciation of the fact that any Christian theology of exile

10. John Howard Yoder, *The Politics of Jesus*, 2d ed. (Grand Rapids: Eerdmans, 1994). See also idem, *The Royal Priesthood: Essays Ecclesiological and Ecumenical*, ed. M. G. Cartwright (Grand Rapids: Eerdmans, 1994); idem, *The Priestly Kingdom: Social Ethics as Gospel* (Notre Dame: Univ. of Notre Dame Press, 1984); idem, *For the Nations: Essays Evangelical and Public* (Grand Rapids: Eerdmans, 1997).

11. John Howard Yoder, "Exodus and Exile: Two Faces of Liberation," *Crosscurrents* (fall 1973) 297–309.

12. Generally to be understood as an appreciation of the artistic, religious, and particularly political debates that were expressed among Eastern European Jews both in Europe and among the immigrant populations of the United States, and conducted largely in the Yiddish language. It is a world known only in small bits and pieces to non-Jewish scholars, particularly in such romanticized forms as the stories of Sholem Aleichem and Isaac Bashivas Singer. But the social and political side of Yiddishkeit was more important to Schwarzschild, especially in its variety of social agendas for diaspora existence, where Zionism was only one of many theoretical formulations.

13. Steven Schwarzschild, *The Pursuit of the Ideal: Jewish Writings of Steven Schwarzschild*, ed. Menachem Kellner (Albany: State Univ. of New York Press, 1990).

will necessarily begin by reviewing nineteenth- and early-twentieth-century internal debates in European Jewish contexts, particularly around the various social and political models that were being advocated in addition to (and often against) the early developments of romantic European nationalism generally, and specifically its influence on the origins of Zionism. Whatever relevance such debates may or may not have in contemporary Jewish debates (which is, of course, not for me to determine),[14] it is quite clear that the various models of territorialism, cultural autonomism, or communal separatism (in addition to Zionism) that were debated in pre–World War II European Jewish contexts—particularly in Germany and Eastern Europe—have an uncanny relevance for any Christian attempt to articulate a normative diasporic Christian theology. To put it simply: listening to the fascinating Jewish debates on religion and nationalism ought to cause Christians to reopen our own debates on faith and nationalism that would force us back to the fourth century when Christianity and nationalism fused—before we arrive back in the present in order to understand twentieth-century Christian theologies, however biblical they claimed to be.[15] Diasporic theology challenges the virtual capitulation to the normative status of nationalism as the only viable context for Christian theology and Christian social existence.

This work is an intentional contribution to that larger project, which is also clearly not only on the agenda of Walter Brueggemann and Stanley

14. A recent comparative work that looked at the lives of Chaim Zhitlowski, Simon Dubnow, and Ahad Ha-Am concluded the section on Zhitlowski (the least Zionist of the three) by stating that his continued significance is quite limited. See David H. Weinberg, *Between Tradition and Modernity* (New York: Holmes and Meier, 1996). Whatever conclusions may be reached in internal Jewish debates on the matter, the significance of Dubnow and Zhitlowski, specifically, for renewed Christian reflection has not even begun to be appreciated. A critical translation of some of Zhitlowski's essays, edited for a Christian readership, would be a worthy project, and may well need to include other Yiddish-writing theorists whose thought would further such a dialogue about their political ideas.

15. I cannot agree more with J. Denny Weaver in regard to significant historical foundational formulations of Christian theology: "these several formulations (Nicaea, Chalcedon, Anselm's) are specific to the church for which Emperor Constantine is a symbol; namely, the church that came to identify its course and purpose with that of the existing social order. That specificity is visible in the Greek philosophical categories and fourth-century world picture of the christological formulas, as well as in the Germanic feudal imagery of Anselm's atonement image, which depicts God as the Lord whose honor is offended. Most importantly, the formulations of Christology and atonement reflect the imperial church, for which the story of Jesus does not supply the particularity of Christian ethics" (*Anabaptist Theology in the Face of Postmodernity: A Proposal for the Third Millennium* [Telford, Pa.: Pandora, 2000] 126).

Hauerwas in the Christian context (see below), but also Daniel and Jonathan Boyarin in the Jewish context. In a very important essay Boyarin and Boyarin "want to propose a privileging of Diaspora, a dissociation of ethnicities and political hegemonies as the only social structure that even begins to make possible a maintenance of cultural identity in a world grown thoroughly and inextricably interdependent."[16] Only a few sentences later, Boyarin and Boyarin offer a prophetic warning that is surely much more relevant to the 1650-year-long Christian nationalist project ("Constantinianism," to use Yoder's term) than it is to the more recent Jewish experiment with nationalism:

> Diaspora can teach us that it is possible for a people to maintain its distinctive culture, its difference, without controlling land, a fortiori without controlling other people or developing a need to dispossess them of their lands. . . . The renunciation of sovereignty (justified by discourses of autochthony, indigenousness, and territorial self-determination) combined with a fierce tenacity in holding onto cultural identity, might well have something to offer to a world in which these two forces, together, kill thousands daily.[17]

I would point out the striking parallel between Yoder's use of "Constantinianism" to question Christian nationalist discourse and the Boyarins' (as Schwarzschild's earlier) open challenges within Jewish debates on Zionism and diaspora existence. Indeed, Yoder was himself aware of these parallels in some segments of Christian and Jewish thought, as is clear in the essay "Galuth as Calling," a prologue to his unfortunately undeveloped Christian theology of exile.

Furthermore, the rise of "post-Zionist" criticism has shed further light on Jewish versions of using the theme of exile for contemporary ideological ends. Both Laurence Silberstein and Yael Zerubavel note the central ideological importance of "exile" as a device for speaking of Jewish history.[18] Defined as the period not only immediately following the ancient Israelite monarchy, the "exile" *(galut)* is typically "read" as the entire period of nonnational Jewish existence—quite literally from 586 BCE until 1948 CE, the founding of the state of Israel. The modern state of Israel is

16. Daniel Boyarin and Jonathan Boyarin, "Diaspora: Generation and the Ground of Jewish Identity," *Critical Inquiry* 19 (1993) 723.

17. Ibid.

18. Laurence J. Silberstein, *The Postzionism Debates: Knowledge and Power in Israelite Culture* (New York: Routledge, 1999); Yael Zerubavel, *Recovered Roots: Collective Memory and the Making of Israeli National Tradition* (Chicago: Univ. of Chicago Press, 1995).

"read" in Zionist polemics as a revival, therefore, of *ancient* nationalist Judaism.

> Zionists, like all nationalists, presume a natural, isomorphic relationship between the nation, its culture, and the space it represents as its homeland. Only in the homeland do conditions exist that are necessary for the growth and flourishing of the nation and its culture. Conversely, spaces outside the homeland, referred to as "exile," are represented as inimical to such growth and dangerous to the health of the nation. Thus, Zionist discourse positions its subjects to accept as true the claim that the "return" of the nation to its homeland is essential to the survival of the nation and the renewal of its culture.[19]

Furthermore, and more to the point at hand:

> The Jew, a product of exile, is thus represented as inauthentic, obsolete, and unproductive. The "new Hebrew" on the other hand, a product and producer of the renewed national life in the homeland, is represented as authentic, modern, and productive.[20]

So, Silberstein concludes, the "binaries" of homeland/exile and exile/redemption are "foundational" to the Zionist historical narrative. Also central to Zionist discourse, therefore, was the importance of such phrases as "negation of the exile" *(shelilat hagalut)* as a central goal for Zionist nationalism.[21]

Zerubavel, however, is even stronger in her analysis of Zionist discourse:

> In spite of . . . diversity, followers of Zionism shared some fundamental views about the Jewish past and the present: they regarded Jewish life in exile as inherently regressive and repressive, and believed in the need to promote some form of revival of Jewish national life *as experienced in Antiquity*. . . .
>   During the centuries of exile, religion functioned as the adhesive bond for the dispersed Jewish communities. But this exilic way of life was a poor substitute for the earlier national phase, thus conveying a process of spiritual degeneration as well as political regression.[22]

19. Silberstein, *Postzionism*, 21.
20. Ibid., 23.
21. Ibid., 29.
22. Zerubavel, *Recovered Roots*, 14 (emphasis mine), 18.

In his recent introduction to a series of essays on Yiddish politics, Emanuel Goldsmith points out that Yiddishkeit failed to develop a viable and sustaining diaspora culture.[23] Historically, this may be a somewhat unfair judgment given the realities of twentieth-century Europe as well as Zionism itself, but there is profound sense in which I agree that Christianity too must find a way to articulate a viable trans- (or non!) national, or diasporic, faith.

Are there potential directions for the development of such an alternative using some resources in Christian history? I see many overlooked areas of potential investigation of Christian "diaspora existence" in nonnational contexts that were, and are, not necessarily to be lamented as periods of weakness, persecution, or cultural depravity. In the context of contemporary nationalist conflicts, of course, it is tantamount to heresy to suggest that some Christian communities actually thrived when they were not themselves in charge. But we rarely reckon with the implication, therefore, that such subcultures are, despite not being dominant, nonetheless still vibrant, living, and creative communities of faith.

In her study of Asia Minor refugees resettling in Greece, for example, Renee Hirschon's now classic ethnography of an immigrant community reveals fascinating memories of a positive Greek Christian ethnic minority existence.[24] The vitality and creativity of the Armenian diaspora communities are also sources of great interest.[25] Certain religious minorities in the West offer examples as well. Anabaptism, in its modern Mennonite, Amish, and Hutterite manifestations, as well as Tolstoyan and related Russian nonconformism (Dukhoborism and Molokanism), are among the richest veins to mine along these lines.[26] The experience of many other Christian minorities, especially outside the West, has yet to be explored for the theological resources available from their often courageous and creative coexistence with, and within, majority cultures.

---

23. Emanuel Goldsmith, "Yiddishism and Judaism," in *The Politics of Yiddish*, ed. Dov-Ber Kerler (Walnut Creek, Calif.: Altamira, 1998) 15.

24. Renée Hirschon, *Heirs of the Greek Catastrophe: The Social Life of Asia Minor Refugees in Piraeus* (New York: Berghahn, 1989).

25. I am impressed, for example, with the work of Ronald Grigor Suny, particularly *Looking Toward Ararat: Armenia in Modern History* (1993); and his essay, "Religion, Ethnicity, and Nationalism: Armenians, Turks, and the End of the Ottoman Empire," in *In God's Name: Genocide and Religion in the Twentieth Century*, ed. Omer Bartov and Phyllis Mack (New York: Berghahn, 2001) 23–61.

26. Modern Quakerism, sadly, is only a minor source in this regard, given the state of its co-opted theological identities in either fundamentalist or New Age expressions.

A few important modern theologians have moved in this direction as well. As we have noted, compatible insights about a potential diaspora theology inform recent Christian theological writings.[27] Further, however, I will defend a view of diasporic theological identity that is not based on a concept of "temporary loss of stature" and thus a ruse for triumphalist calls for "restoration." Much analysis of the Bible in the context of Christian faith traditions in the West has been informed, especially earlier in the twentieth century, by significant ideological presumptions about the Babylonian exile as a time of serious decline, the ossification of religious, "priestly" practices of purity, and the general loss of prophetic energy that was only restored by the rise of Christianity. From the time of Augustine, a major line of Christian tradition has assumed that the health of Christianity and the vitality of its intellectual traditions required what Yoder simply summarized as "being in charge." Yoder, again, has classically referred to this as "Constantinianism":

> After Constantine not only is the ruler the bearer of history; the nonsovereign ethical agent has changed as well. The "Christian" used to be a minority figure, with numerous resources not generally available to all people: personal commitment, regeneration, the guidance of the Holy Spirit, the consolation and encouragement of the brotherhood, training in a discipleship life-style. But now that Christianity is dominant, the bearer of history is Everyman—baptized but not necessarily thereby possessed of the resources of faith. Ethical discourse must now meet two more tests. . . . (1) Can you ask such behavior of everyone? . . . (2) What would happen if everyone did it?[28]

So central is this "being in charge," or "Constantinianism" (to use both of Yoder's phrases, which he used virtually interchangeably), to the commonsense notions of being a modern Christian, as well as writing "relevant" Christian theology (rhetoric most recognizably associated with the twentieth-century works of Reinhold and H. Richard Niebuhr and John Bennett in the American context), that many Western Christians are initially startled to learn that there is a term for such a notion, and further, that there exists the possibility of other ways of conceiving of Christian

---

27. Just to name two works along these lines: Walter Brueggemann, *Cadences of Home: Preaching among Exiles* (Louisville: Westminster John Knox, 1997); Stanley Hauerwas and William Willimon, *Resident Aliens* (Nashville: Abingdon, 1989).

28. John Howard Yoder, "The Constantinian Sources of Western Social Ethics," in *Priestly Kingdom*, 139–40.

faith and practice, and therefore other presuppositions that can inform the conception of theology, ecclesiology, and the analysis of biblical texts. What is interesting, of course, is how this negative appraisal of exile, defined generally as nonstate existence, parallels many Christian theologians' definitions of what constitutes an effective "Christian community." To affirm "exile" from national power, or a chosen "exile" from national existence, is to invite accusations of "sectarian withdrawal from the world" in a (now rather old and tired) Niebuhrian sense. "Sectarian withdrawal," then, plays a similar role in Christian ethical discourse at the end of the twentieth century as "the status of exile" played in early Zionist discourse. In both cases, "responsibility" and "effectiveness" ("entering into history" in Zionist terms) are measured in terms of nationalist or political power. As Yoder suggests, however, another perspective may be not only possible but essential: "If, as the New Testament indicates, extending certain phases of the Old, God calls his people to prophetically critical relationship to the structures of power and oppression, then the alliance between Rome-as-Empire and Church-as-Hierarchy, which the fourth and fifth centuries gradually consolidated, is not merely a possible tactical error but a structured denial of the gospel."[29]

Brueggemann has also determined that exile is a functional category from which to challenge the supposed political theologies of previous Christian ethical discourse: "Reflective Christians find themselves increasingly at odds with dominant values of consumer capitalism and its supportive military patriotism; there is no easy or obvious way to hold together core faith claims and the social realities around us. . . . If it be insisted that church members are still in places of social power and influence, I suggest that such Christians only need to act and speak out of any serious conviction concerning the public claims of the gospel, and it becomes promptly evident that we are outsiders to the flow of power."[30]

Brueggemann articulates the challenge of biblical conceptions of community in the postexilic period: "The most remarkable observation one can make about this interface of exilic circumstance and scriptural resource is this: Exile did not lead Jews in the Old Testament to abandon faith or to settle for abdicating despair, nor to retreat to privatistic religion. On the contrary, exile evoked the most brilliant literature and the most daring theological articulation in the Old Testament."[31]

29. John Howard Yoder, "The Disavowal of Constantine: An Alternative Perspective on Interfaith Dialogue," in *Royal Priesthood*, 245.

30. Brueggemann, *Cadences of Home*, 2.

31. Ibid., 3.

To affirm, in Yoder's terms, "Galuth as Calling," is to question the statist assumption. Significantly, questioning the assumptions of state was part of the (now so clearly prescient) early writings of Jacques Ellul, most notably his two linked volumes, *The Political Illusion* and *Autopsy of Revolution*.[32] Ellul raised serious questions about the dominance of statist, nationalist forms of political and ideological discourse: "Above all, we cannot escape the strange view that history is ultimately a function of the state. . . . When a country has a western model of politics, they have arrived. If one were to reject this form of political involvement, he would be labeled a heretic, a reactionary."[33] Ellul's anarchist-inspired response was a call to local identity and action:

> Nothing short of an explosion will disintegrate the technological society: that is the vital issue. Whatever form the explosion takes (a federalist community, or self-direction hostile to planning, for example) will involve, as always, a sacrifice. A revolution against the technological society (not against technology itself) implies decreased efficiency in all areas (total yield, productivity, adaptiveness, integration), a lowered standard of living, the reduction of large-scale public programs, and the erosion of a mass culture. If we are unwilling to pay the combined price of those four reductions, then we are not ready for revolution, the only revolution that is a necessity today.[34]

Ellul's social analysis is today echoed not only in the increasing interest in diasporic models of Christian ecclesiology, but also in recent trends in postcolonialist study that examine with sophisticated appreciation (and not merely a romantic nostalgia, or sentimental dismissal typical of Niebuhrian criticism) the radical critique embodied in an Amish farm or a Catholic Worker house.

It is critical to note that church history and biblical theology are not the exclusive sources of important discussion and debate on diasporic social formulations. A review of certain lines of cultural studies and post-

---

32. *The Political Illusion*, trans. K. Kellen (New York: Knopf, 1967); *Autopsy of Revolution*, trans. P. Wolf (New York: Knopf, 1971). I must acknowledge that the later writing of Ellul went in objectionable directions, particularly his association with the anti-Islamic polemics of Bat Ye'or, the pseudonym of Gisele Littman, who wrote a series of alarmist attacks on Islam. See the important article by Michael Sells, "Kosovo Mythology and the Bosnian Genocide," in *In God's Name*, 180–205.

33. *Political Illusion*, 14, 18–19.

34. *Autopsy*, 281.

colonialist dialogue is crucial to the task as well and widens the dialogue considerably.

Questioning Nationalism in Cultural and Postcolonialist Studies

An interesting debate now surrounds many older notions of "identity" in cultural studies and postcolonialist analysis. The issues are clearly related to our theological interests, although scholars and writers are often divided into separate "discussions" that tend to take on separate vocabularies of discourse in either cultural studies or theological studies. This separation obviously makes it difficult to see otherwise clearly common threads.

First, the branch of cultural studies we are interested in, postcolonial criticism, is helpfully defined by Bart Moore-Gilbert as "a more or less distinct set of reading practices preoccupied principally with analysis of cultural forms which mediate, challenge or reflect upon the relations of domination and subordination—economic, cultural and political— between (and often within) nations, races or cultures, which characteristically have their roots in the history of modern European colonialism and imperialism."[35]

What is significant for our theological concerns and a reading of the Israelite and biblical literature of exile and diaspora existence, however, is the emergence within these more general lines of discussion of a dialogue on "postnationalism." In her summary of the rise of postcolonial theory, Leela Gandhi devotes an entire chapter to "The Vision of Postnationalism."[36] Gandhi outlines the growing dissatisfaction with postcolonial categories of the "colonizer" and the "colonized" as pure states of identity with entirely separate agendas and norms. There has been so much mixing, resulting in identities best described with terms like "diasporic cultures" or "hybrid cultures," for better or worse, that some have questioned older social analysis that uses stereotyped ("essentialist") class-based categories of the "oppressor" and "oppressed." Such stereotypical, black-and-white generalizations (often now referred to as a false "binary" analysis) only served to perpetuate apartheid regimes (or apartheid theories) of "maintaining the West," "American values," and so on. Gandhi notes that not only do colonized peoples display too many of the elements, both

---

35. "Introduction," in *Postcolonial Criticism*, ed. B. Moore Gilbert et al. (New York: Longman, 1997) 12.

36. *Postcolonial Theory* (New York: Columbia Univ. Press, 1998) 122–40.

negative and positive, of their colonizers, but also that colonizing societies are permanently affected by the colonial enterprise, both materially and culturally. Thus, if "nationalism" is only a transitory tactic of liberation, which can lead uncritically to the same politics of dominance and privilege characteristic of the old colonizing states, what is the potential for avoiding this? Gandhi outlines an ethic of "hybridity" that embraces diasporic existence as a potential source of a new ethic of coexistence among "transnational identities."

But are these debates about "identities" and "critical methodologies" really intended to contribute to some tangible agenda for "social justice"? If so, what are the terms of this tangible benefit? Typically, the assumed categories for social progress (or "liberation") had been thought to be the benefits of existing as a nation-state. "Justice" is thus associated with national independence, especially when the discussion is located in the context of postcolonialism. For example, "justice" in Frantz Fanon's terms, in such postcolonialist classics as *The Wretched of the Earth*,[37] clearly meant independent national existence—apart from colonizing powers. This was mirrored in theological debates. The largely Marxist-informed political categories of debates within Latin American liberation theology also presumed national independence as the "just" goal of "exodus-like" struggles of the poor. But nationalism has a tendency to then dictate the terms and the strategies of defining identity and political agendas. Nationalism has also had the tendency to define the "disenfranchised," as well as how global inequities are to be corrected. Finally, the paradigms of nationalism (especially notable in Fanon) too often served to justify brutal violence as the "only response" to brutal violence. The rhetoric on the left and the right began to blur in the smoking debris of violence.

How has this tended to dictate the terms of both theological and cultural analysis of "identity" and "justice" in relation to a potential diasporic or exilic existence? Nationalism, for example, makes a particular kind of problem out of the status of "refugee." In reflecting on her own work with African refugee communities, Liisa Malkki raises a series of difficult questions about the conception of refugees in contemporary social and political analysis and its implications for practical relief work: "There has emerged a new awareness of the global social fact that, now more than perhaps ever before, people are chronically mobile and routinely displaced, inventing homes and homelands in the absence of territorial, national bases—not in situ but through memories of and claims on

37. Frantz Fanon, *The Wretched of the Earth* (Boston: Grove, 1986).

places that they can or will no longer corporeally inhabit."[38] Malkki argues that refugees are a "problem" *precisely because they are stateless*. Refugees "are not ordinary people but represent, rather, an anomaly requiring specialized correctives and therapeutic interventions. It is striking how often the abundant literature claiming refugees as its object of study locates 'the problem' not in the political conditions or processes that produce massive territorial displacements of people but within the bodies and minds (and even souls) of people categorized as refugees."[39] This can result, paradoxically, in blaming the victim: "Our sedentarist assumptions about attachment to place lead us to define displacement not as a fact about sociopolitical context but as an inner, pathological condition of the displaced."[40]

Interestingly, this has invaded even the legal definitions of refugees, and has become an essential aspect of determining who is actually a "refugee" and thus in need of material (or other) assistance. T. Alexander Aleinikoff writes that the previous "exilic bias" of refugee relief work has changed to an emphasis on *containment*: "Rather than a paradigm shift, then, we may well be witnessing the troubling use of a humanitarian discourse to mask a reaffirmation of state-centeredness."[41]

What are the alternatives to nationalist dominance of the debate about justice or identity that inevitably inform any attempt to write a biblical theology of exile? Is there only one path to social renewal that inevitably includes, for example, reviving older narratives, ethnic identities, or subcommunal consciousness as a basis for state identity, or even as a basis for struggle for justice defined as either "inclusion" or "independent existence"?

Some have called for a radical redefinition of exile and diasporic existence that does not see mobility as pathological, but rather embraces the new realities of transnational identities or celebrates the emergence of global "hybrids." Pnina Werbner helpfully summarizes elements of analysis that has led to the interest in "hybridity" as a potential stance from which to do critical social analysis: "What has evidently rendered

---

38. Liisa H. Malkki, "National Geographic: The Rooting of Peoples and the Territorializing of National Identity among Scholars and Refugees," in *Culture, Power, and Place: Explorations in Critical Anthropology*, ed. A. Gupta and J. Ferguson (Durham, N.C.: Duke Univ. Press, 1997) 52.

39. Ibid., 63.

40. Ibid., 64.

41. T. Alexander Aleinikoff, "State Centered Refugee Law: From Resettlement to Containment," in *Engendering Forced Migration: Theory and Practice*, ed. Doreen Indra (New York: Berghahn, 1999) 265.

holistic models of culture and society unviable is the reality of postwar population movements, transnational capitalism, global telecommunications and the explosion of consumption. What now seems pressing is to theorize the problems of cultural translation and reflexivity, interethnic communication and cross-cultural mobilisation, hybridity and creolisation."[42] Homi Babha agrees, arguing that "the demography of the new internationalism is the history of postcolonial migration, the narratives of cultural and political diaspora, the major social displacements of peasant and aboriginal communities, the poetics of exile, the grim prose of political and economic refugees."[43]

Others have turned to images of rootlessness, using an image of bedouinlike "nomads." In this context, Caren Kaplan outlines an interesting dialogue between those who, largely inspired by the work of Deleuze and Guattari, have been searching "for alternatives to purely nationalist or modernist critical strategies [and] have embraced enthusiastically the generalized figure of the nomad as a symbol of hybridity, mobility, and flux, in short, the metaphorical nomad and theories of nomadology counter assertions of purity, fixed dwelling or being, and totalitarian authorities and social practices."[44]

In short, the use of exile as a trope serves, for some, as a kind of identity or stance from which to engage in critical observation of modern circumstances and their historical precedents. An "exilic," "hybrid," "nomadic," or "diasporic" position enables a critique of the (anthropological) establishment of "categories" (i.e., homeland, nation-states, territories, and sedentary identities) that people "fit into" (or can be bordered into) so that they can be "studied," "counted," "included," or avoided. Such attempts to define static categories is typically pilloried in recent literature as "essentialism," that is, forcing people into a list of traits ("museumed identities") that individuals more or less align with depending on how "genuine" their cultural and ethnic identities are thought to be. In short, the normative state is always an assumption.

But hybridity and exilic existence, not to mention refugee identities, raise serious problems. If people cannot be divided into "national ethnicities" as clear categories, and thus matched to "legitimate homelands,"

---

42. Pnina Werbner, "Introduction: The Dialectics of Cultural Hybridity," in *Debating Cultural Hybridity: Multicultural Identities and the Politics of Racism,* ed. P. Werbner and T. Modood (London: Zed, 1997) 6.

43. Homi K. Bhabha, *The Location of Culture* (New York: Routledge, 1994) 5.

44. Caren Kaplan, *Questions of Travel: Postmodern Discourses of Displacement,* Post-Contemporary Interventions (Durham, N.C.: Duke Univ. Press, 1998) 92.

then much liberal and Marxist political philosophy seems disarmed and unable to articulate a plan of action.

Studying "nationalities," and moving from this to a moral or ideological commitment to "defend national rights," seemed the only viable language for those who looked for alternatives to clear global inequities, suffering, and injustice. But what about the Fourth World? What about identities that are not tied to territory (or perhaps once were, but no longer essentially so)? Since much of the twentieth-century dialogue in cultural studies (if not also in theological studies and social ethics) typically defines "justice" as equal access to commodities, the problem seemed to be one of figuring out how to (often literally) *re-count* authentic nationalities, and then redistribute global commodities accordingly.

But what are "nationalities"? Is this the only existence that is viable? Diaspora studies would suggest otherwise:

> In a world of diaspora, transnational culture flows, and mass movements of populations, old-fashioned attempts to map the globe as a set of culture regions or homelands are bewildered by a dazzling array of postcolonial simulacra, doublings and redoublings, as India and Pakistan seem to reappear in postcolonial simulation in London, prerevolution Teheran rises from the ashes in Los Angeles, and a thousand similar cultural dramas are played out in urban and rural settings all across the globe. In this culture-play of diaspora, colony and metropole, "here" and "there," center and periphery, become blurred.[45]

While there are clear similarities to debates related to multiculturalism, and its challenge against a historical canon that limits itself to the study of "kings and generals," the recent criticism is not merely a question of including "other nationalisms." David Lloyd calls for a revival of interest in the otherwise ignored significance of "subnarratives" (seen as sources of criticism and resistance to a solely nationalist metanarrative). He writes, for example, of the dominance of only one kind of imagined community even in the presence of other possibilities of social configurations of "community": "As the form and end of history, the nation-state in effect regulates what counts as history and gives the law of historical verisimilitude that decides between the contingent and the significant."[46] Reminiscent of Ellul's blistering critique of the virtually unbridled growth

45. Werbner, "Introduction," In *Debating Cultural Hybridity*, 38.
46. David Lloyd, "Nationalisms against the State," in *The Politics of Culture in the Shadow of Capital*, ed. L. Lowe and D. Lloyd (Durham, N.C.: Duke Univ. Press, 1997) 178.

of the power of the modern nation-state since the French Revolution, Lloyd states that "it is a peculiarity of nationalism that of all modes of potentially counter-hegemonic formations none is more thoroughly reinforced or sanctioned by the formations it ostensibly opposes."[47] What is called for, then, is a renewed "critical localism," or, in other terms, a realization that social formations other than nation-states can represent viable social existence. In short, it is a call to recognize diasporic existence as a viable alternative to national existence. Exile becomes a political model.

But are these "localisms" merely a fossilized, idealistic version of pre-existent communal identities or traditions? In his own call for a creative critical localism, Arif Dirlik warns that such local communities are often themselves sophisticated products of the same transnational realities that they are resisting and cannot therefore simply be crude, and naive, attempts to revive a museumed past: "Excluded from this [critical] localism are romantic nostalgia for communities past, hegemonic nationalist yearnings of a new kind, or historicism that would imprison the present in the past."[48]

Masao Miyoshi agrees but seems hesitant about the prospects of developing such a critical localism: "The return to 'authenticity' . . . is a closed route. There is nothing of the sort extant any longer in much of the world. How then to balance the transnationalization of economy and politics with the survival of local culture and history—without mummifying them with tourism and in museums—is the crucial question, for which, however, no answer has yet been found."[49]

But others have suggested that "exile," and particularly models of diasporic existence, are precisely the answer that Miyoshi seeks. But in her analysis of these motifs of travel, exile, nomadic tropes, and "tourism" in connection with romanticized notions of "the creativity of exile," Kaplan properly warns against ignoring the social realities of peripheral regions (made peripheral by oppressive socioeconomic politics): "the desire to become like or merge with the periphery or margin that one's own power has established demonstrates the pitfalls of theoretical 'tourism.' When poststructuralist theory constructs a 'no-man's land' that permits the erasure of the subject positions of the critic in the formation of theory, his-

47. Ibid., 182.

48. Arif Dirlik, "The Global in the Local," in *Global/Local: Cultural Production and the Transnational Imaginary*, ed. Rob Wilson and Wimal Dissanayake (Durham, N.C.: Duke Univ. Press, 1996) 38.

49. Masao Miyoshi, "A Borderless World? From Colonialism to Transnationalism and the Decline of the Nation-State," in *Global/Local*, 95.

torically diverse forms of colonial discourse combine to create a postcolonial postmodern practice of cultural hegemony."[50]

Zygmunt Bauman, too, warns of the inherent dangers of "localism" simply retreating to petty tribalisms:

> To be a born-again communitarian is widely considered today as the sign of a critical standpoint, leftism, and progress. Come back community, from the exile to which the modern State confined you; all is forgiven and forgotten—the oppressiveness of parochiality, the genocidal propensity of collective narcissism, the tyranny of communal pressures and the pugnacity and despotism of communal discipline. It is, of course, a nuisance that one finds in this bed some unwelcome and thoroughly repulsive fellows. How to keep the bed to oneself, how to prove that the unwelcome fellows have no right to be in it—this seems to be the problem.[51]

Finally, we must keep in mind Edward Said's important warning that the first reality for thinking creatively (and for us, theologically) about exile is that it is a form of disaster and trauma that is inseparably connected to human actions related to power, dominance, and brutality:

> To think of exile as beneficial, as a spur to humanism or to creativity, is to belittle its mutilations. Modern exile is irremediably secular and unbearably historical. It is produced by human beings for other human beings; it has torn millions of people for the nourishment of tradition, family, and geography. . . . It is necessary to set aside Joyce and Nabokov and even Conrad, who wrote of exile with such pathos, but of exile without cause or rationale. Think instead of the uncountable masses for whom UN agencies have been created, of refugees without urbanity, with only ration cards and agency numbers.[52]

On a Theology of Exile

Returning to the theological agenda for Christians, our first task following Said's warning is to recount a critical history of the events of the Babylonian exile itself, and some of the more significant socioeconomic realities of postexilic existence in the Babylonian and Persian empires. Furthermore, we will notice that not all the biblical descriptions of

50. Kaplan, *Questions of Travel*, 66.

51. Zygmunt Bauman, "The Making and Unmaking of Strangers," in *Debating Cultural Hybridity*, 56.

52. Edward Said, "The Mind of Winter: Reflections on Life in Exile," *Harpers* (September 1983) 50.

responses to exile are positive models for contemporary faith and practice. This is not to be an uncritical exercise in "the Bible tells me so."
Indeed, in my analysis of the Hebrew responses to exile, and the creative
modeling of their own diasporic existence after the disaster of 587 BCE, I
will have occasion to point out that some of the these objectionable
aspects of a "localism" that amounts to parochialisms are clearly evident
(the Maccabean literature is an excellent case in point). But I maintain that
what many have assumed in their analyses of the exile is that all such communal identity struggles are *retrograde*. At least part of this value judgment
can be attributed to the Western Christian agenda since Augustine's advice
to recently converted Christian soldiers newly perplexed by a commandment about "loving enemies." The great churchman's advice? Look to King
David when Jesus fails to model a viable ethic of asserting Roman military
strength.

To adapt Yoder's term again, a biblical theology along these lines might
be labeled "Constantinian exegesis." Such an exegesis, for example, would
hold not merely that Israel was only viable as a state, but that the only
viable resistance to empire is full-blown military engagements by a Mac-
cabean-style proto-state or reconstructionist state. But as James Scott has
warned, based on his studies of the varieties of covert resistance: "A view
of politics focused either on what may be command performances of
consent or open rebellion represents a far too narrow concept of political
life—especially under conditions of tyranny in which much of the world
lives. . . . We are in danger of making a serious mistake, therefore, whenever we infer anything at all about the beliefs or attitudes of anyone solely
on the basis that he or she has engaged in an apparently deferential act."[53]

The exile represented a nonstate, but not therefore a nonviable existence. The exiles, like modern refugees, however, are problems. Therefore,
biblical theology has too often looked for occasions where either the
Hebrews struggled to restore their own state or thus presumed that they
fully accepted their existence within Babylonian, Persian, and Hellenistic
imperial states.

One can make the case that this statist or Constantinian exegetical paradigm has exercised a tremendous influence on biblical analysis of the
exile and exilic texts. Whereas it was more common earlier in the twentieth century to write off the exilic period as one of "decline" (e.g., Well-
hausen) into priestly sacredotalism and decayed religion, today it is far
more common to read the postexilic community as not only fully co-

---

53. James Scott, *Domination and the Arts of Resistance: Hidden Transcripts* (New Haven:
Yale Univ. Press, 1990) 20, 23.

opted as faithful citizens of the Persian Empire, but also to read Ezra and Nehemiah as official minions, and perhaps the entire Pentateuch as "official Persian documents," suggesting that both the persons and their literary products were involved in willful collaboration with the state structures of Persian imperial rule. Somehow, it seems, there had to be a state—either their own or the Persian Empire, one way or another!

Consider the problem surrounding the vexed question of resistance to imperial rule. If those scholars are correct who read Ezra (and his Pentateuch) as a Persian official who administrated a Persian-authorized document within the boundaries of the Persian province of Yehud, then very little resistance is presumed to exist within biblical documents. This is because, so it is assumed, if the exilic communities really resisted Persian rule, they would logically only be engaged in reviving their old state existence. Thus, if there is no Judas Maccabeus, then there is no resistance. Again, Scott warns against simplistic analysis: "So long as we confine our conception of *the political* to activity that is openly declared we are driven to conclude that subordinate groups essentially lack a political life or that what political life they do have is restricted to those exceptional moments of popular explosion."[54] In short, unless it is statist resistance, it is collaboration. But what if alternative forms of Hebrew existence were being constructed out of the demise of Jerusalem and the Hebrew state? Would other forms of identity besides independent nation-states give rise to other forms of resistance? Is resistance only real when swords are drawn and generals obeyed?

Scott's work would force a serious rereading, however, of texts from Ezra and the Pentateuch (especially for an exilic "J/Yahwist"), if we consider that "we are not, in any case, reduced to waiting for open social protest to lift a veil of consent and quiescence. A view of politics focused either on what may be command performances of consent or open rebellion represents a far too narrow concept of political life—especially under conditions of tyranny or near-tyranny in which much of the world lives. . . . We are in danger of making a serious mistake, therefore, whenever we infer anything at all about the beliefs or attitudes of anyone solely on the basis that he or she has engaged in an apparently deferential act."[55] Working with Asian peasants, Scott came to understand that there was a significant difference between the outward declarations and language of subordinate peoples and the private discussions. He refers to the latter as the "hidden transcript" as opposed to the "public" transcript: "the

54. Ibid., 199.
55. Ibid., 20, 23.

public transcript, where it is not positively misleading, is unlikely to tell the whole story about power relations."[56]

The challenge for biblical analysis of the exile, then, is partly a response to Scott's determination that "a partly sanitized, ambiguous, and coded version of the hidden transcript is always present in the public discourse of subordinate groups."[57] Part of the way forward, I would argue, is to reread texts associated with the Babylonian exile with the *presumption of resistance*, but not necessarily a resistance based on *nationalist* aspiration, even if this was not entirely absent. To anticipate this, one can ask a number of brief questions, some of which will be answered in the chapters that follow.

In surveying the "Jew in the court of the foreign ruler" tradition in the postexilic period (the Joseph narratives, Daniel, Esther, Tobit, etc.), it would be well to keep in mind Scott's observations: "Nothing conveys the public transcript more as the dominant would like it to seem than the formal ceremonies they organize to celebrate and dramatize their rule. Parades, inaugurations, processions, coronations, funerals, provide ruling groups with the occasion to make a spectacle of themselves in a manner largely of their own choosing."[58] If this is so, then one can argue that the audacity to set a story in the court of the invincible Persian ruler—the ability to *see* into the courts of Babylon and Persia—was already to diffuse that aura of invincibility (as Aeschylus would do on the theatrical stages of Athens). It was to crash beyond the public transcript of the powerful and reject the drama of hidden power, hegemony, and control and portray the Imperial Highness as flawed, corrupt, and under the ultimate rule of God. The stories of Daniel and Esther are Hebrew tales of refusing Persian "executive privilege."

As I have noted, in recent work on the Persian period, there is a growing move to read the formation of the Pentateuch as the result of Persian cooperation with a select group of Hebrews to formulate and then administrate a locally based form of Jewish law. But, in his own criticism of the "Persian cooperation" thesis on the origins of the Pentateuch, Jean Louis Ska has raised important concerns.[59] Among those objections, Ska points out: "Some texts contained in the Pentateuch may have raised the suspicion or even the hostility of the Persian authorities. For instance, according to Gn. 15:18, the land promised to Abraham goes from the

---

56. Ibid., 2
57. Ibid., 19.
58. Ibid., 58.
59. While Ska's review is concerned with the versions of the Persian authorization theories associated with the so-called Heidelberg School, similar ideas have appeared in English,

stream of Egypt to the Euphrates. This is a rather ambitious view. The wars of conquest described in Nm 21, 25, and 31 could have raised some perplexities in Persian minds. And what could or would the Persian authorities have said when reading texts such as Dt. 7 (Israel must destroy all the nations occupying the land)?"[60]

Certainly Ezra's (or whoever's) prayer of Nehemiah 9 does not sound like the words of a loyal Persian subject representing Persian interests when he says: "Here we are, slaves to this day—slaves in the land that you gave to our ancestors to enjoy its fruit and its good gifts. Its rich yield goes to the kings whom you have set over us because of our sins; they have power also over our bodies and over our livestock at their pleasure, and we are in great distress" (9:36-37).

Finally, Mark Brett reads the Joseph tales in the context of a presumption that Joseph actually "fell from grace" in accepting the role of an Egyptian governor whose policies led to the enslavement of all Egypt (especially compared to the values expressed in 1 Samuel 8). Then perhaps Joseph is not celebrated in Genesis 41–50 after all, but *lamented* as a corrupted official who ironically was responsible for some of the most oppressive aspects of centralized imperial economies.[61]

I believe that the point is clear without going further. These contemporary concerns, including theological and ethical concerns, are bound up with particular readings of history and particular readings of biblical texts. I offer my critique in this prologue by way of anticipating where my interests lay in the rest of this book.

To summarize: the readings of biblical texts offered in the chapters that follow will presume the viability of a community in exile, and the ability to engage in resistance, even outside of nationalist aspirations or imperial connivance. I then propose that such readings may inform a radical Christian theological resistance to our own history of imperial connivances and the theologies that have so long excused and supported them.

Finally, however, I wish to offer a comment on a debate currently raging in biblical studies as I write my work on exile—namely, the historicity of the monarchical traditions, especially previous to the seventh century.

especially in the work of Jon Berquist, *Judaism in Persia's Shadow: A Social and Historical Approach* (Minneapolis: Fortress Press, 1995); and anticipated somewhat by Kenneth Hoglund's important work, *Achaemenid Imperial Administration in Syria-Palestine and the Missions of Ezra and Nehemiah*, SBLDS 125 (Atlanta: Scholars, 1992).

60. Jean Louis Ska, "'Persian Imperial Authorization': Some Question Marks," in *Persia and Torah: The Theory of Imperial Authorization of the Pentateuch*, ed. J. W. Watts, SBLSymS 17 (Atlanta: SBL, 2001) 169.

61. See Brett, *Genesis*, 109–36.

The suggestions that either the Davidic/Solomonic states did not exist at all or they existed only in a drastically more modest form than the Deuteronomistic History presently suggests are often read as if that idea presents serious challenges to biblical theology. But for whom? Certainly not for an exilic biblical theology. That a diasporic Judean community, or a quasi-political minority under Persian hegemony, may have carefully constructed a militarist and nationalist story only to savagely criticize it as idolatrous and ultimately as disastrous (as the Deuteronomistic Historian clearly does) is an idea that would not spell the end of biblical historiography and most certainly not the end of biblical theology. Rather, it could well be read as a brilliant first move toward the articulation of a community that consists mainly of faithful commitment rather than defined by worldly power. The death of Davidic historicity, if it proves to be the most likely judgment on Israelite history in the tenth and ninth centuries (and while it seems early in the debate, I am not qualified to comment further), is fertile ground for the rise of an exilic biblical theology. I, for one, would not mourn the passing of the king.

2.
VIOLENCE AND EXEGESIS:
The History of Exile

IN ORDER TO ASSESS THE THEOLOGICAL SIGNIFICANCE OF THE
Babylonian exile, it is important to gather information about the
events themselves and their historical context, as well as make some comments about scholarly views on the exile in the past.[1] But to read about
these events in the context of the turn of the twenty-first century, especially as a Western Christian, has its own unique ironies that I believe are
important to recognize at the outset.

The Shadows of Empire: The Exegesis of Violence as Theological Context

Violent crises have become mundane. It no longer matters if crises and
tragedies are meant to be "news" or "entertainment." It is no longer even
shocking that news media literally *project* content to us that is selected by
the maxim: "if it bleeds, it leads."[2] That books can even be published
with titles such as *Studies in Comparative Genocide* or *Small Wars You
May Have Missed* warns us of the possibility of becoming immune to the

---

1. Some of the information in this chapter appeared in "Reassessing the Historical and
Social Impact of the Babylonian Exile," in *Exile: Old Testament, Jewish, and Christian Conceptions*, ed. James Scott (Leiden: Brill, 1997) 7–36. This chapter, however, has been extensively revised and contains additional material more directly relevant to the task of the book
as a whole.

2. This section was largely complete before the tragedies of September 11, 2001. But it is
clear that in the aftermath of these events, the role of the media in literally cashing in on the
spectacle is being debated as this goes to press.

realities of crisis in the lives of hundreds of thousands of people in the twentieth century.[3]

Among other more infamous epithets bestowed upon the twentieth century are "the century of the refugee" and "the century of genocide."[4] Thus, exile is the reality, whether chosen or forced, for an unprecedented percentage of the world's people in movement in the twentieth century, and this reality demands our attention. First and foremost, before any theological statement is made about exile, one must acknowledge that exile is the daily reality for millions of human beings at the opening of the twenty-first century.

Writing for the Survey of International Labour Migration conducted by the United Nations, Peter Stalker rehearses the statistics: 80 million people now live in "foreign" lands. One million people emigrate permanently each year, and another million seek political asylum. At the time he wrote, 1994, there were 18 million refugees from natural disaster or war, but according to the recent report *The State of the World's Refugees 1997-1998*, "50 million people around the world might legitimately be described as victims of forced displacement."[5] When it is added that 20 percent of the world's population control 70 to 83 percent of the global GNP, and that 1.2 billion people live in poverty, we begin to see the results of twentieth-century civilization. Huge population transfers amount to rich nations "penetrating" less powerful nations for labor pools: Arabs in France, Turks in Germany, Mexicans in the United States. "Widening economic gaps between industrialized and developing countries, rapidly increasing populations, the penetration of poor countries by rich ones, the disruption caused by economic development and the web of transport and communications systems all create the 'structural conditions' that might encourage an individual to consider life elsewhere."[6]

Furthermore, political and social decisions impinge on the very meaning of disasters. Even the concept of a "natural disaster" must be questioned if the disaster is thought to be an occasion devoid of power relations and political decisions. The important monograph of Anthony Oliver-Smith, *The Martyred City: Death and Rebirth in the Andes*,[7] represents a school of "disaster studies" that refuses to separate supposedly

3. *Studies in Comparative Genocide*, ed. Levon Chorgajian and George Shirinian (New York: St. Martin's, 1999); Andrew Yooll-Graham, *Small Wars You May Have Missed* (New York: Signal, 2000).

4. *The Century of Genocide*, ed. Samuel Totten et al. (New York: Garland, 1997).

5. Ed. Eric Morris (Oxford: Oxford Univ. Press, 1997) 2.

6. Peter Stalker, *The Work of Strangers A Survey of International Labour Migration* (Geneva: International Labour Office, 1994) 3.

7. Prospect Heights, Ill.: Waveland, 1986.

"natural disasters" from human intervention. In his analysis of the aftermath of a massive earthquake that devastated the Andean village of Yungay on May 31, 1970, Oliver-Smith refers to the "500-year earthquake," suggesting that a large part of the devastation of this "natural disaster" is the legacy of five centuries of Spanish colonialist presence with the accompanying development of social castes and especially the colonizer's rejection of light, indigenous architectural traditions that were suited to the unstable Andean environment. These were replaced by the "superior" heavy, European-style construction of imported Spanish traditions—a monumental architectural tradition that had the unfortunate corollary of transforming homes into death traps: "Colonial governments and their successors, responding to nonindigenous pressures and forces, imposed systems of production, urban and rural settlement, and limits on population mobility that severely undermined indigenous hazard management."[8] The point is simply that disaster studies have come to see that human interaction with the environment—for example, decisions that are made against older wisdom—are inherently a factor in the assessment of "disaster." There is, in short, a politics of disaster that brings it closer to the study of the sociology of human crises of violence, war, and forced population movements.

Such a wider lens is required for a deeper appreciation of the events of the Babylonian exile of the Jews. Thus, the result of an overview of events related to the Babylonian exile of the Jews, beginning even before 597 BCE, will, I hope, shed further light on some of the implications of Neo-Babylonian and Persian hegemony in the Mediterranean rim. Any attempt to clarify the theological significance of Hebrew writings associated with these imperial realities, and for subsequent decades and centuries that followed, needs to consider the massive disruption in the lives of the Judeans who lived in Judah, among others also affected, and the continued realities of living under imperial control and administration.

Although I will subsequently discuss what I see as some of the contemporary theological implications of the ancient Hebrew response to exile, it may thus seem ironic (if not flatly contradictory) that I will in this chapter argue the *negative* significance, and especially the *severity*, of these events. But it is not my intention to argue that a theology of exile arises from the ease of the exilic years or from the exile as a "positive" event.

---

8. Anthony Oliver-Smith, "Anthropological Research on Hazards and Disasters," *ARA* 25 (1996) 315. See also idem, "Peru's Five Hundred Year Earthquake," in *Disasters, Development, and Environment*, ed. A. Varley (London: Wiley, 1994) 3–48. See also *What Is a Disaster? Perspectives on the Question*, ed. E. L. Quarantelli (London: Routledge, 1998), esp. Anthony Oliver-Smith, "Global Changes and the Definition of Disaster," 177–94.

Quite to the contrary, the creativity of the Hebrew theological and social responses to exile is partly appreciated by the reality of these exilic events, as any modern "theology of exile" must be based on a sober reflection of the reality of the nations among whom such a renewed biblical theology of exile must be practiced.

The Problem of Assessing the Importance of the Exile in Biblical Studies

Trying to assess the impact of the Babylonian exile is more controversial than one might first suspect. The importance of the exile, and its impact on the life and faith of ancient Israel, have certainly not been matters of universal agreement. For example, in 1910 C. C. Torrey made the famous comment that the exile, "which was in reality a small and relatively insignificant affair, has been made, partly through mistake and partly by the compulsion of a theory, to play a very important part in the history of the Old Testament."[9]

Torrey's extreme doubts began a tradition of de-emphasizing the exile that would continue (albeit not in the extreme terms Torrey used). More recently, some of this ambivalence about the significance of the exile has been revived. In 1977, for example, in the influential historiography of ancient Israel edited by John Hayes and J. Maxwell Miller, Herbert Donner writes: "It is easy . . . to overemphasize the drastic and debilitating consequences of the fall of Jerusalem and the triumph of Babylonian forces. Various aspects of life certainly were greatly modified, but Babylonian policy was not overly oppressive. The exiles were not forced to live in inhuman conditions . . . [and] remained free and certainly should not be understood as slaves. They would have been under no overt pressure to assimilate and lose their identities."[10] We will soon discover that a reading of biblical texts that presumes a crisis, rather than a sanguine view of exile, reveals a much darker image of exilic circumstances than such assessments allow. But even in earlier twentieth-century views, there were signs of different opinions along the way, even if expressed tentatively. In his *Studies in the Book of Lamentations*, for example, Norman Gottwald considered the reality behind the lamenting poetry to be worthy of notice: "If the enduring memory of events and their impact upon succeeding

9. C. C. Torrey, "The Exile and the Restoration," in *Ezra Studies* (1910; reprint New York: Ktav, 1970) 285.

10. H. Donner, in *Israelite and Judean History*, ed. J. M. Miller and J. H. Hayes, OTL (Philadelphia: Westminster, 1977) 421, 433.

generations is the major criterion of historical importance, then there can be no doubt that the sequence of happenings from 597 to 538 B.C. were among the most fateful in all Hebrew-Jewish history. Is it far wide of the mark to recognize in the sixth century B.C. the severest test which Israel's religion ever faced?"[11]

But research on the exile did not share Gottwald's early suggestion about the central importance of these events, and his own views have changed somewhat on the impact of the exile.[12] Opinions remained mixed for some time. An excellent indication of this is the ambiguity in John Bright's influential *History of Israel*. On the one hand, Bright would write: "Although we should not belittle the hardships and the humiliation that these exiles endured, their lot does not seem to have been unduly severe"; and yet two pages later he writes: "When one considers the magnitude of the calamity that overtook her, one marvels that Israel was not sucked down into the vortex of history along with the other little nations of western Asia."[13]

This ambiguous assessment is shared in many of the recent works on the impact of the exile on biblical literature.[14] Peter Ackroyd's work, still considered by many to be the major analysis of the exile, was written in conscious awareness of the neglect of the exilic and postexilic periods in biblical analysis.[15] But even this work, which dealt with the exile as its main subject of investigation, reflected an ambiguity about the actual conditions of exile. In his assessment of the conditions of the exiles in Babylon, for example, Ackroyd writes that indications "are of reasonable freedom, of settlement in communities—perhaps engaged in work for

11. Norman K. Gottwald, *Studies in the Book of Lamentations*, SBT 1/14 (Naperville, Ill.: Allenson, 1954) 19.

12. See, for example, his comments in the text, *The Hebrew Bible: A Socio-Literary Introduction* (Philadelphia: Fortress Press, 1985) 418–39, which reflects his later views that one of the most important factors of the exilic community was their "higher class" status. I will have occasion to dispute the significance of this and the implication that their experiences were somehow mitigated by their previous status in Palestine.

13. John Bright, *History of Israel*, 3d ed. (Philadelphia: Westminster, 1981) 345, 347, respectively.

14. Studies include Raymond S. Foster, *The Restoration of Israel: The Return from the Exile* (London: Darton, Longman and Todd, 1970); Ralph W. Klein, *Israel in Exile: A Theological Interpretation*, OBT (Philadelphia: Fortress Press, 1979); P. R. Ackroyd, *Exile and Restoration*, OTL (Philadelphia: Westminster, 1968). To this must now be added two important and more recent collections of essays, Scott, ed., *Exile*; and Lester L. Grabbe, ed., *Leading Captivity Captive: The Exile As History and Ideology*, JSOTSup 278 (Sheffield: Sheffield Academic, 1998).

15. Ackroyd, *Exile and Restoration*, esp. "The Exilic Age," 1–16.

the Babylonians, but possibly simply engaged in normal agricultural life—of the possibility of marriage, of the ordering of their own affairs, of relative prosperity."[16] Yet, a few lines later, Ackroyd also acknowledged that the "uncongenial nature" of the situation should not be "understated." Finally, consider the view of Bustenay Oded that the exiles were "certainly put to forced labor . . . [but] it is highly unlikely that they were assigned the status of imperial slaves in perpetuity or that they were conscripted permanently to hard labor."[17] Nevertheless, Oded observes, slave status is recognized in the Murashû documents.[18] While each of these, in turn, attempts to present a balanced picture, the presumed "lack of evidence" seems inevitably to push the scholars toward a benign assessment of the human and social impact of the exile. A more severe impact, they seem to presume, would have left more evidence. We will see that there is considerable evidence to consider in any case—but it begs the question of what does, in fact, constitute acceptable evidence. In chapter three I examine some of the recent work on the books of Ezekiel and Lamentations as examples of scholarly tendencies to forthrightly dismiss evidence of severe treatment during and after the exile. Furthermore, Scott's work[19] alerts us that "resistance" rarely takes the form of outright revolution or open warfare in history, and to assess resistance only by these rarely effective events is to misconstrue the nature of human responses to oppression and suppression.

The arguments of this chapter, however, that the exile was both catastrophic and transformative for Hebrew existence (and thus for biblical theology) are not entirely unprecedented. For example, one important essay that challenged the prevailing assumptions about the generally light treatment of exiles was J. M. Wilkie's 1951 article asking whether we may need to reassess the attitude toward the treatment of the exiles in the light of Deutero-Isaiah's concept of the "suffering servant": "there is independent evidence to suggest that Second-Isaiah's language is neither metaphorical nor at variance with the actual conditions, but is an accurate description of conditions which he knew only too well."[20] Note, by

---

16. Ibid., 32.

17. Oded, "Observations on the Israelite/Judean Exiles in Mesopotamia During the Eighth-Sixth Centuries BCE," in *Immigration and Emigration within the Ancient Near East, Festschrift E. Lipinski,* ed. K. van Lerberghe and A. Schoors, OLA 65 (Leuven: Peeters, 1995) 205–12.

18. Ibid., 209.

19. James C. Scott, *Domination and the Arts of Resistance: Hidden Transcripts* (New Haven, Conn.: Yale Univ. Press, 1990).

20. See J. M. Wilkie, "Nabonidus and the Later Jewish Exiles," *JTS* 2 (1951) 36–44. See also W. G. Lambert's descriptions of the violent claims of Nebuchadnezzar, "Nebuchadnezzar King of Justice," *Iraq* 27 (1965) 1–11.

the way, an interestingly similar debate about the impact of the earlier Neo-Assyrian conquest of the Northern Kingdom in 722. Here the debate centered on assessing the impact of the earlier Assyrian crisis, and particularly whether the Assyrians imposed religious restrictions on the northern Israelite cult. Morton Coogan, for example, argued in a manner similar to benign assessments of the later Babylonian exile, stating that the Neo-Assyrian conquest had minimal impact on the faith and life of those who remained in the land after the exiles were taken. But Hermann Spiekermann later gave much more attention to Neo-Assyrian imperial practices and documents, leading to his suggestions of much more severe treatment by the Neo-Assyrian conquerors.[21]

Absent from most of the discussions of the later Babylonian exilic experience, however, is any attempt to assess the extent of the human crisis itself, because of a bias toward measuring human impact based solely on the theological changes, or lack of changes, found in the text. It is my intention in this chapter to argue along similar lines as the early suggestions of Wilkie and the later work of Spiekermann, namely, that the assessment of the impact of the Babylonian exile must make far more use of nonbiblical documents, archaeological reports, and a far more imaginative use of biblical texts read in the light of what we know about refugee studies, disaster studies, postcolonialist reflections, and sociologies of trauma.

I should mention that recent work complicates the question of the impact of the Babylonian exile by taking a radically skeptical view of the possibility of reconstructing historical events before, and even during, the exile with any confidence whatsoever. When this is combined with a skepticism about "highly stereotyped literary forms," the result is to dismiss the exile's central significance and theological impact. Indeed, I think it is fair to say that in some circles the exile was being reassessed in the 1990s as not so much a political, human, and theological crisis, but rather as the geopolitical maelstrom out of which the entire biblical "mythology" arises. We must take into consideration, however briefly, two discussions that relate directly to recent scholarly analysis of this time period in biblical history. These two will be called, for purposes of summary, (1) the "Persian authorization" thesis and (2) the discussion arising from the publication of Hans Barstad's work, *The Myth of the Empty Land*.[22]

---

21. Coogan, *Imperialism and Religion: Assyria, Judah and Israel in the Eighth and Seventh Centuries BCE*, SBLMS 19 (Missoula, Mont.: Scholars, 1974); and Hermann Spieckermann, *Juda unter Assur in der Sargonidenzeit*, FRLANT 129 (Göttingen: Vandenhoeck & Ruprecht, 1982).

22. The classic text is Peter Frei and Klaus Koch, *Reichsidee und Reichsorganisation im Perserreich*, OBO 55 (Göttingen: Vandenhoeck & Ruprecht, 1984; 2d ed. 1996). Compare a

Persian Authorization of the Pentateuch?

In one variation, this view suggests that postexilic "Judaism" created, virtually ex nihilo, the entire biblical preexilic tradition, from the patriarchs, through the exodus, and even through the monarchical period. The work of Thomas Thompson, John Van Seters, and Philip Davies (whose book is provocatively titled *In Search of Ancient Israel*) suggests that Israelite history really begins only after the rise of the Persian Empire, and any events previous to this is questionable history at best.[23] If such views are combined with those of the so-called Heidelberg School (Peter Frei, Klaus Koch, Erhard Blum, etc.) that the Pentateuch is itself in some significant sense an "authorized" document of Persian rule,[24] or even that the Torah is, for all intents and purposes, an outright creation of the Persian court, then one can surmise that the biblical authors are an enthusiastically pro-Persian group of settlers who need a basis for their claim to Yehud in the Western coastal satrap "Beyond the River." In this case, the exile becomes not so much a crisis in the development of ancient Israelite identity and theology as the occasion for its being invented. Gary Knoppers has summarized the central thesis: "Frei's provocative thesis . . . draws upon primary texts from a number of different centuries and from a variety of ancient Mediterranean sites to argue for a consistent and highly structured Persian legal policy toward the tremendous range of local communities within its domain."[25] In short, Persian "authorization" of the Jewish law for its Jewish citizens is, according to Frei and others, consistent with

similar thesis, apparently argued quite independent of the Heidelberg scholars, in Jon Berquist, *Judaism in Persia's Shadow: A Social and Historical Approach* (Minneapolis: Fortress Press, 1995).

23. The list of materials in this debate has grown rather lengthy, but the standard works include the earlier work by Thomas L. Thompson, *The Historicity of the Patriarchal Narratives: The Quest for the Historical Abraham*, BZAW 133 (Berlin: de Gruyter, 1974); and his more recent work; *The Mythic Past: Biblical Archaeology and the Myth of Israel* (London: Basic, 1999); as well as Philip R. Davies, *In Search of Ancient Israel*, JSOTSup 148 (Sheffield: JSOT Press, 1992); and an important collection of essays edited by Lester L. Grabbe, *Can a "History of Israel" Be Written?* JSOTSup 245 (Sheffield: Sheffield Academic, 1997). Related to this is the work of John Van Seters, *In Search of History: Historiography in the Ancient World and the Origins of Biblical History* (New Haven: Yale Univ. Press, 1983). Among the more vocal responses to this line of investigation is William G. Dever's polemical work, *What Did the Biblical Writers Know and When Did They Know It?* (Grand Rapids: Eerdmans, 2001).

24. The work that set off the discussion was Frei and Koch, *Reichsidee und Reichsorganisation*, but is helpfully summarized and critically reviewed in English in James W. Watts, ed., *Persia and Torah: The Theory of Imperial Authorization of the Pentateuch*, SBLSymS 17 (Atlanta: SBL, 2001).

25. Gary N. Knoppers, "An Achaemenid Imperial Authorization of Torah in Yehud?" in *Persia and Torah*, ed. Watts, 115.

Persian policies elsewhere. However, Knoppers, Joseph Blenkensopp, Jean Ska, and others have expressed serious skepticism about a thesis that Ska noted was received with "a first flush of enthusiasm [but] came under soft or sharp criticism from several sides."[26] Ska further suggests that Persian "authorization" of Hebrew pentateuchal writings would seem odd, given the hints here and there of negative attitudes toward Persian rule—what Scott would call a "hidden transcript" of complaint against imperial authority. Why do there remain such obviously negative views expressed in Scripture toward Persian rule?

Resistance in the Persian Period

The "Persian authorization" theory is not dissimilar to the assumption of most scholars of the twentieth century that Jewish attitudes toward Persian rule were generally compliant, indeed grateful. In his popular commentary, Fred Holmgren reflects this general perspective in an interesting manner. In his comment on Neh 9:36-37, one of the most significant complaints against the Persians, Holmgren recognizes that this passage indicates a measure of resentment and unrest: "To be 'almost free' is never enough; if you are a slave, 'almost free' means that you are still a slave. Under Persian rule the Jews were 'almost free.'"[27] But inexplicably Holmgren then continues at some length to maintain the general assumption about Jewish attitudes to Persian rule: "Jews did not despise this 'almost free' existence, however, because under benevolent monarchs the Jews were free to return to the land and there to rebuild the temple and the city of Jerusalem. The writings of both Ezra and Nehemiah portray the Persian rulers as cooperative and fair ... toward the Jewish community."[28] The key, then, is the supposed benevolence of the Persian emperors. It is true that some biblical passages would seem to support such assumptions—perhaps most powerfully in Deutero-Isaiah's (or some later editor's) enthusiastic bestowal of the term "Messiah" on Cyrus in Isa 45:1.[29] It is furthermore true that Jewish names turn up among the Murashû

---

26. Jean Louis Ska, "'Persian Imperial Authorization': Some Question Marks," in *Persia and Torah*, ed. Watts, 164.

27. Fredrick Carlson Holmgren, *Ezra and Nehemiah: Israel Alive Again*, ITC (Grand Rapids: Eerdmans, 1987) 134.

28. Ibid., 134–35. See similarly F. Charles Fensham, *The Books of Ezra and Nehemiah*, NICOT (Grand Rapids: Eerdmans, 1982) 10, 15, 89, 150–60.

29. Blenkinsopp, for example, summarizes positive views of Cyrus, even though he also notes that this is limited somewhat to Isa 40–48; see his "Second Isaiah—Prophet of Universalism," in *The Prophets*, ed. Philip R. Davies (Sheffield: Sheffield Academic, 1996) 186–206.

documents, leading many scholars to conclude that under the Persians, business must have been good for at least some of the community members.[30] Finally, in research on the court tales of the book of Daniel, one notes the frequently presumed positive view of Persian rulers. Even if Daniel is written after the Persian period, its benign view of Darius is typically considered a reliable collective memory of the Jews in diaspora.[31]

I must contend, however, that allowing such a perspective drawn from these few sources to dominate the interpretation of all Persian period biblical literature, and the Jewish experience of Achaemenid rule, would lead us to overlook important sociological and sociopsychological factors that are crucial for a modern assessment of the historical and ideological understanding of the Persian period. To begin, let us consider the recent revisions to the historical picture of the Achaemenid rulers themselves.

Margaret Root contrasts the Persians' own self-image and propaganda, as portrayed on official carvings, against actual practice: "The world was at peace on the walls of Persepolis as it never was in actuality. While news of the Persian sack of Miletus was striking terror in the Athenian soul, artisans from near and far were carving dreams in stone for Darius. It is easy to be cynical about this paradox between the actuality and the art of 'Pax Persiana.' And yet, even to have conceived this vision of an imperial cosmos where the Four Quarters sing harmonious praises to the power of the king was something unprecedented in the ancient world: a haunting finale for the Pre-Hellenic East."[32]

In her important reassessment of the implications of the famous Cyrus Cylinder, Amélie Kuhrt concludes: "The assumption that Persian imperial control was somehow more tolerable than the Assyrian yoke is based, on the one hand, on the limited experience of one influential group of a very small community which happened to benefit by Persian

---

30. Ran Zadok, *The Jews in Babylonia during the Chaldean and Achaemenid Periods according to the Babylonian Sources* (Haifa: Univ. of Haifa Press, 1979). Zadok, however, notes that very few Jewish names turn up as officials or members of the upper echelons of society. Nehemiah, he argued, was a clear exception to the rule; see 86–87.

31. So John J. Collins, who writes that "the benevolence of the king is assumed," *Daniel*, FOTL 20 (Grand Rapids: Eerdmans, 1984) 72. In an otherwise very interesting study, Lawrence Wills, *The Jew in the Court of the Foreign King: Ancient Jewish Court Legends*, Harvard Dissertations in Religion 26 (Minneapolis: Fortress Press, 1990), further presumes the positive view of the foreign rulers. This view is maintained in commentaries such as André LaCocque, *The Book of Daniel* (Atlanta: John Knox, 1979) 113; Norman Porteous, *Daniel*, OTL (Philadelphia: Westminster, 1965) 90; and Otto Plöger, *Daniel*, KAT (Leipzig: Gütersloher, 1965) 98.

32. Margaret Cool Root, "The King and Kingship," in *Achaemenid Art: Essays on the Creation of an Iconography of Empire*, Acta Iranica, Textes et Memoires 9 (Leiden: Brill, 1979) 311.

policy and, on the other, on a piece of blatant propaganda successfully modeled on similar texts devised to extol a representative and practitioner of the earlier and much condemned Assyrian imperialism."[33]

In an academic forum where the historical image of Cyrus was examined again, R. J. van der Spek repeats the older view and then takes issue with it on the basis of the historical sources:

> In modern literature he is praised as an innovator who ruled an empire in a new way, and exercised religious tolerance and liberality towards the subjugated. This policy would have contrasted very favourably with the attitude of the Assyrian kings, who were notorious for their cruelty, their mass deportation and their imposition of Assyrian cults. . . .
>
> This contrasting view, however, is quite incorrect. Cyrus and the other Persian kings ruled their empire in a way which was quite common in antiquity. . . .
>
> Cyrus introduces no new policy towards subdued nations, but acted in conformity with firmly established traditions, sometimes favourable, sometimes cruel. Under his responsibility temples were destroyed, Ecbatana was plundered, after the battle of Opis Cyrus "carried off the plunder (and) slaughtered the people."[34]

That Cyrus is called a messiah in Isa 45:1 should not be overread, K. D. Jenner suggests, since even this notion could have involved a far less enthusiastic perspective than many modern interpreters assume: "Cyrus, being in a position of dependency and obedience to JHWH, was no more than a useful tool in the service of Jerusalem."[35]

Finally, Kenneth Hoglund argues convincingly for a reassessment of the role of Nehemiah as a Persian official, whose task was more military than spiritual, and as concerned with the further imposition of Persian control over Judah as it was with any free expression of local religion by the Jewish residents there: "The enlargement of military activity in the Levant in the mid-fifth century is only a signal of deeper changes taking place within the administration of the western Imperial holdings. These fortresses, built upon standardized plans, were staffed with imperial forces drawn from all over the empire. As such, they were garrisons,

33. Amélie Kuhrt, "The Cyrus Cylinder and Achaemenid Imperial Policy," *JSOT* 25 (1983) 94–95.

34. R. J. van der Spek, "Did Cyrus the Great Introduce a New Policy Towards Subdued Nations? Cyrus in Assyrian Perspective," *Persica* 10 (1982) 278–79, 281–82.

35. K. D. Jenner, "The Old Testament and Its Appreciation of Cyrus," *Persica* 10 (1982) 284.

pockets of concentrated force established by the imperial system to maintain the empire's interests within the Levant. . . . There is some evidence to suggest that the appearance of these garrisons was directly related to the collection of revenues and the maintenance of the administrative machinery over the territory."[36] In short, as Hoglund summarizes, "The appearance of these garrisons in the mid-fifth century is the indelible fingerprint of the hand of the Achaemenid empire tightening its grip on local affairs in the Levant."[37] None of this *proves* that the Jews resisted or even resented Persian involvement in local affairs. But are there signs of a negative Hebrew response to Persian rule?

The Culture of Permission and the Royal Correspondence of Ezra 1–7

The royal correspondence in the book of Ezra is clearly an important source, since Persian and local Palestinian officials are presented in dialogue about the Jewish fate.[38] A careful examination of this correspondence, however, reveals an ambiguity precisely on the issue of the attitude of the Jewish community toward the Achaeminid emperors. When one considers these documents as expressions of foreign prerogative over Jewish destiny, in short, as symbols of dominance, then an entirely different light is shed on their assessment.[39]

But how can letters of permission, for which one would presumably be very grateful, be symbols of dominance? One need only remind oneself of the ever-present requirement to carry "papers" in authoritarian regimes—and the resentment of the ubiquitous demand to produce them. Such registration papers became symbols of dominance and resistance in

---

36. Kenneth G. Hoglund, "Achaemenid Imperial Administration in Syria-Palestine and the Missions of Ezra and Nehemiah," 1989, 351. Although now published (same title, SBLDS 125 [Atlanta: Scholars, 1992]), I used Hoglund's dissertation for this study, for which I am grateful to him. Beyond Hoglund, also see Kuhrt, "Cyrus Cylinder"; and van der Spek, "Did Cyrus."

37. Hoglund, "Achaemenid Imperial Administration," 433.

38. This is emphasized by Tamara Eskenazi: "Instead of dismissing this characteristic as a clumsy splicing job, we must recognize it as one of the book's central themes: Ezra-Nehemiah is a book of documents . . . they demonstrate the power or propriety of documents as causative principles and significant forces in human events. The ultimate power behind the documents . . . is God. But God's messages, in Ezra-Nehemiah, are transcribed by divinely appointed human subjects . . . into writings which become the definitive forces in the unfolding reality" (Tamara Cohn Eskenazi, *In an Age of Prose: A Literary Approach to Ezra-Nehemiah*, SBLMS 36 [Atlanta: Scholars, 1988] 41–42).

39. The question of dating this material would take us deep into another argument. Suffice it to say at this point that an "oral stage" of the Daniel and Esther stories has been argued

campaigns such as Mahatma Gandhi's early symbolic act of burning the registration cards that were required of Asians in South Africa in 1906.[40] In his classic analysis of confinement, Erving Goffman mentions aspects of what I have called a Persian-induced "culture of permission": "One of the most telling ways in which one's economy of action can be disrupted is the obligation to request permission or supplies for minor activities that one can execute on one's own on the outside."[41] Furthermore, "total institutions disrupt or defile precisely those actions that in civil society have the role of attesting . . . that he is a person with 'adult' self-determination, autonomy, and freedom of action."[42]

My thinking about the royal correspondence in Ezra 1–7 was further inspired by interviews conducted in Los Angeles with Japanese Americans who were internees during World War II. In these conversations, I was struck by the frequent mention of letters of permission allowing these men to leave the camps and travel within the United States on personal or educational business. When I asked them what their attitude toward these letters was, they uniformly expressed gratitude and appreciation—but then made an intriguing reference to the contempt that their children felt for these same documents of permission. For the children, these letters were insulting documents that "permitted Americans to be citizens of their own country." One thinks immediately of the phrase in Neh 9:36, which has Ezra saying: "Here we are, slaves to this day—slaves in the land that you gave to our ancestors." In short, attitudes toward these documents differ radically between those who originally carried them and those who stand and read them in the Japanese-American Museum of Los Angeles.

With this in mind, rereading the entire set of letters gives an interesting impression. Simply to note the appearance of the term *decree* in these letters, and elsewhere in the Bible, is immediately revealing. The term appears forty-two times in the Old Testament (NRSV) (typically $t^e\bar{e}m$ or $pitg\bar{a}m$), of which fourteen occur in Ezra 1–7, an additional nine in Esther,

in some detail by Ernst Haag and Lawrence Wills; and establishing the earlier forms of Ezra and Nehemiah, but especially Nehemiah, is a central task of Ulrich Kellerman's important monograph, *Nehemia: Quellen, Überlieferung und Geschichte*, BZAW 102 (Berlin: Töpelmann, 1967).

40. For the purposes of this study, I refer to Louis Fischer's more popular work, *The Life of Mahatma Gandhi* (New York: Harper, 1950).

41. Erving Goffman, *Asylums: Essays on the Social Situation of Mental Patients and Other Inmates* (Chicago: Aldine, 1961). Goffman also cites Gresham Sykes, *The Society of Captives* (Princeton: Princeton Univ. Press, 1958); Elie Cohen, *Human Behaviour in the Concentration Camp* (London: Grosset & Dunlap, 1953); and Eugen Kogon, *The Theory and Practice of Hell: The German Concentration Camps and the System behind Them*, trans. H. Norden (London: Secker & Warburg, 1950).

42. Goffman, *Asylums*, 43.

and nine in Daniel 1–6. The vast majority of these (thirty-two instances) are commands of foreign emperors dealing with the Jewish minority. The terms translated into English as "decree" in Ezra-Nehemiah, Daniel, and Esther are loanwords from the political and administrative vocabulary of Imperial Aramaic. This is hardly surprising, since minorities quickly learn words like "police," "immigration authorities," "papers," "command," "order," and "authorized." But what do these "decrees" do? Clearly, they largely control the life of the rebuilding community.

The Jewish community is trapped by the competing claims to authority made by the local non-Jewish officials and the Persian court ("Who gave you a decree to build this house?" Ezra 5:3). The correspondence itself does not involve the Jewish community, but takes place, as it were, "over their heads," between the local authorities and the central Persian administration. These local non-Jewish leaders tell the Persian court, "We also asked them their names, for your information" (Ezra 5:10). The implied threat is obvious. The books exhibit a heightened consciousness of a people not in control of their own lives: "I, Darius, make a decree," "You are permitted to go to Jerusalem," "I decree that any of the people . . . ," and so on. The Jewish community must appeal to the Persian court for permission at every turn, although they attempt to ease the sting by referring constantly to prophetic authority as important before mentioning Persian authority.

Given this sociological context, a consideration of some of the editorial insertions surrounding the correspondence should serve to illustrate the ambiguity of the Jewish attitude toward the Persian ruler and warn us against hasty assumptions about positive implications. As examples, consider the following four rhetorical devices.

1. *God "stirred" the heart of the Persian official.* Already in Ezra 1:1, it is stated that the Lord "stirred" the heart of King Cyrus. Too much, and too little, can be made of this. The term certainly does not suggest a special relationship with Cyrus; rather, it is merely a conventionalized manner of speaking of God's ultimate control even of enemies. (The same Hiphil form of the verb "to stir" is found in 1 Chron 5:26, where Tiglath-Pileser III's heart is "stirred" by God, and in Isa 19:2, where Egyptians are "stirred" against Egyptians. David wonders why Saul's heart is "stirred" against him in 1 Sam 26:19, and Ezra 4:15 speaks of sedition being "stirred up" in the city of Jerusalem.)

2. *The authority of Haggai and Zechariah.* In Ezra 5:1-2, and in reference to the temple work in 6:14, the prophetic authority of Haggai and Zechariah is specifically mentioned before recognizing any authority of the Persian rulers. The indication seems to be that for the exilic community, the true authorities are the prophets, and the Persian

monarch is secondary. Indeed, after a lengthy demonstration of the power of the emperor to allow the temple construction to get underway, it seems a bit ungrateful to suggest that the elders of the Jews "prospered through the prophesying of the prophet Haggai and Zechariah" (Ezra 6:14; cf. 5:1-2). Furthermore, attention to the rebuilding of the temple as a theme in both Haggai and Zechariah should not distract us from the strongly independent, if not nationalist, language used in both prophets. Haggai refers to God's plan to "overthrow the throne of kingdoms; I am about to destroy the strength of the kingdoms of the nations." This is followed by the historically significant allusion to God's overthrowing "the chariots and their riders; and the horses and their riders" (Hag 2:22). Zechariah, too, may refer to punishment of the nations that caused the exile rather than the Persians (2:8, "the nations that plundered you"), but the implications of the rise of Jerusalem's notoriety and majesty, though peaceful, are surely the reduction in importance of other nations and peoples (as in Zechariah 14).

3. *To stand before the king.* Far too little attention has been paid to the fact that the opening sequence of the Nehemiah stories—namely, Nehemiah's relationship with the Persian monarch—sounds very much like the folklore tradition of "the Jew in the court of the foreign ruler," and ought to be compared to the Persian period folklore of Esther, Daniel, and probably Joseph. Yet rarely do scholars of Nehemiah question the historicity of Nehemiah's official standing, while radically doubting the historicity of the tales of Daniel, Esther, and Joseph. But if we do read Nehemiah in the light of Persian period folklore motifs, some interesting aspects of the story come into clearer focus.

For example, note the frequency with which the narrators of Persian period stories emphasize the significance of "standing before" the foreign king. In Dan 1:5 and 19 the appearances before the king are the frame scenes for the story as a whole. In Dan 2:2 Nebuchadnezzar's advisers come into his presence and *stand before the king* before the Jewish resisters are introduced. These resisters "stand" rather than bow before the image of the king. Similarly, in Dan 10:11-12 Daniel is to stand before God's messenger. Furthermore, Esther and Mordecai (who "stands" rather than bows before Haman), as well as Ezra and Nehemiah, had their turn to "stand before the king." These scenes are dramatic and crucial. Rarely do these figures "stand before" some lower official (which would more likely have been the case, historically).[43] That these scenes are significant is

43. There are some "standing before the king" scenes in the Deuteronomistic History (note 1 Kgs 1:28, Bathsheba called to stand before the king; 3:16, two prostitutes stand before the king; in 18:15 Elijah points out that he stands before God (rather than merely the king?);

clearer when compared to the mention of "bowing" or (as the NRSV translates it) "doing obeisance," which is more common in the Deuteronomistic History (1 Sam 24:8; 28:4; 2 Sam 1:2; 9:6, 8; 14:4, 22, 33, etc.). The point is that these are dramatic moments precisely because they would incite great fear in the hearers of the story.

Both the Ezra and Nehemiah stories include significant appearances before the king. In the Nehemiah text, the supposed relationship of Nehemiah to the king should not distract us from the language in Neh 2:2, Nehemiah is "very much afraid." Fear of the authorities and their opposition appears in 4:8 (Eng. 14), and Nehemiah's own fear of local opposition is mentioned in 6:14, 16. The fear of the king is mentioned in Dan 1:10. Nehemiah is granted "mercy" before "this man."[44] The term for "mercy" is found also in 1 Kgs 8:50; 2 Chron 30:9; Ps 106:46; and Dan 1:9 in cases of God's assurance before intimidating power. We ought to remind ourselves, also, that if Nehemiah was some kind of a wine taster in the story, then the Persian monarch's concern with the appearance of Nehemiah may have been motivated by self-interest rather than any concern for his Jewish servant. The monarch "honors" Nehemiah by placing this foreigner in a clearly expendable position.

When, in Ezra 7, the letter from Artaxerxes is completed, there is a significant response on the part of the writer (vv. 27-28) that is frequently taken to indicate the favorable attitude of the Jews toward the Persian monarch. See Blenkinsopp, for example: "we note once again the theme of the benevolence of the Persian kings."[45] Hugh Williamson states that this reaction is one of "praise and thanksgiving."[46] On the other hand, Wilhelm Rudolph commented on a certain "characteristic" attitude of Ezra, who spontaneously broke into thanks at hearing the orders of Artaxerxes, but his thanks are directed to God rather than the king, who was, after all, simply influenced by God's power.[47]

Rudolph's comment points in an interesting direction. I would argue further that, especially in the Ezra material, a more forceful picture emerges from a consideration of this passage. In Ezra, as in other post-

note also 17:1. Elisha says the same in 2 Kgs 3:14. In the narratives, it is more typical to mention that someone was "before" the king (no mention of standing), or simply going to the king, with no court scene mentioned at all.

44. Blenkinsopp wonders if the use of "this man," is a slightly pejorative term (*Ezra-Nehemiah*, OTL [Philadelphia: Westminster, 1988] 210). Kellerman, however, compares it to other uses of courtroom language where one imagines a gesture toward the person being accused (*Nehemia*, 8, 11).

45. Blenkinsopp, *Ezra-Nehemiah*, 160.

46. Williamson, *Ezra, Nehemiah*, WBC (Waco, Tex.: Word, 1985) 105.

47. Rudolph, *Esra und Nehemia*, HAT 20 (Tübingen: Mohr/Siebeck, 1949) 77.

exilic works, we are invited to picture the lowly exile (always introduced as a member of the minority Jewish race) standing before the majestic presence of the Persian monarch: "Blessed be the Lord, the God of our ancestors, who put such a thing as this into the heart of the king to glorify the house of the Lord in Jerusalem, and who extended to me steadfast love before the king and his counselors, and before all the king's mighty officers. I took courage, for the hand of the Lord my God was upon me" (Ezra 7:27-28a).

Three elements of this passage are worthy of note. First, briefly, that Ezra was protected by "the hand of God" is an aspect of the Ezra narrative material that we encounter in other places, especially in 8:22-24, where God's hand protects Ezra from enemies (!), and seems an interesting version of the Deuteronomistic phrase referring to God's "mighty hand and outstretched arm" (e.g., Deut 4:34; 5:15; 7:19; 11:2; 26:8; 2 Kgs 17:36; cf. Neh 2:8).

Second, Ezra "took courage." This may simply be a manner of speaking about "being encouraged," of having one's spirits lifted. But it can easily be a more serious matter, suggesting that God "strengthened" Ezra during a life-threatening encounter. After all, the Hithpael (reflexive) form of $\d{h}zq$, "to be empowered," is often used in preparation for warfare, particularly in late Hebrew sources. In 2 Chron 15:7 Asa is to "take courage" in a time of danger (note the similarity of 15:2 and Ezra 8:22-24). In 2 Chron 23:1 Jehoida "takes courage" as preparation for battle, and similarly with Amaziah in 25:11 (so also 2 Chron 19:13). Israel is to "take courage" because of their near relief in Isa 41:6-7. In short, such a phrase is indeed curious if Ezra was to appear before a sympathetic, enlightened Persian ruler. More likely, he feared for his life (note the specific mention of the "mighty officers" in the king's presence). The military imagery that the narrator uses suggests a form of "spiritual warfare" against an enemy that is feared.

Third, Ezra was the object of ḥesed, which is typically translated as "steadfast love."[48] In Psalms 118, 106, 107, and especially in 136, note that ḥesed is the particular power of God to deliver Israel from their enemies (also Ps 143). The shout of praise for God's ḥesed is associated with the miraculous defeat of enemies in 2 Chron 20:21, which is also associated (by the act of fasting) with God's deliverance from enemies in Ezra 8:21-23.[49] Similarly, in Dan 1:9 God made Daniel the object of ḥesed and mercy

48. Katherine Doob Sakenfeld, The Meaning of Ḥesed in the Hebrew Bible: A New Inquiry, HSM 17 (Missoula, Mont.: Scholars, 1978) 233.

49. My study on fasting and its military associations in this material appears as "Hebrew Satyagraha: The Politics of Biblical Fasting in the Post-Exilic Period," Food and Foodways: An Interdisciplinary Journal (1993) 5:3, 269–92.

before the head of the eunuchs. An analysis of the militant use of *ḥesed* in the context of Ezra's (and, in a similar phrase, "mercy" in Neh 1:11) appearance before the Persian monarch forces one to conclude that the passage assumes the necessity for God's delivering action against an enemy. That the result was the king's permission should not minimize the implied spiritual warfare in the Ezra passage. Praise was directed to God's delivering power, not to the Persian monarch's good intentions.

4. *"We are slaves."* Finally, in both Ezra 9:7-8 and Nehemiah 9, the editors have Ezra referring to the condition of the Jews as "slavery." So startlingly abrupt is Neh 9:36-37, with its complaint of the burden of Persian taxation and its mention of enslavement, that many modern scholars place this entire prayer into a later era than the rest of Ezra-Nehemiah. Hoglund, for example, suggests: "It is this enhanced control and domination of the community that resulted in the anti-Persian sentiments scattered throughout the narratives of Ezra-Nehemiah. The author . . . holds the empire responsible for the sense of powerlessness that pervades the community."[50] Thus, when taking on the idea that the missions of Ezra and Nehemiah were intended to induce loyalty in the Jewish community, Hoglund dryly comments, in reference to Ezra 9:8-9 and Neh 9:36-37: "If the missions of Ezra and Nehemiah were commissioned by the Achaeminid court to induce loyalty in Yehud, the narratives of Ezra-Nehemiah suggest that the reformers themselves were unaware of this goal . . . [texts such as Ezra 9:8-9 and Neh 9:36-37] hardly seem conducive to engendering greater loyalty toward the empire."[51] As noted, Blenkinsopp also leans toward a reassessment of the Persian policies:

> In spite of the pro-Persian sentiments in Isa 40–48 and favorable allusions to the Persians' providential role in Ezra-Nehemiah, there is no reason to believe that their rule was significantly more benign than that of their Semitic predecessors. The allusion to military conscription, forced labor, and the requisitioning of livestock recall references elsewhere to the heavy burden of taxation during the early Persian period (Ezra 4:13; 7:24; Neh 5:4). One of the worst aspects of imperial policy under the Achaemenids was the draining away of local resources from the provinces to finance the imperial court, the building of magnificent palaces, and the interminable succession of campaigns of pacification or conquest. . . . The prayer is therefore, by

50. Hoglund, "Achaeminid Imperial Administration," 436.
51. Ibid., 144.

implication, an aspiration toward political emancipation as a necessary precondition for the fulfillment of the promises.[52]

Summary: Ezra-Nehemiah, Religious Resistance, and Persian Authorization?

The arguments presented here may not be convincing when considered in isolation—no one nuance or phrase serves clearly to establish a hostile attitude toward Persian rulers. Taken as a whole, however, these arguments lead me to conclude that the attitude of the editors of Ezra-Nehemiah toward their Persian overlords is neither gratitude nor warmth. Their attitude is both the realistic assessment of forced subservience, and in response, a faithful nonviolent resistance to any idea that Persian power or authority is greater than God's spiritual armament of the faithful. Thus, the editors of Ezra-Nehemiah represent a subversive theology, a hidden transcript, that reserves recognition of authority to God alone, while maintaining a necessarily polite demeanor to the imperial representatives.

The Myth of the Empty Land: Doubts about the Exile

Other debates have centered on our ability (or inability) to write with much confidence about the exile at all. A frequent (and accomplished) participant in discussions that express serious skepticism about modern attempts to reconstruct history from biblical texts, Lester Grabbe is nonetheless among the few scholars who have recently hazarded an attempt to write a history of the Babylonian exile.[53] It is an interesting comparison to read Ackroyd's older classic, *Exile and Restoration,* which offered a confident rehearsal of historical events based largely on the Bible, and Grabbe's far more tentative and careful attempt to risk a few guesses about what might have happened. Consider the apologia given at the conclusion of his recent examination of the question of whether biblical history can be written at all: "In many periods of history, we often do not have enough information to come to certain conclusions. Our reconstructions may be tentative at best; our actual work will be relativistic. . . . In that

---

52. Blenkinsopp, *Ezra-Nehemiah,* 307–8.

53. Lester L. Grabbe, *Judaism from Cyrus to Hadrian,* 2 vols. (Minneapolis: Fortress Press, 1991); and also his work *An Introduction to First Century Judaism: Jewish Religion and History in the Second Temple Period* (Edinburgh: T. & T. Clark, 1996).

case, the historian is best described as a juggler. The secret is to keep as many balls as possible in the air at once without dropping any."[54] I believe that more can be said than Grabbe is confident with saying, just as more biblical texts need to be now read under a critically informed social analysis of exilic events than Ackroyd thought were relevant. This is because I am interested not only in what biblical and nonbiblical evidence there is for exilic events, but also in making observations that may assist us in assessing the *significance* of these events. It is this last notion that has become problematic in recent biblical discussion, particularly in the debates and discussions that frequently cite the work of Hans Barstad, *The Myth of the Empty Land*. Since this debate, too, has implications for our ability to speak of exilic events, it is important to summarize this work as well.

Barstad's 1996 work has provided grist for the mill in a number of discussions that attempt to assess (and often dismiss) the actual significance of the events brought about by Nebuchadnezzar's military actions along the Mediterranean coast in the late seventh and early sixth centuries BCE. Barstad's short monograph has one central point that seems valid in and of itself, but the further, elaborated conclusions that he draws from his main argument are problematic.

In my view, Barstad's central point amounts to a restatement of Enno Janssen's views in his 1956 monograph, *Juda in der Exilzeit*.[55] Janssen had maintained that there was an important community that carried on in Judah after the events of 597–587 BCE, and that the Chronicler's use of the image of the land being "emptied" was an exaggeration that may well be part of an ideological prejudice of the exiled communities against those who were left behind. Part of the motivation may have been the claiming of certain property and economic rights as a result of their continued existence in the land. As Barstad argues, the biblical mentality of a humiliation of Judah led to the belief that Palestine was "completely depopulated and in ruins."[56] This can be seriously questioned as an accurate picture of Palestine after 586. So far, so good.

Can we, however, make reliable judgments about the size and vitality of the community back in Judah based on some notion of the literary quality of their writing? Believing that we can, Barstad points out that "no

---

54. Grabbe, "Introduction," in *Can a History of Israel Be Written?* ed. L. L. Grabbe, European Seminar in Historical Methodology 1, JSOTSup 245 (Sheffield: Sheffield Academic, 1997) 36. See also Grabbe, *Judaism from Cyrus to Hadrian*.

55. Enno Jannsen, *Juda in der Exilzeit*, FRLANT 69 (Göttingen: Vandenhoeck & Ruprecht, 1956).

56. Hans Barstad, *The Myth of the Empty Land: A Study in the History and Archaeology of Judah during the "Exilic" Period*, Symbolae Osloenses 28 (Oslo: Scandinavian Univ. Press, 1996) 20.

one, to my knowledge, has ever disputed either the fact that Lamentations represents outstanding literary quality, or that it is a product of Palestine. When we find that poetry of such high quality as Lamentations was actually produced in Judah after the disaster of 586, there is no reason whatsoever why similar poetry or other kinds of texts could not likewise have been written during the exilic period."[57]

But how can we laud the *quality* of the poetry and ignore the *subject* of that poetry? The poetry of Lamentations is about horrific devastation, yet because it is well written, are we to assume that the destruction described must not have been that bad? Barstad seems to argue precisely this: "We should keep in mind that we are dealing with a small, basically agricultural society, in a Mediterranean climate. With life going back to normal fairly soon, it would represent a fatal misunderstanding of how ancient agricultural societies functioned to perceive any fundamental changes in every life or culture."[58] Is Barstad correct? Did life carry on, as he says, in "much the same way" as before? In a recent public forum, Schniedewind briefly reviewed the wealth of archaeological evidence that starkly contradicts Barstad's assumptions of "normal life" after 587 BCE: "The end of the Davidic monarchy and the destruction and pillaging of the Jerusalem Temple alone suggests that all the basic organizations did not continue in 'much the same way.' Certainly government and religious institutions did not continue in 'much the same way.' . . . In the seventh century, at the end of the monarchy, there are at least 116 sites in Judah (cities, towns, and villages). In the 6th century (in the Babylonian Period) the number drops to 41 sites. . . . 92 of the 116 sites of the monarchic period were abandoned in the Babylonian Period."[59]

The data continue to be damaging to Barstad's thesis. Eighty percent of the cities, towns, and villages were abandoned or destroyed in the sixth century, and 42 percent of the towns and villages of the Persian period were on previously unsettled sites. Schniedewind also pointed out that "there is a steep drop in the number of public works, luxury items, and writing. . . . In the last days of the Judean monarchy, we have a relatively densely populated, economically prosperous urban state. This picture radically changes in the Babylonian period. . . . So did life continue in

57. Ibid.
58. Ibid., 43.
59. William Schniedewind, "In Search of the Exile," 4-5, SBL annual meeting, Boston, 1999. I would like to thank Schniedewind for providing me with copies of his presentation, which drew heavily, and with appreciation, on the work of David W. Jamieson-Drake, *Scribes and Schools in Monarchic Judah: A Socio-Archeological Approach*, JSOTSup 109 (Sheffield: Almond, 1991).

'much the same way'? I think not."[60] In his recent survey, Ephraim Stern is direct and clear in reference to archaeological evidence: "The Babylonian conquest clearly brought total destruction to Jerusalem and the Judean Hill sites to the south of Jerusalem."[61]

Barstad argues that the continued production of certain exportable commodities after 587 BCE (Barstad cites olive oil and wine) can be taken as "continuity" of a presumably healthy economy. But without information as to who received the results and economic benefits of such continued production—the indigenous population, or the occupying power—this observation means very little. Indeed, the famous prayer in Neh 9:36-37 strongly suggests otherwise: "Here we are, slaves to this day—slaves in the land that you gave to our ancestors to enjoy its fruit and its good gifts. *Its rich yield goes to the kings whom you have set over us* because of our sins; they have power also over our bodies and over our livestock at their pleasure, and we are in great distress" (my emphasis). However, how much economic production did continue?

In his recent overview of Neo-Babylonian policies toward their western regions, David Vanderhooft replies to what he called the "deeply flawed" thesis of Barstad: "The material culture of Judah and adjacent regions in the first half of the sixth century points to a sharp contraction in demographic terms and to reduced economic activity, signaled, for instance, by the virtual disappearance of Greek ceramics. This evidence for a massive disjunction can hardly sustain the argument that the Babylonians under Nabuchadnezzar implemented a rational economic policy for exploiting a provincialized Judah. . . . Some people remained in Judah after 582 . . . [but] the evidence for Babylonian destruction of cities and towns in Judah and adjacent regions is overwhelming."[62] Indeed, Vanderhooft simply does not believe that there is evidence of much Babylonian interest in the western regions. He disputes that there was any serious provincial administration in place in this region, partly resulting from Nebuchadnezzar's rather brutal policies for dealing with Egyptian incursions into this area between 605 and 601. The emperor "considered the economic viability of the region secondary to the imperative of pushing the Egyptians out by razing their client cities. Such a polity had another benefit for the Babylonians: it eliminated the necessary expense of

60. Schniedewind, "In Search of Exile," 6.

61. Ephraim Stern, *Archaeology of the Land of the Bible*, vol. 2: *The Assyrian, Babylonian, and Persian Periods, 732–332 BCE*, ABRL (New York: Doubleday, 2001) 323.

62. David Stephen Vanderhooft, *The Neo-Babylonian Empire and Babylon in the Latter Prophets*, HSM 59 (Atlanta: Scholars, 1999) 106.

installing garrisons in this distant region to patrol the southern border."[63] Ultimately, then, any attempt to reduce the impact of the exilic events on the life of the Hebrew people founders on the evidence.

But Barstad's work contains not only a consistent attempt to minimize the tragedy of Babylonian hegemony, but quite unexpectedly goes so far as to ask for an odd sympathy for the imperial problems of a Nebuchadnezzar:

> When reading the commentators on the biblical texts relating to these events, one sometimes gets the Sunday school feeling that they regard the Babylonians as an evil people who came to destroy the true believers in Judah out of sheer wickedness, and that the bringing of Judeans into exile was a mean punishment or base revenge following the uprising of the Judean king. It is high time that we start thinking about the whole matter from a rather different perspective. The Neo-Babylonian empire represented a highly developed civilization, with an advanced political and economic structure. . . . Having no natural resources of its own, the whole existence of the empire depended entirely upon the import of materials like metals, stone, and timber, and all sorts of food and luxury items.[64]

It would be hard to imagine a perspective more at variance with the theses proposed in the present work, as I hope will be clear in the summary of scholarly work that follows.

The Shadow of Empire: A Survey of Recent Literature

What was the nature of imperial economics in the ancient Near East? A survey of recent historical analyses of ancient Near Eastern regimes is enlightening. With regard to the Neo-Babylonian policies under Nebuchadnezzar, Vanderhooft writes of the "brute facts of subjugation" and surmises that Nebuchadnezzar's western ventures had monetary motivations as well: "The procedure of funneling resources from the subject populations of the empire to the heartland through seizure and exaction was no less important to the Babylonians than it had been to the Assyrians, and the massive building projects of the Neo-Babylonians, and those of Nebuchadnezzar II in particular, indicate how well these practices were refined in the sixth century. Nebuchadnezzar campaigned almost yearly

63. Ibid., 83.
64. Barstad, *Myth of the Empty Land*, 63–64.

in the west, in part to insure order, but also to fill the royal coffers."[65] On this there is an interesting consensus of critical opinion in regard to the social and economic goals of ancient Near Eastern empires. See, for example, Gerdien Jonker on the Neo-Assyrian Empire:

> In the first part of the first millennium the surrounding lands, including Babylonia, were terrorized by the Assyrians. Their diplomatic policy of "peace" involved deportation and demolition. . . . Deportations totally disrupted life in the inhabited world in the first millennium. It was not enough for the conquerors to raze every sign of human habitation to the ground, not enough to cut down the trees and burn the crops in what today would be described as a scorched-earth policy; they disinterred the dead and denuded the earth by removing the fertile topsoil, loading it on to carts and taking it back home with the expressed aim of ensuring that, ". . . their name and that of the descendants, their remains and those of their offspring, should no longer be on the lips of humanity." We know of 157 mass deportations undertaken by Assyrian dictators, by means of which they intended to do their utmost to eradicate any traces of the memory of their opponents; they were not content "until nothing remained."[66]

Mogens Larsen summarizes the central goal of the Assyrian Empire: "a huge military and administrative apparatus designed to secure a constant flow of goods from the periphery to the center."[67]

Finally, in his fascinating monograph on *Siege in Ancient Warfare*, Paul Kern has tersely summarized the role of warfare in the Assyrian economy:

> Much of the organization of the Assyrian Empire came to depend on a military system that could provide the resources necessary to sustain the Empire. Military campaigns not only served to protect and expand the empire, but they also augmented its material and human resources. Money to fill the royal treasury and support the temples came from the tribute the Assyrians imposed on the cities of its expanding empire. . . . Manpower for the army, horses for the cavalry, and scarce goods such as precious metals also flowed into Assyria through this system. . . . The general prosperity of the Assyr-

---

65. Vanderhooft, *Neo-Babylonian Empire*, 61–114.

66. Gerdien Jonker, *The Topography of Remembrance: The Dead, Tradition, and Collective Memory in Mesopotamia*, Studies in the History of Religions 68 (Leiden: Brill, 1995) 47–48.

67. Mogens Larsen, "The Tradition of Empire in Mesopotamia," in *Power and Propaganda: A Symposium on Ancient Empires*, ed. M. Larsen, Mesopotamia: Copenhagen Studies in Assyriology 7 (Copenhagen: Akademisk Forlag, 1979) 100.

ian people also depended on this system. Soldiers carried the booty they had seized in conquered towns back to Assyria, where it enriched the general economy of Assyria.[68]

The propaganda and ideological supports for these policies in Assyrian inscriptional evidence are equally clear. According to Jonker, "The Neo-Assyrian kings legitimized the only sort of contact that they felt justified in developing with neighboring countries, namely their policies of conquest and deportation, by referring to the historical Sargon. The theatre of the past was formed by the memory of the supremacy of Akkad and of the achievements of its legendary kings."[69] Finally, Mario Liverani points out that the main recipients of the Assyrian propaganda were the Assyrian masses themselves: "It is essential to get the instruments of imperialism to be efficient, self-convinced and enthusiastic, as if they were working in their own interest against the foreigners, whilst in fact they are working with the foreigners to the advantage of the ruling class."[70]

Barstad spoke of a "highly sophisticated culture" of the Neo-Babylonian Empire, whose emperor apparently needed more "lebensraum." But recent assessments of the Chaldean Empire are similar to those offered for their brutal Assyrian forebears.[71] Amélie Kuhrt, for example, notes: "The most spectacular evidence of Nebuchadnezzar's extraordinary military successes can be found in the remains of his building-works in Babylonia. All the great old cities were extensively rebuilt, their shrines repaired and beautified. Most notable in this massive effort at reconstruction is the development of Babylon into the immense and beautiful city of legend. . . . The many lengthy, royal inscriptions and stamped bricks show that most of this building was the work of Nebuchadnezzar during his long reign of forty-three years (605–562)."[72]

But at what human cost? Writing of "The Fury of Babylon," Lawrence Stager summarizes the scorched-earth policy of the Neo-Babylonian Empire as evident in the remains of Ashkelon: "Archaeology cannot be so precise as to date the destruction of Ashkelon to 604 BCE, but the

---

68. Paul Bentley Kern, *Ancient Siege Warfare* (Bloomington: Indiana Univ. Press, 1999) 58.

69. Jonker, *Topography*, 63.

70. Mario Liverani, "The Ideology of the Assyrian Empire," in *Power and Propaganda*, 297–317.

71. On the similarity of Neo-Assyrian and Neo-Babylonian tactics and policies, see Stern, *Archaeology*, vol. 2, 309.

72. Amélie Kuhrt, *The Ancient Near East*, vol. 2: *From c. 1200 BC to c. 330 BC*, Routledge History of the Ancient World (London: Routledge, 1995) 593.

Babylonian Chronicle leaves little doubt that the late seventh-century destruction we found all over the site, followed by a 75-80 year gap in occupation until the Persian period, was the work of Nebuchadnezzar in 604 BCE."[73] Stager observed that Nebuchadnezzar's policy created "a veritable wasteland west of the Jordan River," and then notes evidence of fiery destruction, and even—in a sentence that holds a moment of human tragedy frozen in time—the remains of a woman whose skull reveals that she died by being clubbed to death. So much for the imperial administration of central Mesopotamian warlords.

The claim is often made that the Persians were far more humane. Were the Jewish diaspora communities better off under the Achaemenid administrations? Matthew Stolper's analysis of the Murashû archive is suggestive: "In both . . . tenure and commercial practice, Achaemenid administration put new faces on old patterns. The Murasu texts point to some results of this policy: a tendency toward concentration of wealth, and a tendency toward relative impoverishment at the lowest ranks of the state-controlled agricultural sector, despite indications of overall prosperity in the province."[74] The Persian "economy" was essentially a system designed to horde precious metals. Alexander was apparently stunned by the amounts of bullion he found stashed at Susa, Ecbatana, and Persepolis, but it can hardly be said that the Persian or the Hellenistic rulers were interested in encouraging business or spreading wealth among the populace. The rare comment from standard histories of the Persian Empire on matters of economics are interesting. For example, Richard Frye states:

> Taxes . . . abounded in the Achaemenid empire. It seems there were harbour fees, market taxes, tolls on gates and roads and frontiers of various kinds, a tax on domestic animals, perhaps ten per cent, and other taxes as well. Gifts were received by the king on New Year's day, and when he travelled extra hardships were placed on the population. Most of these gifts and sundry taxes, were mainly paid in kind rather than specie. Corvée labour, for roads, public buildings and the like, was employed extensively by satraps as well as the king. So life for the common person must have been at times oppressive. The local public works were probably financed by local taxes, while gold and silver streamed into the king's coffers.[75]

73. Lawrence Stager, "The Fury of Babylon: Ashkelon and the Archaeology of Destruction," *BAR* 22.1 (1996) 69.

74. Matthew Stolper, *Entrepreneurs and Empire: The Murāšû Archive, the Murāšû Firm, and Persian Rule in Babylonia,* Uitgaren rau het Nederlands Historisch-Archaeologisch Instituut te Istanbul (Leiden: Brill, 1985) 154.

75. Richard Frye, *The Heritage of Persia* (London: Weidenfeld & Nicolson, 1962) 114–15.

J. M. Cook adds: "Labour and production in Persis were organized on a huge scale by the central administration in a way that would seem to leave relatively little scope for what we should call modest private enterprise. . . . Sheep raising was also organized on a large scale. The Persians' criticism of Darius that he made a business of everything is not belied by the evidence from the one province of the empire that in theory was not subject."[76] Finally, I note Peter Green's significant observations about the Hellenistic period under the Ptolemies and Seleucids: "one central fact conditioned the conduct, outlook, and administration of both the Ptolemaic and Seleucid dynasties for the entire course of their existence: they treated the territories they controlled, however they might assign them, as royal estates."[77]

The point was to facilitate the gathering of enormous amounts of precious metals in the treasuries of the rulers who would provide the occasional public displays, but who usually maintained large armies of mercenaries to ensure the constant flow of goods. Green further summarizes: "To take your own superiority for granted does not necessarily, or even commonly, imply that you are altruistically eager to give others the benefit of it, especially when you are busy conquering their territory, exploiting their natural resources and manpower, taxing their citizens, imposing your government on them, and unloading their accumulated gold reserves into the international market in the form of military loot. The main, indeed the overwhelming, motivation that confronts us in these Greek or Macedonian torchbearers of Western culture, throughout the Hellenistic era, is the irresistible twin lure of power and wealth, with sex trailing along as a poor third and cultural enlightenment virtually nowhere."[78] Green describes Antiochene tastes for excess: "The same kind of ostentation as Ptolemy II had affected was clearly a crowd-pleaser in Antioch, too. We find the same thousands of extras with gold shields and crowns, the same horses and elephants and ivory tusks, the gold jars of saffron ointment, the twelve-pound silver dishes, the thousand-table banquets, gigantism and vulgarity triumphant."[79]

The point is simply this: irrespective of the very real differences between the political and ideological regimes from before 587 BCE until, and after, 164 BCE, we must always attend to the stubborn similarities of

76. J. M. Cook, *The Persian Empire* (New York: Shocken, 1983) 89–90.

77. Peter Green, *Alexander to Actium: The Historical Evolution of the Hellenistic Age* (Los Angeles: Univ. of California Press, 1990) 157, quoting A. T. Olmstead, *History of the Persian Empire: Achaemenid Period* (Chicago: Univ. of Chicago Press, 1948) 297–99.

78. Green, *Alexander to Actium*, 187.

79. Ibid., 386.

ancient imperial designs toward power and control over wealth, territory, and human resources. On this, there appears to have been little diversity in practice and results.

A Theology of Victims of Exile

In writing about the exile, I chose to write from the perspective of an empathy, if not open sympathy, with the attempts of refugee Hebrews to rebuild a social life from the pieces left by the Chaldean militias of the sixth century, the Persian militias of the fifth and fourth centuries, the Hellenistic phalanxes of the third and second centuries, and so on. Interestingly, in his monograph on ancient siege warfare, Kern also notes that as a historian, he does not wish to forget the horrific realities of his subject:

> Although I have tried to avoid exaggerations, I confess that I have endeavored to arouse the pity of my readers for the women and children caught in siege warfare and that I have found literary sources, most especially the tragic poets, useful for that purpose. Women and children were an essential part of siege warfare. Their presence threatened the notion of war as a contest between warriors, undermined the conventional standards of honor and prowess that governed ancient warfare, and paradoxically made war less restrained by creating a morally chaotic cityscape in which not only the walls collapsed but deeply rooted social and moral distinctions as well. We cannot understand siege warfare without understanding the plight of women and children and the effect of their presence on war.[80]

This perspective is not unlike Malkki's criticism of *contemporary* studies of refugee populations, particularly when she notes how often such studies end up implicitly blaming the victims: "They [refugees] are not ordinary people but represent, rather, an anomaly requiring specialized correctives and therapeutic interventions. It is striking how often the abundant literature claiming refugees as its object of study locates 'the problem' not in the political conditions or processes that produce massive territorial displacements of people but within the bodies and minds (and even souls) of people categorized as refugees."[81] How might a reading of exilic events on the side of the victims read?

---

80. Kern, *Ancient Siege Warfare*, 4.
81. Liisa H. Mallki, "National Geographic: The Rooting of Peoples and the Territorializing of National Identity among Scholars and Refugees," in *Culture, Power, and Place: Explorations in Critical Anthropology*, ed. A. Gupta and J. Ferguson (Durham, N.C.: Duke Univ. Press, 1997) 63.

Martin Noth perceptively commented that the Babylonian exile of 587/586 BCE ought to be seen as the final event, or "merely the conclusion of a long historical process," of the fall of the independent states of Israel and Judah in the western sector of the Near East.[82] Even the "rise" of these small states in ancient Palestine, argues Benedikt Otzen, was possible only because of a vacuum of power among the larger warring states after the decline of Egyptian hegemony over Palestine, and until the eventual rise of Neo-Assyrian power followed quickly by Neo-Babylonian usurpation after the rise of the aggressive Chaldean tribes to power.[83] The most significant, and for Israel most ominous, development in the "fall" of the Hebrew states was the reign of Tiglath-Pileser III (745–727). He reformed Assyrian power and organization, including a breakup of governmental units to reduce the threat of local rulers; strengthened the control of the central bureaucracy, and streamlined the process whereby new lands were incorporated into the Neo-Assyrian orbit. By 738 Tiglath-Pileser (known in the Bible by his Babylonian throne name, "Pul") had received tribute from the Syrian states (Hamath, Tyre, Byblos, Damascus) and already from Israel—although Israel would not be openly annexed to Assyrian territory until 722.

According to the biblical traditions, the so-called Syro-Ephraimite War (2 Kings 15–16) brought about the direct interference of Assyrian power in Israel. Pekah of Israel joined Edom and Damascus in an anti-Assyrian coalition and attempted to force Ahaz of Judah to join. Ahaz (2 Kgs 16:5-9) determined that the coalition was futile and appealed for Assyrian assistance. The result of Ahaz's meeting with the Assyrian monarch included Ahaz installing an additional altar in the temple (v. 10). The reference to this altar has invited interesting debate. Some scholars contend that it was not imposed by the Assyrians even though the altar is discussed in the context of a condemnation of Ahaz by the Deuteronomistic Historian (v. 2, "He [Ahaz] did not do what was right in the sight of the Lord his God").

In the northern territories of Israel, Hoshea tried to break free from Assyrian control by appealing to Egypt for assistance (2 Kgs 17:4). The Assyrian response was swift. There is some dispute as to who conquered Samaria in 722: the Assyrian monarch Shalmaneser or Sargon II, who claimed to deport 27,290 people in his conquest of this territory.[84] There

---

82. Martin Noth, *The History of Israel*, trans. P. R. Ackroyd, 2d ed. (New York: Harper & Row, 1960) 289. Oded also begins his analysis of the exile by reviewing the events under the Neo-Assyrian Empire, in *Israelite and Judaean History*, ed. J. H. Hayes and J. M. Miller, OTL (Philadelphia: Westminster, 1977) 435–88.

83. Benedikt Otzen, "Israel under the Assyrians," in *Power and Propaganda*, 251–62.

84. *ANET*, 284.

56 A BIBLICAL THEOLOGY OF EXILE

soon followed a massive upheaval in the population of the northern territories. Archaeological evidence suggests that there were many refugees
who fled south into the kingdom of Judah at this time, but surely many
thousands were deported to other areas of the Assyrian territories.

The fanciful legends surrounding these so-called lost tribes of Israel
contain at least one basic truth—we have no idea what became of those
northern Israelites who were deported. The Bible, as it is, contains no
record of northern, Assyrian exiles (the late book of Tobit is of no historical value in this regard). Furthermore, attention quickly turns in the
Deuteronomistic Historical works to the Assyrian harassment of Judah,
especially given Egypt's attempts to lure some of the smaller states into
their orbit of influence. It is likely that the siege of Jerusalem, when
Hezekiah was king of Judah (2 Kings 18–20) was brought about as a result
of Hezekiah's listening to Egyptian promises of support (and contrary to
the apparent warnings of Isaiah not to trust that "broken reed of a staff,"
Isa 36:6).

Geopolitical circumstances would shift significantly with the rise of
the Chaldean tribes to power in Babylon. Kurt Galling refers to "an
unprecedented rearrangement of circumstances" in the second half of
the sixth century.[85] When Ashurbanipal died, the Babylonians under
Nabopolassar rose in revolt against the northern Assyrians. When the
Medes entered the battle as allies of the Babylonians, the fate of Assyria
was virtually sealed. The Medes began to invade Assyrian territory in 626
BCE, and Nineveh, the capital, fell by 614 (although 612 is also mentioned
by some scholars).

In 609, when the last of the Assyrian armies were stranded in Harran,
Pharaoh Necho II (609–595) attempted to shore up the failing Assyrian
forces (although Mary Gyles reviews the evidence for arguing that Necho
did, in fact, fight the Assyrian forces, rather than assist them[86]). If the biblical account is to be trusted, it is likely that Necho saw the advantages of
a weakened buffer state between Egypt and the rising Neo-Babylonian
Empire, but the expedition failed, and Nebuchadnezzar succeeded in
removing the Assyrians as a factor in future imperial politics. Carchemish, however, was held by the Egyptians, thus blocking Babylonian trade
interests. At the famous battle of Carchemish in 605, Pharaoh Necho's
forces were decimated, and the way was clear for Nebuchadnezzar to proceed southward, perhaps even attempting to enter Egyptian territories as

85. Kurt Galling, *Studien zur Geschichte Israels im persischen Zeitalter* (Tübingen:
Mohr/Siebeck, 1964) 1.
86. Mary Francis Gyles, *Pharaonic Policies and Administration, 663 to 323 BC* (Chapel
Hill, N.C.: Univ. of North Carolina Press, 1959) 27ff.

the Assyrians had earlier done (and as Nebuchadnezzar tried in 601 as well as 568/567).[87]

From 609 to 605, Egypt exercised its control of these narrow land areas by installing its own puppet ruler in Jerusalem, Eliakim, who was given the regnal name Jehoiakim. Citing 2 Kgs 23:35 and Jer 22:13-19, many scholars assume that Jehoiakim's rule was oppressive. When the Egyptians were defeated at Carchemish in 605, their hold on Palestine was permanently weakened, and Nebuchadnezzar was in control. According to 2 Kgs 24:1, Jehoiakim was under Babylonian rule for three years. Nebuchadnezzar, who as the prince had taken control of the army,[88] was involved in numerous campaigns in the west. Ashkelon fell in 604, but in 601 Nebuchadnezzar failed to take Egypt—which may have been the occasion for unrest and even open rebellion in Palestine.[89] In any case, in 600 Nebuchadnezzar was back in Babylon, rallying his armies for another attempt on Egypt.[90] Nebuchadnezzar was able to exercise full control over this area in 598/597, when Jehoiachin, the young son of the Egyptian-installed ruler Jehoiakim, surrendered (D. J. Wiseman comments that the presence of a precise date for the capture of Jerusalem reveals the importance of Jerusalem to the Babylonians[91]).

Nebuchadnezzar's siege of Tyre undoubtedly took place in 598 (although some want to suggest that it was later), and it lasted thirteen years (Ezek 29:17-18). According to Nebuchadnezzar's inscriptions, he appointed in Jerusalem "a king of his liking, took heavy booty from it, and brought it into Babylon."[92] According to 2 Kgs 24:14, the number of exiles taken at this time was 10,000, and then adding in v. 16 the numbers of 7,000 artisans and 1,000 "smiths," in all 18,000. This does not match Jer 52:28, which notes 3,023 persons carried into captivity. Scholars have debated whether this number counts only men; if so, the total numbers of these initial exiles in 597 would have been considerable (15,000-30,000?). Even if the smaller number of Jeremiah (3,023) is accepted, one must still multiply by some kind of average family size. Assyrian sources clearly identify families

---

87. D. J. Wiseman, *Nebuchadrezzar and Babylon,* Schweich Lectures 1983 (Oxford: Oxford Univ. Press, 1985) 28.

88. Ibid., 14. Nebuchadnezzar claims to have "finished them off completely" (ibid., 14–15).

89. Oded, in *Israelite and Judaean History,* ed. Hayes and Miller, 470.

90. This information is provided by the "Wiseman Chronicles" in D. J. Wiseman, *Chronicles of Chaldaean Kings (626–556 B.C.) in the British Museum* (London: Trustees of the British Museum, 1956).

91. Wiseman, *Nebuchadrezzar and Babylon,* 32.

92. *ANET,* 564—thus March 15/16, 597?

accompanying exiles.[93] There is little reason to doubt that Babylonian policies were the same, irrespective of the historical reliability one places in Jeremiah's advice to "marry your sons and daughters" in exile (Jeremiah 29). Kern helpfully summarizes the similar tactics of siege warfare: "it is apparent that all conquerors of cities considered both people and property at their disposal. Looting was universal, massacres or transportation common."[94]

Mattaniah, third son of Josiah, was renamed "Zedekiah" and placed on the throne as a puppet ruler of the Babylonians (further supporting the contention by many scholars that Josiah's line had a definite pro-Babylonian bias. Such a political leaning may partially explain Josiah's campaign to Megiddo in 609 to stop the advance of Pharaoh Necho northward). Jehoiachin himself, recognized by the Deuteronomistic Historian and by Zedekiah as the true ruler, was deported to Babylon. Walther Zimmerli notes Ezek 17:13 as a reference to Jehoiachin's imprisonment: "He took one of the royal offspring and made a covenant with him, putting him under oath (he had taken away the chief men of the land)."[95] Among the more striking archaeological confirmations of biblical historiography was the discovery of a ration list in the ruins of Babylon—a text that mentions Jehoiachin himself.[96] Zedekiah, on the other hand, eventually fell prey to the promises of Hophra, son of Psammetichus II of Egypt, and withheld tribute to Babylon. Tyre may have joined in this resistance (Josephus, *Ant.* 1.21).

The biblical books of Jeremiah and Ezekiel give further evidence for the emergence of political, ideological, and theological splits that were emerging in the Jewish communities with regard to Babylonian rule. Jeremiah 26–29 contains the "prophetic debate" between Jeremiah, a "pro-Babylonian" prophet,[97] and Hananiah, clearly disposed toward Egypt.

93. The best source on the Assyrian deportation practices is B. Oded, *Mass Deportations and Deportees in the Neo-Assyrian Empire* (Wiesbaden: Reichert, 1979). See now also idem, "Observations," in *Immigration and Emigration*, ed. Van Lerberghe and Schoors, 205–12.

94. Kern, *Ancient Siege Warfare*, 25.

95. Walther Zimmerli, *Ezekiel 1*, Hermeneia, trans.R. E. Clements (Philadelphia: Fortress Press, 1979) 13.

96. E. F. Weidner, "Jojachin, Koenig von Juda," in *Mélanges Syriens Offerts à Monsieur René Dussaud* (Paris: Geuthner, 1939) 927. W. F. Albright concluded that Jehoiachin was recognized as ruler by the Babylonians, in "The Ration Lists," *BA* 5 (1942) 49–54, which is an opinion now widely held, even though Weidner himself, noting that Jehoiachin was called "*mar sarri* (prince)," thought that the Babylonians recognized their puppet king Zedekiah as legitimate ruler (926).

97. While it may not be fair to suggest that Jeremiah was actually favorably disposed to the Babylonians, his view was certainly considered such by the Babylonians themselves

Jeremiah's famous "Letter to the Exiles" and the response to it in Jeremiah 29 reveal further divisions.[98]

There are clear suggestions of Egyptian interference in a possible revolt of Zedekiah in the eleventh year of Nebuchadnezzar that required Nebuchadnezzar's return to reassert control. Wiseman, however, suggests that Zedekiah may have initiated contacts among many western states in hopes of building a coalition against Babylon.[99] Nebuchadnezzar finally returned to Jerusalem and laid siege to the city in 587/586. In August 5, 587 (or August 15, 586, according to Abraham Malamat[100]), the city fell to Nebuchadnezzar's siege, Zedekiah's halting resistance was crushed, and he was captured at Jericho. His sons were killed before his eyes, and then his eyes put out before he was taken "in fetters" (2 Kgs 25:7) to Babylon.

It seems beyond dispute that Jerusalem was treated severely. Nearby towns show total cessation of occupation (Lachish and Beth-Shemesh), and Wiseman noted ash layers at Gezer and Tell el-Hesi indicating Babylonian battles.[101] In addition to the summaries provided by Schniedewind based on more recent archaeological evidence, older works speak with an interesting consensus. S. S. Weinberg writes: "Excavations by Kathleen Kenyon yield a picture of ruin and desolation that confronted the first returnees of 539/8. While some people had no doubt continued to live in Jerusalem, the archaeological picture is one of their squatting among the rubble, which increased as the terrace walls . . . collapsed through lack of care and the debris accumulated in impassable piles on the lower slopes. No great change in the condition of the city occurred until the time of Nehemiah's arrival in 445."[102] Weinberg further considers it unlikely that in these circumstances any viable material culture could have been

(Jer 39:11-14). There is a good review of the issues in M. B. Rowton, "Jeremiah and the Death of Josiah," *JNES* 10 (1951) 128–30.

98. One frequently sees a reference to Jeremiah's advice to "build houses, plant gardens, and marry your sons and daughters" as an indication of a tolerable life in exile. I have argued, however, that this should not be taken literally, but as an allusion to the laws of "Yahweh war" in Deut 20, where soldiers who have just built a home, planted a garden, or become engaged must not go to war. Thus Jeremiah was proclaiming an armistice on the exiles using the stereotypical Deuteronomic images of "seeking the peace of the city where you are." See Daniel Smith, "Jeremiah as Prophet of Nonviolence," *JSOT* 43 (1989) 95–107.

99. Wiseman, *Nebuchadrezzar and Babylon*, 36.

100. Abraham Malamat, "The Twilight of Judah: in the Egyptian-Babylonian Maelstrom," in *Congress Volume: Edinburgh 1974* , VTSup 28 (Leiden: Brill, 1975) 123–45.

101. Wiseman, *Nebuchadrezzar and Babylon*, 38.

102. S. S. Weinberg, "Post-Exilic Palestine: An Archaeological Report," in *Proceedings of the Israel Academy of Sciences and Humanities* 4 (1971) 80.

maintained: "We must think more in terms first of squatters and then of people able to maintain only a mere subsistence level."[103]

More recent assessments concur. Gösta Ahlström states that the destruction of Jerusalem was "thorough. The walls were broken down and the city was plundered. . . . Arrowheads of northern origin and destroyed buildings that have been unearthed in excavations from this period bear witness to the disaster of the city."[104]

It is difficult to estimate the human extent of the crisis. Just arriving at a credible number for the population of Jerusalem is controversial. Magen Broshi estimated that Jerusalem would have occupied five hundred to six hundred dunams in the seventh century, and that forty to fifty inhabitants per dunam was a "reasonable" estimate. This results in a population estimate of nearly 24,000.[105] W. S. LaSor, however, notes that highly accurate population figures from Ebla result in 446 persons per dunam, which would force a much higher estimate for Jerusalem if the two cities were in any way similar in population density.[106] Indeed, LaSor tends to concur with W. F. Albright's estimate of 250,000 before the exile. Obviously, these estimates vary so greatly as to make confident assessments of a quantitative impact on Judah extremely difficult. But combining the archaeological evidence of destruction with any of these population estimates begins to draw a picture of horrific events that not surprisingly become permanently etched into the historical lore of the Hebrew Bible (e.g., Ps 137; Lamentations; see also the Lachisch Ostraca[107]).

The temple, of course, was destroyed, and many of the religious implements of worship were carried into exile with the people. It appears that the policy of Nebuchadnezzar was to place captured religious implements or statues in the temple of Marduk in the city of Babylon in order to symbolize the capture of the people and the defeat of their gods. In the case of the Jews, a capture of temple vessels served the same purpose and may well be the tradition underlying the story of Belshazzar's feast in Daniel 5, as well as the ability of Cyrus to magnanimously return them in Ezra 1–6.

---

103. Ibid., 81.

104. Gösta Ahlström, *The History of Ancient Palestine* (Minneapolis: Fortress Press, 1993) 798. According to Philip J. King, "Shiloh found evidence of the Babylonian destruction everywhere: thick layers of dark ash, scattered iron and bronze arrowheads, and collapsed structures" ("Jerusalem," in *ABD* 3:757).

105. See population discussions, including the sudden growth of southern settlements after the fall of the north, in M. Broshi, "Estimating the Population of Ancient Jerusalem," *BAR* 13 (1978) 46–57.

106. See W. S. LaSor, "Jerusalem," in *ISBE* 2:1001–30.

107. *ANET*, 322.

The taking of temple vessels, however, has been disputed as a literary trope. I. Kalimi and J. D. Purvis have argued that the Chronicler wants to use the idea of "returned temple vessels" to establish continuity with the Solomonic temple, but this certainly does not mean that such a sacking of the temple did not take place.[108] References to the symbols of Jewish worship having been taken from the temple are widespread, not only limited to texts influenced by the Chronicler.

The Babylonians moved the local administrative center of their conquered Palestinian territory north from Jerusalem to Mizpah, a further comment on the viability of Jerusalem after the destruction. Accounting for the exaggeration of Chronicles generally (2 Chron 36 portrays the land as virtually emptied), the numbers of the exiles must have been larger than the estimates of the book of Jeremiah and closer to the estimates in 2 Kings 24. After all, if the chronological sequence of 2 Kings can be trusted—and we note that the number 18,000 is associated with the surrender of Jerusalem in 597—how much more must we contend with after the destruction of the city ten or eleven years later? The biblical text, notably, does not even attempt to estimate the numbers of those who fled, were killed, or taken as deportees (note the tripartite description of the fate of Judeans in Ezek 5—the sword, fire, and deportation). Finally, however, it is not likely that we can use the postexilic number supplied for us in Ezra-Nehemiah (the so-called Golah lists, which place the postexilic community at over 42,000 persons) since we are not certain if these numbers reflect the postexilic community of Yehud (if such a province existed early in Persian rule), whose numbers could include many who did not go into exile. Note, however, that Oded has suggested the possibility that Babylonian exiles joined with the northern Israelite communities that were earlier deported by the Neo-Assyrian Empire, thus contributing to higher postexilic numbers.[109]

We are well aware that both the Neo-Assyrian and Neo-Babylonian rulers knew the significance of making examples of rebellious cities (note A. T. Olmstead's famous observation in 1918 about Neo-Assyrian "calculated frightfulness"[110]). Sociologists of disaster inform us of the

---

108. See I. Kalimi and J. D. Purvis, "King Jehoiachin and the Vessels of the Lord's House in Biblical Literature," *CBQ* 56 (1994) 449–57.

109. Oded, "Judah and the Exile," in *Israelite and Judaean History*, ed. Hayes and Miller, 480–85.

110. Olmstead, *JAOS* 38 (1918), 209–63, quoted to good effect in Hayim Tadmor, "Assyria and the West: The Ninth Century and Its Aftermath," in *Unity and Diversity*, ed. Hans Goedicke and J. J. M. Roberts (Baltimore: Johns Hopkins Univ. Press, 1975) 36–48.

significance of memories of such trauma, especially when they come in series of disasters,[111] and I have argued elsewhere that we do not even begin, for example, to fairly assess common themes such as the behavior of Ezekiel until we consider the extent of the trauma of 586.[112]

There would have been a succession of crises for those back in the land as well. Josephus (*Ant.* 10.9.7) alludes to a campaign of Nebuchadnezzar in Palestine in 582, probably in reprisal for the murder of Gedaliah. The historical evidence, then, suggests a series of traumatic events experienced by both communities, those in exile and those back in the land.

The last Neo-Babylonian ruler was the enigmatic Nabonidus, an Aramean who ruled the Babylonian Empire from 556 to 539. The events between these two rulers, Nebuchadnezzar and Nabonidus, are not reflected in many biblical texts. Nebuchadnezzar died in 562 and was succeeded by Awil-Marduk (Evil-Merodach). His reign lasted only an unstable two years before Neriglissar unseated him (559–556). His son, Labashi-Marduk, was the last of the line of Nebuchadnezzar, and he reigned only three months before the revolt occurred that placed the Aramean Nabunaid (555–539) on the throne. Nabunaid, or Nabonidus, was an officer in Nebuchadnezzar's service and was certainly a very elderly leader. Our sources about Nabonidus are almost all hostile, emphasizing his absence from Babylon and his favoritism to gods other than Marduk (specifically Sin, the moon god). Marduk was the central Babylonian deity,[113] and the priests of Marduk were clearly inflamed against Nabonidus. The stories of madness and the emotional instability of the Babylonian monarch that are portrayed in the first six chapters of Daniel are normally thought to be modeled on the historical ruler Nabonidus, particularly since the publication of an otherwise unknown Daniel-like tale among the Dead Sea texts known as "The Prayer of Nabonidus," which—as the title suggests—explicitly names Nabonidus

111. In the older classic, M. Barkun, *Disaster and the Millennium* (New Haven: Yale Univ. Press, 1974) 77. See my sociological overview of these issues in D. Smith, *The Religion of the Landless* (Bloomington: Meyer-Stone, 1989) 49–68.

112. A helpful introduction to the implications of such a study is H. A. Bulhan, *Frantz Fanon and the Psychology of Oppression* (New York: Plenum, 1985) and E. and B. Duran, *Native-American Postcolonial Psychology* (New York, SUNY Press, 1995). I draw on both of these as suggestive for my own study of Ezekiel: "Ezekiel on Fanon's Couch: A Postcolonialist Critique in Dialogue with David Halperin's *Seeking Ezekiel*," in *Peace and Justice Shall Embrace: Power and Theopolitics in the Bible: Essays in Honor of Millard Lind*, ed. T. Grimsrud and L. Johns (Telford, Pa.: Pandora, 1999) 108–44, some of which appears in ch. 3 below.

113. *ANET*, 308–15.

in the context of a story that has an impressive number of the familiar elements of the stories of Daniel 1–6.[114]

As I have had occasion to suggest, the condition of the land and community back in Palestine after the crisis of 587 is also difficult to assess. It is often presumed that some form of religious life continued in the ruins of the temple, but there is no direct evidence. Janssen also claims that, among other works, the Deuteronomistic History was completed in Palestine, showing a very active community there. According to Ephraim Stern: "we can conclude that in the Babylonian period, despite the destruction of the temple, the culture of the Israelite period continued. Some 70-80% of every pottery group from this time consists of vessels which are usually attributed to the latest phase of the Israelite period."[115] The Chronicler's claim that religious life virtually ended back in Palestine is hotly contested, particularly since Janssen's early arguments and Barstad's recent revival in more extreme forms.

The Chronicler's agenda is clearly to denigrate the communities of people remaining in the land, reflecting what had later become a serious division among the people whose roots were associated with various deportations; this is reflected in the intracommunal tensions recounted in Ezra 1–6, when there was conflict over who was, in fact, authorized by the Persians to rebuild the temple.

Certainly the evidence for conflict between those left behind and those taken to Babylonian territories suggests some form of active and organized life back in Palestine. As noted, archaeological evidence points to continued economic activity, which would, of course, be precisely in the interests of the Neo-Babylonian regime to encourage. If Lamentations is in any way historically reliable, however, there is evidence for a depressing condition back in Palestine. The rubble of destroyed buildings is referred to (2:2), and 5:2-5 suggests strongly a regimented economic activity in the land:

> Our inheritance has been turned over to strangers
>> our homes to aliens
> we have become orphans, fatherless;
>> our mothers are like widows

---

114. 4QPrNab, available in a recent translation by F. García Martínez, *Qumran and Apocalyptic: Studies on the Aramaic Texts from Qumran*, Studies on the Texts of the Desert of Judah 9 (Leiden: Brill, 1992) 119–20.

115. Ephraim Stern, *Material Culture of the Land of the Bible in the Persian Period, 538–332 BC* (Warminster: Aris & Phillips, 1982) 229.

We must pay for the water we drink
the wood we get must be bought
With a yoke on our necks we are hard driven
we are weary, we are given no rest.

Violence in the area suggests lawlessness and danger from brigands (5:9, 11):

We get our bread at the peril of our lives
because of the sword in the wilderness. . . .
Women are raped in Zion
virgins in the towns of Judah.

Finally, the evidence of conflict in Ezekiel between exiles and those back in the land suggests organized life in both locations as well as deeply dividing ideas about land possession (e.g., Ezek 33:23-29; compare the "good" vs. "bad" figs in Jer 24:1-10).[116] Whatever our assessment of the damage back in Palestine, Ahlström warns: "The archaeological material has not yet been systematized in a way that provides a clear picture of how destructive the Babylonian campaigns (598–570 BCE) against Judah, Tyre and Transjordan really were."[117]

To conclude this brief historical survey, the Persian conquest and the end of the Neo-Babylonian regime came with legendary swiftness (Isa 45). Cyrus the Persian, after unifying the Persian tribes and defeating the Medes, conquered the city of Babylon in 539. According to classical sources (Herodotus 1.788-91), Cyrus was able to conquer the city without violence because the Persians surprised the Babylonians during the celebrations of the New Year (a historical memory probably also reflected in the story of Belshazzar's Feast, Dan 5). Cyrus himself boasts that he entered the city with no violence[118] but attributes this accomplishment to his being selected by Marduk to be the legitimate successor.

The biblical sources about the early Persian period, inexactly discussed in Ezra 1–6, indicate that the Persians were relatively benign in their return of exiles to their homelands, including the Jews. As noted, however, recent work on the Persian period reveals that this supposed "enlightened

---

116. W. H. Brownlee, "The Aftermath of the Fall of Judah according to Ezekiel," *JBL* 1970 (89) 393–404.

117. Gösta Ahlström, *The History of Ancient Palestine* (Minneapolis: Fortress Press, 1993) 805. Ahlström also (807) speculates about the possibility of Babylonian garrisons in many of the Judean locations, but there is no firm evidence of this.

118. *ANET*, 315–16.

rule" of the Persians (including Cyrus) can be greatly exaggerated.[119] Hoglund has invited modern scholars to a deeper appreciation of the missions of Ezra and Nehemiah as elements of a Persian imperial policy of increased military presence in the west in order to shore up the western flank facing the Greek enemies, particularly after the Egyptian revolt in 460 (Inarus Revolt) that involved Greeks. This revolt was eventually crushed by Artaxerxes I in 454.[120]

Part of the myth of Persian benevolence is the idea of an end to the exile in 539. But all that ended was Neo-Babylonian hegemony, to be replaced by that of the Persians.[121] Ezra would point out, in his public prayer, that the Jewish people were "slaves in our own land" under the Persians (Neh 9.36-37). "Postexilic" Hebrew writings, like Daniel, would go so far as to reinterpret Jeremiah's predicted "70 years" into 490 years— effectively implying that the people were still in exile in the Persian and Hellenistic periods.[122]

The Status and Treatment of the Exiled Community

In his analysis of the conditions of exile, Noth had already suggested that "the exiles were not 'prisoners' but represented a compulsorily transplanted subject population who were able to move about freely in their daily life, but were presumably compelled to render compulsory labor service."[123] More recently, Bustenay Oded suggests that the exile community became land tenants of royal land, that craftsmen were involved in projects, and that the religious personnel were able to conduct aspects of Jewish religious ritual at sites such as Casiphia (Ezra 8:15-20). In sum, Oded believes that there is no evidence of suppression or religious persecution, and that the community members had "a certain internal

---

119. See my "Resistance in a 'Culture of Permission,'" in *Truth's Bright Embrace: Essays and Poems in Honor of Arthur O. Roberts*, ed. H. Macy and P. Anderson (Newberg, Ore.: George Fox Univ. Press, 1996) 15–38; also Kuhrt, "Cyrus Cylinder"; and two summaries of papers: van der Spek, *Persica* 10 (1982) 278–83; Jenner, *Persica* 10 (1982) 283–84.

120. Hoglund, *Achaemenid Imperial Administration*. An alternative perspective is taken by J. Berquist, *Judaism in Persia's Shadow: A Social and Historical Approach* (Minneapolis: Fortress Press, 1995), which is more along the lines of Ruben Richard's challenging dissertation, "The Role of the Imperial Decrees in Ezra-Nehemiah," Univ. of Cape Town, 1995.

121. S. Herrmann effectively reminds us of this fact in *A History of Israel in Old Testament Times*, trans. J. Bowden (Philadelphia: Fortress Press, 1975) 289.

122. On this matter, see the important essay by Michael Knibb, "The Exile in the Intertestamental Period," *Heythrop Journal* 17 (1976) 253–72.

123. Noth, *History of Israel*, 296.

autonomy and that they enjoyed the freedom to manage their community life (Ezek. 33:30-33)."[124]

But notable in Oded's sanguine picture of exilic life is a reference to the Murashu texts, and the terms "assume," "presume," and "no clear and explicit evidence."[125] It is precisely these tendencies to presume a tame, even if not entirely comfortable, existence that needs to be challenged in the light of an analysis informed by the experience of exiles throughout history and the evidence of trauma in the Hebrew literature after the experience.

A good example of this assumption is the view, nearly obligatory in the literature about the exile, that the exiles were not "slaves." This is hardly a precise observation, however, given the wide variety of slave systems in human history and the typical lack of definition given for this term among biblical scholars who use it.[126] Further, one must contend with the reality that the Bible certainly did consider the term to be appropriate to the condition of the Jews living under Persian rule (Neh 9:36), and may be an element of the significance of the exodus stories that were very much part of the Isaiah and Ezra-Nehemiah textual traditions.[127]

Furthermore, to say with M. A. Dandamaev that they were not "slaves" in the technical Neo-Babylonian sense is only to describe a detail of Neo-Babylonian jurisprudence.[128] This does not tell us very much about the human conditions of the exiles. For this we must pull together circumstantial evidence from the biblical and nonbiblical texts, including the following important points.

In 1938 F. H. Weissbach discussed a cuneiform inscription of Nebuchadnezzar II that reads, in part: "the lands of Hattim, from the upper sea to the lower sea, the land of Sumer and Akkad, the land between the two rivers, . . . the rulers of the lands of Hattim across the Euphrates where the sun sets, whose rulership, at the bidding of Marduk my lord, I overcame, and the mighty cedars of the mountain of Lebanon were brought to the city of Babylon, the whole of the races, people from far places, whom Marduk my lord delivered to me—I forced them to work on the building

---

124. B. Oded, "Judah and the Exile," in *Israelite and Judaean History*, ed. Hayes and Miller, 483.

125. Ibid.

126. It is important to see the wide diversity in slave systems as carefully documented in Orlando Patterson, *Slavery and Social Death* (Cambridge: Harvard Univ. Press, 1985).

127. This is argued to great effect by Williamson, *Ezra, Nehemiah*.

128. Among many of Dandamaev's sources, one may cite "Social Stratification in Babylonia 7th to 4th Centuries BC," *Acta Antiqua* 22 (1974) 437: "The forced labour sector in Babylonia, in contrast to Greek and Roman antiquity, was not able to absorb such masses of captives."

of Etemenanki—I imposed on them the brick-basket."[129] Inscriptions are not to be taken as dispassionate historical documents, of course. But note the terms used in this inscription: "I forced them to work" refers clearly to corvée labor, and "I imposed on them the brick basket" further employs strong terms of subservience. Moshe Weinfeld relates Akkadian *tupshikku* to the Hebrew term *sabbāl, siblâ* ("bearing burdens"; see 1 Kgs 5:27-32 [ET 5:13-18] and 11:28 of Solomon's forced labor) and points out that the terms *ilku* and *tupshikku* are two variants of forced labor—*ilku* involving travel (connecting with the verb *alaku*, "to go"), and *tupshikku* "refers specifically to bearing burdens and construction work done locally."[130] Similar differentiation in the types of forced labor are seen in Hittite and Egyptian nomenclature. The two terms, however, are used interchangeably of corvée labor.

This is even more likely given the facts of labor use in siege warfare itself. Again, Kern reminds us, using Assyrian sources: "The heart of the old Assyrian army was a corps of professional soldiers who did the fighting in war and carried out police duties in peacetime. For military campaigns, a muster swelled the army by a factor of perhaps four. These militia troops served less as a fighting force than as a labor force, providing logistical support to the army and hauling dirt for siege ramps."[131]

Other Neo-Babylonian texts assert Nebuchadnezzar's claim to authority over conquered peoples. Langdon's early translation of one of these texts effectively illustrates this: "I called into me the far dwelling peoples over whom Marduk my lord had appointed me and whose care was given unto me by Šamaš the hero, from all lands and of every inhabited place from the upper sea to the lower sea from distant lands the people of far away habitations kings of distant mountains and remote regions who dwell at the upper and the nether seas with whose strength Marduk the lord has filled my hands that they should bear his yoke and also the subjects of Šamaš and Marduk I summoned to build E-tem-in-anki."[132]

It is significant how often labor is associated with rule over varied peoples in the Neo-Babylonian inscriptions. Furthermore, Robert McCormick

129. F. H. Weissbach, *Das Hauptheiligtum des Marduk in Babylon* (Leipzig: Hinrich, 1938) 46–47. The translation from Weissbach's German is my own. See the older translation in Stephen Langdon, *Building Inscriptions of the Neo-Babylonian Empire*, Part 1: *Nabopolassar and Nebuchadnezzar* (Paris: Leroux, 1905) 59 and 149. I wish to thank Fr. William Fulco, S.J., for his helpful advice on many of the linguistic features of this text.

130. M. Weinfeld, *Social Justice in Ancient Israel and in the Ancient Near East* (Minneapolis: Fortress Press, 1995) 85.

131. Kern, *Ancient Siege Warfare*, 18.

132. Langdon, *Building Inscriptions*, 149.

Adams's archaeological survey of the central flood plain of the Euphrates in 1981 led him to conclude: "There is no doubt about the rapid, continued growth that got under way, during, or perhaps even slightly before, the Neo-Babylonian period. This is most simply shown by the rising number of sites . . . the total increases from 143 in the Middle Babylonian period to 182 in the Neo-Babylonian period, to 221 of Achaeminid date . . . the available documentary evidence suggests that large masses of people were involuntarily transferred as part of intensive Neo-Babylonian efforts to rehabilitate the central region of a domain that previously had suffered severely."[133]

Such evidence should not be overlooked when considering the impact and conditions of the Babylonian exile (Jer 51:34-35). We now have cuneiform documents that confirm the existence of "Judean villages" among the Neo-Babylonian settlements of deported peoples. That these documents mention settlements of specifically Jewish people already communicates that peoples were settled together (an essential sociological component to ethnic survival, incidentally) and that their ethnic identity was a matter of record. In their analysis, F. Joannes and A. Lemaire conclude: "Independent of the precise location of this 'Judean village,' this term establishes that the deported Jews regrouped, or reconstructed themselves, in Babylonia (perhaps in part according to their place of origin) in new groupings or associations. . . . This regrouping allowed the maintenance of a communal life almost as intense as in Judea. . . . This tablet . . . confirms completely what historians have previously surmised about the life of the exiles in Babylon."[134] It seems clear, then, that the exiles were not simply mixed together with other peoples in hopes that all would be "citizens of the empire"—an assumption that seems behind the many attempts to suggest that life was surely not "so bad" for the deported peoples.

When this evidence of identity and work details is combined with biblical references to "slavery" and conditions of exile, the emerging picture is painted in dark colors, even if we must carefully work with the use of metaphors and allusions rather than precise historical observation.

---

133. R. McCormick Adams, *Heartland of Cities: Surveys of Ancient Settlement and Land Use on the Central Floodplain of the Euphrates* (Chicago: Univ. of Chicago Press, 1981) 177.

134. F. Joannes and A. Lemaire, "Trois tablettes cunéiformes a onomastique ouest-sémitique (collection Sh. Moussaieff) (Pls. I-II)," *Transeu* 17 (1996) 27. I wish to thank the authors for their kind remarks about my own work on the exilic community listed among those scholars whose previous suggestions have been at least partially confirmed by this tablet.

The Murashu Archive and the Elephantine Community as Evidence for Exilic Conditions

Before continuing this line of investigation, it is important to address a common response to the suggestion that the exile involved a severe and traumatic experience—namely, the evidence of the Murashu archive, and less frequently, the Elephantine colony.

It is frequently pointed out that many Jewish names appear in the Murasu archive from Nippur, texts that were found in 1893,[135] and already being analyzed in print by 1898. As these are business documents that appear to show Jews involved in commerce, the conclusion was quickly determined that life in exile was obviously not so bad. Two matters must be immediately clarified. First, and most important, the Murashu archive date from the reigns of Artaxerxes I and Darius II (464–404 BCE). While these texts reflect the Persian period, how much can we assume this to be a reflection of the earlier Neo-Babylonian period? Second, however, is the controversy about what these Jewish names do reveal about socioeconomic activity and social standing. Michael Coogan notes that Jews appear as agriculturists, fishermen, sheepherders, and cocreditors in contracts.[136] Ran Zadok, however, challenges any assumptions about an image of comfortable Jewish communities in exile: "The highest positions in the Achaemenian administration of Babylonia were held by Persians and to some extent by Medes. The lower positions were manned mainly by Babylonians who constituted the majority. . . . Judging from their names, few officials were Arameans, Arabians and Phoenicians; nonetheless, collectively, these officials still largely outnumbered the Jews. Much like their Jewish colleagues . . . these officials were mostly minor functionaries. Nehemiah, who held a senior position, was an exception."[137]

---

135. H. V. Hilprecht and A. T. Clay, *Business Documents of Murashû Sons of Nippur Dated in the Region of Artaxerxes I (464–424 BC)*, Babylonian Expedition Series A (Philadelphia: Dept. of Archaeology and Paleontology, Univ. of Pennsylvania, 1898).

136. Michael D. Coogan, "Life in the Diaspora: Jews at Nippur in the Fifth Century BC," *BA* 37 (1974) 10.

137. Zadok, *Jews in Babylonia*, 87. In *Myth of the Empty Land*, Barstad cites two further works by Zadok in an attempt to establish a conclusion quite at variance with our view of the lower status of the exilic community. See R. Zadok, *The Pre-Hellenistic Israelite Anthroponomy and Prosopography* (Leuven: Peeters, 1988); idem, "Onomastic, Prosopographic and Lexical Notes," *Biblische Notizen* 65 (1992) 47–54. After examining both works, however, I find nothing that emends or contradicts Zadok's earlier general conclusions. In the last article, for example, Zadok certainly does comment that Jews were well represented among interpreter-scribes at Nippur, but that "there were almost no Jewish high officials there" (52). Work as interpreters, incidentally, rather neatly confirms the general traditions suggested by the folklore of Dan 1–6.

In a later work, Coogan also tried to refine the analysis of the names themselves, hoping to tease out information about the exiles from the selection of names. Conclusions around names using the root *šlm*, for example, reveal the lines of this kind of analysis: "In the biblical sources the use of the root in personal names is suggestive. . . . Beginning in the late seventh century . . . the root occurs with such frequency in personal names that we may speak of a fad in the naming of children, a euphemistic tendency related to the absence of *šalom* in the last decades of Israel's history."[138] Such attempts to glean information from choice of names, however, has revealed little that is useful for our analysis of the impact of exile.

The Elephantine colony is an entirely different matter, of course, as it was a military garrison in the era for which we have significant numbers of texts. Irrespective of the time of its founding, one can presume that attitudes toward the Persians would be different among those already disposed to serve the Persian Empire, and that this colony would have little helpful information for drawing conclusions about the treatment of exiles under the Chaldeans. What is most clear in these texts, however, is local trouble with the indigenous Egyptian "Khnum priests," who apparently are implicated in the destruction of the Jewish shrine built there.[139]

Further evidence that the Jews of the Elephantine colony had serious theological differences and disagreements with the Jerusalem community makes this a case with little direct relevance for any discussions of the conditions of exiles except by rough analogy.[140] Finally, however, and most importantly, it is likely that the Egyptian Jewish diaspora was formed at the time when a significant number of Jews opposed the Chaldeans and escaped to Egypt as a refuge.[141] If this is the most likely origin for the Elephantine community, then the dynamics of a chosen "exile" to Egypt as a benign refuge, as opposed to a forced relocation, make this community virtually irrelevant for any discussion of the impact and trauma of the Babylonian exile.[142]

138. Michael D. Coogan, *West Semitic Personal Names in the Murasu Documents*, HSM 7 (Missoula, Mont.: Scholars, 1976) 85.

139. "B19" in B. Porten, *The Elephantine Papyri in English: Three Millennia of Cross-Cultural Continuity and Change* (Leiden: Brill, 1996) 139–44.

140. See B. Porten, *Archives from Elephantine: The Life of a Jewish Military Colony* (Berkeley: Univ. of California Press, 1968); idem, *The Elephantine Papyri in English*.

141. Oded, "Judah and the Exile," 486–87.

142. Cf. Smith, *Religion of the Landless*, 50–65. In this earlier work I give a detailed sociological examination of the psychosocial dynamics of chosen versus forced relocation and explain why examples of chosen relocation are not a significant source of comparative information.

Finally, were Jews "drafted" by the Babylonians in the period of Nabonidus? In 1958 C. J. Gadd published an important article analyzing D. S. Rice's discovery, in 1956, of inscriptions from the court of Nabonidus, found on stones that were used to build a mosque in Iraq. Included in these inscriptions was Nabonidus's claims to have "committed to my hands" the people of "Hatti-land" (among others), who also "kept guard for me." Because of the alienation between Nabonidus and the people of Babylon that is reflected in the anti-Nabonidus texts that we have, Gadd considers it "unlikely that the army of Nabonidus, when he withdrew to Arabia, could be composed mainly of native Babylonians (using this term to describe inhabitants of the ancient cities and country of lower Iraq).["]143

Gadd went on to point out that the list of places occupied by Nabonidus—namely Taima, Dedan-al-'Ula, Fadak, Khaybar, Yadi', Yathrib-Medina—is a list that coincides, with one exception, to lists of oases where Jewish communities prospered at the time of the rise of Islam. When this observation is combined with the inscriptions, it suggests that Nabonidus drafted residents of the western sector of the empire. Gadd believed that "short of actually naming the Jews . . . [the implication of his using Jews in his militia] could scarcely be stronger."144

The Lexicography of Trauma
Anticipating somewhat the following chapters, here I briefly consider selections from the harsh vocabulary of defeat that lead to an initial sobering judgment of the impact and experience of exile. Chains and bonds are spoken of with at least three different major terms and frequently associated with the Babylonian conquest whether literally or figuratively: (1) *môsēr*, masculine noun, from *'āsar*, "to tie, imprison," is usually translated "bonds" in Nah 1:13: "And now I will break off his yoke from you and snap the bonds that bind you"; significantly of the Babylonian exile in Isa 52:2: "Shake yourself from the dust, rise up, O captive Jerusalem, loose the bonds from your neck"; and Ps 107:14: "He brought them out of darkness and gloom, and broke their bonds asunder." (2) "Fetter" (always in plural, *zîqqîm*); Nah 3:10: "Yet she became an exile, she went into captivity . . . all her dignitaries were bound in fetters"; Isa 45:14 (of foreigners coming as prisoners, a reversal of fortune motif): "[they] shall come over in chains and bow down to you"; Psalm 149 echoes the treatment of the dignitaries: "to bind their kings with fetters and their nobles with chains of iron [a

143. C. J. Gadd, "The Harran Inscriptions of Nabonidus," *Anatolian Studies* 8 (1958) 85.
144. Ibid., 86.

fourth term, *kebel*, used of Joseph[145] in Ps 105:18]." Note the form in Jer 40:1: "when he took him bound in fetters." The Septuagint has *chairopedais*, literally "foot shackle." (3) *Neḥūštîm*, "bronze fetters," from the root *neḥōšet*, "bronze/copper"; notably Jer 39:7 uses this term to refer to the bonds on Zedekiah (cf. 2 Kings 25). 2 Chron 36:6 speaks of such fetters on Jehoiachin. Finally, Lam 3:7 speaks of siege and chains in reference to reflections on the conquest of Jerusalem after the event.

Further insights can be gained from a brief examination of three terms for "imprisonment": (1) *kelî* from the verb *kālāʾ*, "to hold back," in 1 Sam 25:33; Ps 119:101; Jer 32:2; and notably of exiles in Isa 43:6. (2) *Bôr ʾên mayîm*, "pit with no water," occurs in the late Joseph material in Gen 37:24, but see Jer 38:6 and Zech 9:11, where the reference is closer to exile. (3) *Bêt ʾābdîm*, "house of slavery," the image used of Egyptian bondage: Exod 13:3, 14; 20:2; Deut 5:6; 6:12; 7:8; etc., but note also Jer 34:13 and Mic 6:4.[146]

Clearly, various forms of the Hebrew terms normally rendered "imprisonment" turn up as metaphors for exile, along with the various use of terms of binding and fetters. Can all of this be dismissed as mere stereotyped metaphor?

In more detail, however, note the frequent biblical motif that relates "sight to blind" and "release of prisoners" as metaphors of exile. This is found in many exilic and postexilic passages (e.g., Ps 146:7-8; Isa 42:7; 61:1; Zech 9:12). Indeed, this may be a Babylonian motif borrowed by those who experienced aspects of the Babylonian tradition. Consider a Šurpu Hymn, an incantation to Marduk, the patron god of the Babylonians:

> [It rests with you, Marduk . . .]
> to set free the prisoner, to show (him) daylight
> him who has been taken captive, to rescue him
> him whose city is distant, whose road is far away
> let him go safely to his city
> to return the prisoner of war and the captive to his people . . .
> may the sick get well, the fallen get up

---

145. Note the significance of the Joseph stories being postexilic. See Donald B. Redford, *A Study of the Biblical Story of Joseph (Genesis 37–50)*, VTSup 20 (Leiden: Brill, 1970).

146. Serious questions can be raised about the application of this terminology to the Egyptian bondage before the exodus. If Redford is correct that the tradition of the Hebrew "slaves" working in Pithom and Raamses can be no older than the late sixth century BCE, then we cannot discount an "exilic" redaction of the exodus traditions that may well reflect the Babylonian experience with more accuracy than the Egyptian experience. See Redford, *Joseph*; and esp. idem, *Egypt, Canaan, and Israel in Ancient Times* (Princeton: Princeton Univ. Press, 1992).

the fettered go free, the captive go free
the prisoner see the light (of day).[147]

If there is a line of dependence here on Babylonian sources, then we cannot discount the possibility of rich irony in the borrowing of this phrase—God will accomplish the "freedom" about which the Babylonians only wax eloquent. Alternatively, the motifs of release from captivity and prison, so obviously applied to the conditions of exile by the biblical writers, may be borrowed from standard royal formulas for expressing great largesse at special occasions, or at the enthronement of new rulers throughout the ancient Near East;[148] but nonetheless they are terms clearly and easily applied by the biblical writers to the memories of the conditions of exile. In short, the metaphor of imprisonment and references to places of imprisonment do not grow more plentiful during the exilic period by pure chance, especially in view of its foreignness to the Israelite judicial system.[149] Contemporary assessments of the exile must not simply dismiss this imagery as purely metaphorical with no historical basis.

In the chapters that follow, then, I try to establish ways that the biblical literature arises from the experience of these events, as well as being deeply influenced by these social, economic, and political contexts. I maintain that the critical point is that the ancient Hebrew "theology of exile" arose from these circumstances, and therefore any modern "theology of exile" must carefully recall their context, as well as our own context, for any theological reflection on the biblical experience.

147. Erica Reiner, Šurpu: A Collection of Sumerian and Akkadian Incantations (1958; repr. Osnabrück: Biblio, 1970) 26–27.
148. Weinfeld, Social Justice, 75–96.
149. Smith, Religion of the Landless, 174. There is a considerable literature on prisons in antiquity. A special issue of the Journal of the Economic and Social History of the Orient 20 (1977) included a number of important articles: J. Renger, "Wrongdoing and Its Sanctions: On Criminal and Civil Law in the Old Babylonian Period," 65–77; T. S. Frymer, "The Nungal-Hymn and the Ekur Prison," 78–89; J. Sasson, "The Treatment of Criminals at Mari," 90–113; K. K. Riemschneider, "Prison and Punishment in Early Anatolia," 114–26. Like Renger, Riemschneider does not believe that prisons as institutions existed in the ancient Near East (114).

3.
LISTENING TO CRIES
FROM BABYLON:
On the Exegesis of Suffering in Ezekiel and Lamentations

Judah has gone into exile with suffering
    and hard servitude;
she lives now among the nations,
    and finds no resting place;
her pursuers have all overtaken her
    in the midst of her distress.

—Lamentations 1:3

It is so obvious as to be a certainty that Ezekiel was first and foremost a prophet for the exiles.

—Walther Eichrodt, *Ezekiel*

WE HAVE SURVEYED SOME OF THE DEBATES REGARDING THE EXILE AS a historical event. It remains to ask whether we hear any biblical voices from this event. Two biblical books famously claim to come directly from the experience of the exile—one from Babylon and one back in Palestine. Ezekiel, the priest/prophet, was apparently taken with the first deported groups around 597 BCE and only heard of the destruction of Jerusalem in 587 BCE from that great distance. Lamentations, on the other hand, is a short collection of poetic cries of pain from an apparently devastated city and surrounding countryside. But are we really listening to the voice of Ezekiel? Do we hear the songs of Lamentations rising from the debris of Jerusalem?

All biblical books are products of a community of transmission, and the communities of the books of Ezekiel and Lamentations are clearly communities that are struggling with crises, personal and social, that include dealing with suddenly mobile identities and transnational culture and theology. They are voices of traumatized communities, and our analysis of the biblical response to exile, after outlining the events of the exile, must begin here. In this chapter I contend that in Ezekiel and Lamentations, specifically, we have early and important reactions to the trauma of exile from home and from the exiles, and that any theological arguments using these materials must also take this wider context of the tragic events into account. I propose to illustrate how this may affect doing theology with these texts.

Ezekiel, Lamentations, and Refugee Studies

As I have argued in the previous chapter, it was economics and power politics that dragged Ezekiel and his compatriots to Babylon, as it was also economics and political control that reduced Jerusalem to devastation. What has all this to do with Ezekiel and Lamentations? If we speak of the typical Ezekiel of biblical studies, or the frequent dismissal of Lamentations as stereotyped poetry, the answer is simple: not much. But when these texts are read with an eye to the study of refugee culture (to take only one related social science discipline that may shed light on the impact of traumatic events like the Babylonian conquests), these social and political observations can mean a great deal. Consider the implications of reading the books of Lamentations and Ezekiel as, among other things, products of "state-sponsored terrorism." Caroline Gorst-Unsworth, who works on treatment of terror and torture victims, defines this phrase as:

> essentially the act of a state against an individual or group, with the aim of achieving specific psychological changes (directly) in their victims and often (indirectly) in their communities . . . the survivor of torture has not merely been the accidental victim of physical injury or threat of death such as might occur, for example in a natural disaster or accident. . . . He or she has received the focussed attention of an adversary determined to cause the maximal psychological change. . . . Neither is it the individual who suffers. For every person tortured there are mothers and fathers, wives, husbands and children, friends and relatives who wait in uncertainty and fear. . . . Torture has effects on communities and on whole societies.[1]

1. Caroline Gorst-Unsworth, "Psychological Sequelae of Torture: A Descriptive Model," *British Journal of Psychiatry* 157 (1990) 475–76.

When we read Ezek 5:12: "One third of you shall die of pestilence or be consumed by famine among you; one third shall fall by the sword around you; and one third I will scatter to every wind and will unsheathe the sword after them," do we have any substantive reason to excuse Mesopotamian regimes from the accusation of state-sponsored terrorism merely because it is ancient history we speak of rather than the twenty-first century?

In reference to the Neo-Assyrian Empire, Amélie Kuhrt writes of reliefs depicting its kings reclining near the severed heads of enemies, as well as Assyrian inscriptions boasting of the dead rebels draped on their city walls, and rebellious rulers entrapped with wild animals in cages that are then suspended at the entrance to cities. The king "was awe-inspiring; the fear that filled his enemies was the terror of those knowing that they will be ruthlessly, but justly, punished. The royal power to inspire fear was visualized as a shining radiance . . . a kind of halo, that flashed forth from the royal face. . . . It made him fearsome to behold and it could strike his enemies down, so that they fell to their knees before him, dazzled by the fearful glow."[2]

It is interesting to note that in his recent work, David Vanderhooft wants to carefully distance Neo-Babylonian inscriptions from the sheer cruelty of Neo-Assyrian rhetoric. But even at that Vanderhooft, as we have seen in the previous chapter, must refer to the "brute facts of subjugation," and writes that the Neo-Babylonian Empire under Nebuchadnezzar II was "at base, focused on domination and exploitation of non-Babylonian populations for the benefit of a ruling elite."[3]

Biblical materials do not present a different picture. Even in the context of legends, the suddenness of executions demanded by the "mad king" is an essential element in the drama of the tales in Daniel 1–6, Esther, and the Joseph story (Gen 37–50), even if we are dealing with late Persian period collective memories of the Neo-Babylonian experience. But we have seen this view "of the top," that is, from the perspective of the empires, in the previous chapter. In this chapter we approach the question from the perspective of the victims themselves. Such an investigation is deeply enhanced by a reading of modern refugee studies.

2. Amélie Kuhrt, *The Ancient Near East c. 3000-330 BC*, 2 vols. (London: Routledge, 1995) 2:517.

3. David Stephen Vanderhooft, *The Neo-Babylonian Empire and Babylon in the Latter Prophets*, HSM 59 (Atlanta: Scholars, 2000) 6.

A Survey of Refugee and Disaster Studies in Preparation for Reading Ezekiel and Lamentations

In her summary of refugee studies, Liisa H. Malkki notes that there are considerable difficulties simply defining the term *refugee*,[4] especially given the context of the rise of refugee studies in the immediate postwar years of the first half of the twentieth century. This becomes interesting for our analysis in the way that refugee studies have been separated from a wider study of social and political contexts: "If nothing else, the development of the discourse on refugees has sometimes facilitated the continued depoliticization of refugee movements; for instead of foregrounding the political, historical processes that generated a given group of refugees, and that reach far beyond the country of asylum and the refugee camp, development projects tend to see a whole world in a refugee camp."[5]

Malkki, notably, refers in her work to a "sedentarist bias" that now defines the refugee as a "problem" precisely because the refugee is stateless. Thus, this bias suggests the presumed necessity of territory and sealed borders; a presumption that invites xenophobic reactions to the presence of such refugee groups.[6] Malkki calls for an approach to the study of the phenomenon of refugees that also incorporates a study of what "being home" is. But what is particularly suggestive is her questioning of the territorial, nationalist bias of present refugee research: "a denaturalizing, questioning stance toward the national order of things, presents itself as a promising site from which to identify new research directions in the study of refugees, exile, displacement, and diaspora—as well as for imagining new forms of political engagement."[7]

Given these cautions, however, it is possible to note that studies of refugee events and groups reveal an interesting tension between those who emphasize the creative ability of traumatized populations to reconstruct, or even maintain, precrisis identities, and those who emphasize the debilitating conditions of not having sufficient stability to maintain identity, culture, and rationality. These two directions of emphasis can be readily illustrated. For example, in their own introduction to an important series of essays considering identity, gender, and change in refugee settings, Ruth Krulfeld and Linda Camino observe: "Despite experiences of being violently or forcibly uprooted and plunged into discord and dis-

4. Liisa H. Malkki, "Refugees and Exile: From 'Refugee Studies' to the National Order of Things," *ARA* 24 (1995) 496.
5. Ibid., 507.
6. Ibid., 511
7. Ibid., 517.

order, refugees demonstrate the strengths of innovation for survival, as well as the vitality to create and negotiate new roles and behaviour to achieve both necessary and desired ends. By doing so, they reveal the multi-layered, richly contextualized meanings of their lives and traditions as they act to re-affirm self and community."[8]

Here the generalized studies of "disaster" more generally defined may assist us, especially when we can cite disaster theorists such as Claude Gilbert, who has revived older views about how "disasters" only become "disastrous" for people when the events exceed the ability of the group to cope, redefine, and reconstruct: "we may speak of disaster when actors in modern societies increasingly lose their capacity to define a situation that they see as serious or even worrying through traditional understandings and symbolic parameters."[9] Studies of Palestinian experiences in prisons, for example, suggest that coping strategies help to put negative experiences into meaningful frames, such as suffering for the "political cause," for the love of one's friends and families, for heroic fulfillment, and through a deepening sense of religious devotion.[10] Indeed, it has often been noted that reconstructing some of the structural and social elements of previous existence can assist in this process. Palestinians in refugee camps continue to use village designations and re-create neighborhoods. Julie Peteet observes: "If one wished to locate the home of a person who is from Safed, one could ask, 'Where do the people of Safed live?' In short, the camps were structurally arranged to mirror rural Palestine in a desire to re-form a physical and social geography of trust."[11]

Another way that this reconstruction process has been observed in refugee study literature is in the forging of new histories in the process of

8. Ruth M. Krulfeld and Linda A. Camino, "Introduction," in *Reconstructing Lives, Recapturing Meaning: Refugee Identity, Gender, and Culture Change*, ed. R. M. Krulfeld and L. A. Camino (Basel: Gordon and Breach Science, 1994) xv.

9. Claude Gilbert, "Studying Disaster: Changes in the Main Conceptual Tools," in *What Is Disaster: Perspectives on the Question*, ed. E. L. Quarantelli (Routledge: London, 1998) 17.

10. See Samir Quota, Raija-Leena Punamaki, and Eyad El Sarraj, "Prison Experiences and Coping Styles among Palestinian Men," *Peace and Conflict: Journal of Peace Psychology* 3, no. 1 (1996) 19–36. Cf. Lucie Kassabian, "Displacement and Bicultural Integration: Factors Contributing to the Psychological Well-Being of Armenian-Americans," in *CORI–The American Anthropological Association*, Selected Papers on Refugee Issues IV (Arlington: American Anthropological Assn., 1996) 73–104; and Lucia Ann McSpadden, "Negotiating Masculinity in the Reconstruction of Social Space: Eritrean and Ethiopian Refugees in the United States and Sweden.," in *Engendering Forced Migration: Theory and Practice*, ed. Doreen Indra (New York: Berghahn, 1999) 242–60.

11. Julie M. Peteet, "Transforming Trust: Dispossession and Empowerment among Palestinian Refugees," in *Mistrusting Refugees*, ed. E. Valentine Daniel and John C. Knudsen (Berkeley: Univ. of California Press, 1995) 174.

reconstructing identity. E. Valentine Daniel and John Chr. Knudsen observe:

> Several anthropologists working with refugees have found that one of the important components in the recovery of meaning, the making of culture, and the reestablishment of trust is the need and the freedom to construct a normative picture of one's past within which "who one was" can be securely established to the satisfaction of the refugee. The refugee's self-identity is anchored more to who she or he was than what she or he has become. . . . "Individualities" constructed in oral autobiographies are deemed irrelevant by many caseworkers whereas for the refugee this is the foundation on which a meaningful world may be rebuilt.[12]

Included among the options of this reconstruction of history, however, is the possibility that cultures can be reconstructed on negative terms, such as being considered cursed, sinful, or doomed. In her study of Cambodian refugee narratives, for example, Marjorie Muecke observed: "In an attempt to comprehend the heinousness of the mass persecution of Cambodians in the late 1970s, many Cambodians have raised the possibility that Cambodian culture itself had a bad karma. Belief in karmic explanation of their misery could enable Cambodians to sustain the legitimacy of Buddhism and to rebuild their confidence in their future by virtue of having now expiated their karmic demerit through their massive sufferings. But belief in a karmic explanation could also justify a belief in the imminence of Armageddon. Fear of extinction is not new among the Khmer."[13]

Future writing on the theological viewpoint of the Deuteronomistic Historian, and the influence of similar perspectives from the prophets Jeremiah and Ezekiel, for example, ought to consider this widely observed phenomenon, especially given the generally recognized *negative* evaluation of the previous monarchical history typical of all three of these biblical sources. Similarly, in my own field studies,[14] I have heard many Cree Indian Christians in Canada lament that their shamans have no powers any more because these powers were abused in the past by the shamans

12. "Introduction," in ibid., 5.

13. Marjorie Muecke, "Trust, Abuse of Trust, and Mistrust among Cambodian Refugee Women: A Cultural Interpretation," in *Mistrusting Refugees*, 40.

14. My field studies have involved interviewing Lakota (U.S.), Cree (Canada), and Aboriginal Australian Christians about their own interpretations of stories from the book of Daniel. While I have drawn on these field experiments for much of my written work, esp. my commentary on Daniel (*NIB* 7:19–194), I plan to publish a short monograph on the entire experiment of doing field interviews as a part of biblical analysis.

themselves for self-gain before the whites arrived. Finally, the noted scholar of Armenian history, Ronald Suny, mentions a similar controversial view among some Armenian clergy who explained some of the suffering at the hands of the Turks as a result of "our sins."[15] Surely the frequency of the motif that "it's all because of our sins" in cross-cultural settings would lead one to reconsider the possibility that it is among the effective coping strategies of a people in crisis. After all, if one's suffering is because of one's own oversights, and not because of the power of the emperor and his armies, then this holds out considerably more hope about a future restoration, given appropriate spiritual recovery.

As noted, however, other refugee theorists emphasize the *destructive* behavioral patterns that are frequently observed. Patrick Matlou, for example, emphasizes the destructiveness of flight and the ensuing divisions and internal factions that can result: "During the processes of forced migration that so often result, ongoing social structures and institutions undergo significant changes. As the state disintegrates, its monopoly over the instruments of power and the allocation of resources disappears. Warlords, praetorian guards, religious zealots, and crime bosses take over the shattered shells of now weakened states and societies. Development recedes, what progress had been made is lost, and violence becomes the order of the day as the weak are further subjugated."[16] When one considers the divisions between those Judeans who seemed to gravitate toward Egypt and those (like Josiah) who seemed to have a preference for dealing with Babylon, such internal divisions sound familiar.

Furthermore, in a series of observations that seem deeply suggestive for the shrill oracles of judgment by Ezekiel aimed, at least partially, at fellow exiles, Matlou adds: "The deprivation and uncertainty that refugees often suffer sometimes lead them into conflict with each other over scarce rewards. In this regard, exile often serves as an arena for the continuation of conflicts begun at home and leads to the intensification of discriminatory practices that were already in place."[17] Many scholars of Daniel, for example, have noted the strange ambiguity of diaspora narratives like those of chs. 1–6 with regard to the view of the foreign rulers. There appear to be alternating views of near positive feelings about the emperor

---

15. See Ronald Grigor Suny, "Religion, Ethnicity, and Nationalism: Armenians, Turks, and the End of the Ottoman Empire," in *In God's Name*, ed. O. Bartov and P. Mack (New York: Berghahn, 2001) 23–61.

16. Patrick Matlou, "Upsetting the Cart: Forced Migration and Gender Issues, the African Experience," in *Engendering Forced Migration*, 133.

17. Ibid., 136.

(e.g., Darius in ch. 6), but at the same time the fear of spectacular death by burning, maiming, mauling, and impaling (virtually all six stories refer to such horrific forms of capital punishment at the whim of the emperor).

Such uncertainty, interestingly enough, turns out to be a conscious strategy in the imperial repertoire of modern terrorist regimes. In his study of Latin American persecution of peasant societies, Stuart Turner notes that "brutal actions were carried out on a few individuals in such a way that the wider population was literally terrorized. For this to be successful, the state had to make sure that the population was well informed about the violence taking place and was maintained in a state of fear by a sequence of unpredictable actions involving acts of intimidation alternative with conditional protection."[18] Thus, the occasions of vaguely positive evaluation of emperors in regimes that we know from archaeological and textual evidence to be brutal certainly does not mean that the biblical texts reveal positive feelings about living in the shadows of empires. It merely reveals the ambiguity of living under a regime that calculates public relations as an element of domination.

Life under these regimes can have other internal consequences as well. In a fascinating analysis of refugee cultures, Barbara Harrell-Bond and Eftihia Voutira speak of the realities of the notion expressed by many refugees that "to be a refugee means to learn to lie."[19] One of the most important "divides," therefore, is between the officials and the refugees. Based on his work with Vietnamese refugees in Norway, John Knudsen observes that the refugees "often stress that the brutality of the wars has engendered suspicion, individuality, and distrust rather than forthrightness, cooperation, and trust. Hence even daily communication is described as more indirect than direct and often accomplished."[20]

Although I will have occasion to develop this point further below, this is an appropriate place to raise once again the closely related observations in the pioneering work of James Scott. Scott noted the difference between the "hidden transcript," the opinion genuinely held by the subordinated groups, which is often encoded in the "public transcript." Clearly, biblical exegesis of the texts of the Diaspora must take into consideration the reality of "official correspondence" being an element of biblical documents,

---

18. Stuart Turner, "Torture, Refuge, and Trust," in *Mistrusting Refugees,* 57.

19. Eftihia Voutira and Barbara E. Harrell-Bond, "In Search of the Locus of Trust: The Social World of the Refugee Camp," in *Mistrusting Refugees,* 216.

20. John C. Knudsen, "When Trust Is on Trial: Negotiating Refugee Narratives," in *Mistrusting Refugees,* 18.

and not conclude too quickly that the necessity of dealing with officials therefore establishes positive and working relations with the regime. Scott's work, with Harrell-Bond and Voutira's observations about refugee culture noted above, forces us to read with considerable awareness of the subtleties of living under dominant regimes. With these preliminary observations in mind, let us move toward some observations on two cases: reading Ezekiel in a psychological context, and reading Lamentations and treaty-curse literature (especially Deuteronomy 28) as "stereotypical" literature. As in the previous chapter, I will note how the debates on both these subjects have contributed to working assumptions about the exilic circumstances.

Ezekiel on the Couch?

What are the implications of these brief observations from refugee studies for reading Ezekiel? One way to approach this issue is through a discussion of the frequent theme of Ezekiel's psychological state, which has once again been raised by David Halperin.[21] Halperin's work is a fascinating contribution to the collection of efforts by scholars, whether versed more in biblical or in psychological disciplines, to analyze the behavior and attitudes of the priest/prophet Ezekiel through a close examination of selected texts. Halperin himself states that his work is an attempt to revise, correct, but in general to renew the psychoanalytical suggestions originally made by E. C. Broome.[22] Although Halperin acknowledges that psychological interpretations of Ezekiel go back at least as far as A. Klostermann's 1877 essay,[23] it is Broome's more Freudian approach that Halperin is particularly interested in revising and reviving.

One should note that many scholars resist psychological interpretations of Ezekiel. Eichrodt protests: "Never at any point . . . do we find any trace of mental abnormality or even disease. In spite of all his frequently bizarre symbolic actions and the often overstrained excitability of his speech, Ezekiel's message is everywhere seen to be well thought out and directed towards a single end, which is in keeping with his conception of God, of the world, and of human nature."[24] Further, Brevard Childs noted

---

21. David J. Halperin, *Seeking Ezekiel: Text and Psychology* (University Park: Pennsylvania State Univ. Press, 1993).

22. E. C. Broome, "Ezekiel's Abnormal Personality," *JBL* 65 (1946) 277–92.

23. A. Klostermann, "Ezechiel: Ein Beitrag zu besser Würdigung seiner Person und seiner Schrift," *Theologische Studien und Kritiken* 50 (1877) 391–439.

24. Eichrodt, *Ezekiel*, 26.

that "various theories have been suggested to explain the peculiarities of Ezekiel's ecstatic behaviour in terms of psychological disturbances or physical illness . . . but in general these attempts have met with little positive reception by critical commentators and have left only an indirect influence on the history of research."[25]

But even in the context of rejecting specific psychological explanations, there are notable strains in this resistance to psychologizing in the scholarly interpretations of Ezekiel, especially when confronted with what Georg Fohrer designated as the twelve "sign-actions" of the prophet, for example, the famous enactments of silent tableau scenes of Jerusalem, the packing of an "exile's bag," symbolic cutting of his own hair, binding his own hands, and so on. Walther Zimmerli varies between seeing these actions as conscious efforts to "set forth in a visible action the event announced by Yahweh as something already begun," and those actions that may result from events that "overtake him and which make him appear to be overpowered by these experiences . . . [such as] the tragic loss of his wife."[26] In other words, Zimmerli concedes that such events make it difficult to avoid some kind of psychological or psychotheoretical notions for fully appreciating Ezekiel.[27]

Halperin's Analysis of Ezekiel: Some Sample Arguments
Halperin states that the "centerpiece" of his arguments about the psychological nature of Ezekiel is Ezek 8:7-12, the account of "digging through the wall" during the visionary return to Jerusalem that occupies one of the most important "visions" of the first half of the book, chs. 8–11. Halperin's central assertion is that this digging in the wall "is a symbolic representation of sexual intercourse," and his entire psychoanalytical interpretation of Ezekiel and his sexuality follows from this initial interpretation.

Three Hebrew terms appear to be the center of Halperin's argument about sexuality and Ezekiel's digging in walls. The term *ḥôr*, "hole,"

25. Brevard S. Childs, *Introduction to the Old Testament as Scripture* (Philadelphia: Fortress Press, 1979) 359.

26. Walther Zimmerli, *Ezekiel*, Hermeneia, vol. 1, trans. R. E. Clements (Philadelphia: Fortress Press, 1979) 29.

27. As Halperin himself acknowledges, any voyages into the study of Ezekiel today must steer a steady course between Walther Zimmerli and Moshe Greenberg, and are likely to need to do so for some time to come, although Block's recent two-volume work is a significant contribution to general Ezekiel studies. Zimmerli, on the one hand, has provided us with a commentary deeply informed by the history of twentieth-century Christian critical studies in the book of Ezekiel, particularly those tendencies to seek a more consistent reading of the Hebrew by pointing out the various layers of textual emendations and occasionally eliminating selected sections of text as later intrusions; on the other hand, Greenberg has taken a more cautious approach, wanting to avoid the frequent recourse of tearing into the fabric of the present text. These general tendencies of two modern Ezekiel scholars serve

appears in Ezek 8:7, the relatively rare verb *ḥātar*, "to dig, bore through," and *petaḥ*, "opening, entrance." Part of the interest in this passage is, of course, the great difference between the Masoretic text and the shorter Septuagint text.

Halperin translates the Hebrew text of Ezek 8:7-8 as follows: "And he brought me to the opening of the court. And I looked, and behold, one hole in the wall. And he said to me, 'Son of man, dig in the wall.' And I dug in the wall, and behold, one opening." Halperin translates the Greek as follows: "And he led me in to the entry spaces of the court. And he said to me, 'Son of man, dig.' And I dug, and behold, one door."

Now, some problems are already evident here. Halperin translates the Hebrew terms as the specific "one opening." But here is an example of the use of *'eḥad* as an indeterminate—"a hole." Notably, Gesenius lists Ezek 8:8 as an example of precisely this phenomenon of *'eḥad* as indeterminate.[28] Furthermore, the Greek reflects the same phenomenon, and so *petaḥ* need not refer to an actual door, but could be the more ambiguous "opening" or "entryway." *Petaḥ* can be something other than a door, as noted in Ps 77:23 and on many occasions in the New Testament. F. C. Conybeare and S. G. Stock note several examples of an indeterminate use of the numeral *eis*, which changes "under the influence of the Hebrew."[29]

But what did Ezekiel actually see? "Door," in English, is hopelessly ambiguous. This can well be illustrated with the English translation of

as helpful counterweights in an examination of just a few sample texts in this essay. Cf. Leslie Allen, *Ezekiel 20–48*, WBC (Waco: Word, 1990); Ellen Frances Davis, "Swallowing Hard: Reflections on Ezekiel's Dumbness," in *Signs and Wonders*, ed. J. C. Exum, Biblical Texts in Literary Focus (Decatur, Ga.: Scholars, 1989) 217–37; William H. Brownlee, *Ezekiel 1–19*, WBC (Waco: Word, 1986); Meindert Dijstra, "The Glosses in Ezekiel Reconsidered: Aspects of Textual Transmission in Ezekiel 10," in *Ezekiel and His Book: Textual and Literary Criticism and Their Interrelation*, ed. J. Lust, BETL 74 (Leuven: Leuven Univ. Press, 1986) 55–77; J. Van Goudoever, "Ezekiel Sees in Exile a New Temple-City at the Beginning of the Jobel Year," in *Ezekiel and His Book*, ed. Lust, 344–49; Moshe Greenberg, "What are Valid Criteria for Determining Inauthentic Matter in Ezekiel?" in *Ezekiel and His Book*, ed. Lust, 123–35; R. E. Clements, "The Ezekiel Tradition: Prophecy in a Time of Crisis," in *Israel's Prophetic Tradition: Essays in Honour of Peter R. Ackroyd*, ed. R. Coggins, A. Phillips, and M. Knibb (Cambridge: Cambridge Univ. Press, 1982) 119–36; Iaian M. Duguid, *Ezekiel and the Leaders of Israel*, VTSup 56 (Leiden: Brill, 1994); Joseph Blenkinsopp, *Ezekiel*, Interpretation (Louisville: John Knox, 1990); Bernhard Lang, "Street Theatre, Raising the Dead, and the Zoroastrian Connection in Ezekiel's Prophecy," in *Ezekiel and His Book*, ed. Lust, 297–316; Susan Niditch, "Ezekiel 40–48 in a Visionary Context," CBQ 48 (1986) 208–24; Moshe Greenburg, *Ezekiel 1–20*, AB 22 (Garden City, N.Y.: Doubleday, 1983); idem, *Ezekiel 21–37*, AB 22A (1997).

28. E. Kautzsch and A. E. Cowley, eds., *Gesenius' Hebrew Grammar*, 17th ed. (Oxford: Clarendon, 1982).

29. F. C. Conybeare and St. George Stock, *Grammar of Septuagint Greek* (1905; repr. Peabody, Mass.: Hendrickson, 1988) 25.

Gen 19:6, "Lot went out of the door to the men, and shut the door after him." The first use of "door" is *petaḥ*, "entryway," while the second is *delet*, the actual device of closure, presumably a wooden door on some kind of hinge. Halperin, not catching the indeterminate use in both the Greek and Hebrew, appears to presume that Ezekiel sees a door (he translates "one door"), rather than an opening—a hole in the wall.

The more generalized view of a hole in the wall invites speculation. Halperin earlier contends with C. G. Howie, who presumed that Ezekiel was digging a hole in the wall: "Let us grant, for the sake of argument, Howie's rather curious assertion that digging holes in walls was a 'common process' in Ezekiel's time. (It is hard to imagine who, aside perhaps from a burglar, would have had use for such an operation.)"[30] I suggest that there may be another occasion for holes in walls: the results of battering rams during the siege of the city. To begin, consider a series of other uses for the term *ḥôr*. When we read these occasions, we should ask, What are the occasions for digging holes? Some of the uses of the term are as follows: 2 Kgs 12:10, a hole made in a box to collect money; 1 Sam 13:6, the Hebrew people hid themselves in holes, caves, rocks, tombs, etc. for fear of the Philistines; 1 Sam 14:11, Hebrews coming out of "holes" where they have hidden themselves; Job 30:6, hiding in holes from poverty and disaster; Nah 2:13 (ET 2:12), caves and dens (holes); Zech 14:12 (day of the Lord), eye rots in their "holes"; Isa 11:8, the nursing child shall play over the hole of the asp. Note especially Isa 42:22: "But this is a people robbed and plundered, all of them are trapped in holes and hidden in prison; they have become a prey with no one to rescue."

Halperin is on somewhat stronger ground when he claims a sexual association with the somewhat rare term *ḥātar*, "to dig, bore through." Adultery is nearby in two cases: Job 24:16 and Jer 2:34, but so is the "digging" of thieves or the poor. Amos 9:2 refers to digging to Sheol to escape judgment, rather like the uses of *ḥôr* noted above: Note that the term *ḥātar*, is translated into Greek as *oryssō*, which is generally used for "hew, dig (tombs, wells, graves, etc.)"; see Gen 21:30; 26:15, 18, 19, 21; Exod 7:24; 2 Chr 16:14; Tob 2:7; 8:9.

Halperin cites only one other occasion of the use of the term *ḥôr* in a decidedly sexual context, Cant 5:4. But an expanded survey of the use of the term would have suggested much stronger associations with disasters—judgments of God, confrontation with military enemies, or poverty. Surely this suggests these "holes" as places of refuge or safety in times of disaster rather than sexual imagery. I am not saying that "digging holes" is a technical term always associated with warfare or disasters—I am simply

---

30. Halperin, *Seeking Ezekiel*, 22.

stating that this usage in connection with wars and disasters, whether real or threatened, is much more common than a sexual usage. Attentiveness to this point would have suggested something other than repressed sexuality in a reading of Ezek 8:7-8.

When we do consider the historical and social context of Ezekiel, however, other associations suggest themselves. Ezekiel, by most modern estimates, was among the first exiles taken from Jerusalem. This exile occurred after a siege of the city by Nebuchadnezzar. Now that we have Paul Kern's systematic discussion of the subject of ancient siege warfare, we note that throughout the Bible there are references to sieges involving siege engines and battering rams from at least as early as the Assyrian Empire.[31] Amos 4:3 speaks of defeat by the Assyrians: "Through breaches in the wall you shall leave" (see also Ps 144:14, which compares a breach with exile). Isa 30:13 goes into graphic detail: "Therefore this iniquity shall become for you like a break in a high wall, bulging out, and about to collapse, whose crash comes suddenly, in an instant." The passage 2 Kgs 25:4 directly attests to battering rams in the Babylonian arsenal during the siege of 587. In two separate texts, Ezekiel also refers to battering rams: in his tableau where he sets up the model of the siege of Jerusalem in 4:2, 3; and in pronouncing the disaster in 21:27 (Eng. 22). They are implied in 26:9, where the walls of Jerusalem are being "struck" and towers broken down. Thus, an image of Ezekiel digging through walls ought to suggest damage done to Jerusalem walls in a siege, and all Ezekiel must do is dig a bit further, and "behold," an opening!

But which wall are we talking about? Ezekiel says only that he is placed on the north entrance to the temple court. This seems to imply that Ezekiel imagines himself standing outside the city of Jerusalem. This view is shared by Iaian Duguid in his study of Ezekiel and the elders; he suggests that the sequence of moving inward toward the temple supports this reading.[32]

Estimates of Jerusalem's perimeter wall before the exile are varied, but the temple court clearly represents the extreme northern end. 2 Chr 25:23 presumes that King Joash of Jerusalem broke down 400 cubits of northwestern wall, and then immediately seized "vessels of the house of God." No further destruction of walls appears to be necessary. According to W. S. LaSor, the "Sheep Gate" is so named because here sheep are brought in from outside the city wall, in preparation for sacrifice at the temple.[33] It seems clear, then, that the northeastern segment of the city wall was also the

---

31. Paul Bentley Kern, *Ancient Siege Warfare* (Bloomington: Indiana Univ. Press, 1999) 29–61.

32. Duguid, *Ezekiel and the Leaders of Israel*, 112.

33. W. S. LaSor, "Jerusalem," *ISBE* 2:1001–30.

northeastern wall of the temple complex and therefore would most likely show the damage of the siege of 597, when Ezekiel was taken into exile. Finally, I would note that in his discussions of Nehemiah's survey of the damaged walls of Jerusalem almost 150 years later, Joseph Blenkinsopp points out that the northern, as well as eastern, section of Jerusalem would have borne the brunt of attacks by Mesopotamian regimes, and thus Nehemiah finds this section in the greatest state of destruction, and more workers are employed in this section than at the other sections.[34]

As Zimmerli and others note, the Hebrew text's additional discussion of digging in the walls does, in fact, relate to 12:1-16, which alludes to Zedekiah's attempted escape from Jerusalem. Most scholars see 12:13 as a post-587 insertion regarding Zedekiah's blindness and capture, and my reading would make this a natural association.

One can argue similarly with other examples in Halperin's analysis. For example, Halperin believes that Ezekiel's turning a sword on himself to shave the hair of his beard is a veiled reference to pubic hair, and off we go into an analysis of the psychosexual implications of this. But swords are used throughout the prophetic literature as metaphors for conquering armies—as Halperin knows: "Let us grant that Ezekiel . . . inspired by a still earlier prophet, turned Isaiah's razor on himself. What might have driven him to [do this]?"[35]

What drove him indeed! What appears to have driven Ezekiel the man to act out the horrors of conquest—the scattering of refugees in fear, the butchering of those captured, and the taking of exiles—is what causes thousands upon thousands of traumatized humans to relive memories that can literally drive them to despair, alcoholism, silence, and suicide. When analyzing a refugee's paranoia, surely a sword is sometimes actually a sword.

Now, one could back up on the historical literalism here and simply say that this is what Ezekiel imagined even if he is not reflecting the actual condition of the wall or actual use of swords. The point is, however, that reading Ezekiel in the context of the sociopolitical events of the time suggests that his behavior and observations can, and probably should, be read in the light of these actual traumatic circumstances as a prerequisite to any assessments of the behavior, much less the textual reconstruction of a problematic passage, in Ezekiel.

Further, I must say that the results of Halperin's analysis of Ezekiel the man are not pleasant. Halperin himself states: "Ezekiel 'as he really was'—

---

34. Blenkinsopp, *Ezra-Nehemiah*, OTL (Philadelphia: Westminster, 1988) 232. Compare the emphasis on foes from "north" in Jer 1:13-15.
35. Halperin, *Seeking Ezekiel*, 27

as I imagine him—is very far from being a lovable person. He emerges in these pages as an extreme exemplar of a morbidity that afflicts many and perhaps all human societies."[36] Furthermore, Halperin ends his analysis of Ezekiel by stating that the prophet "died as he had lived: wretched, hateful, tormented by rages and longings which he could not possibly have understood."[37] I maintain, quite to the contrary, that Ezekiel knew at least one major source of his torment (and so do we)—the tortuous brutalities of ancient siege warfare and the trauma of destruction. Yet Halperin mentions the exile two times in his entire book, and then only in passing. Such tendencies to read the psychological state of Ezekiel totally apart from the social and political experiences he suffered are symptoms of the same avoidance in other biblical scholarly analyses of the exile as a real event where human beings deeply suffered. Any psychological assumptions about Ezekiel derived apart from serious attention to the exile are thus tantamount to blaming the victim.

Trauma Studies and Posttraumatic Stress Disorder: Ezekiel the Refugee

Attention to the social, economic, and traumatic factors at work in circumstances and contexts of subordination, disaster, warfare, or political oppression (either individually or a group) has led in recent years (at least since the 1970s) to increased attention to Posttraumatic Stress Disorder (hereinafter PTSD). It was only in 1980 that the widely cited *Diagnostic and Statistical Manual of Mental Disorders* (DSM) of the American Psychiatric Association listed a symptomology of "Post-Traumatic Stress Disorder." Among the indications of PTSD appearing in the latest edition of DSM, we find: "recurrent and intrusive distressing recollections of the event, including images, thoughts, or perceptions ... recurrent distressing dreams of the event ... acting or feeling as if the traumatic event were recurring (includes a sense of reliving the experience, illusions, hallucinations, and ... flashbacks) ... intense psychological distress at exposure to internal or external cues that symbolize or resemble an aspect of the traumatic event ... efforts to avoid thoughts, feelings ... associated with the trauma ... feeling of detachment or estrangement from others."[38]

Since this symptomology has entered DSM, however, interest in trauma studies and related psychological and sociological studies have

36. Ibid., 5.

37. Ibid., 225.

38. Cf. John B. Murray, "Posttraumatic Stress Disorder: A Review," *Genetic, Social, and General Psychology Monographs* 118, no. 3 (1992) 316.

increased dramatically.[39] This interest has not come without a serious backlash. To suggest that (for example) warfare, both shooting and being shot at, can have serious and debilitating psychological consequences has obvious implications for governments and industries who are determinedly attempting to spend as much money as possible on the causes of destruction and as little as possible on its results, both human and environmental. In a recent review of the history of PTSD, John Wilson points out:

> Viewed from a historical perspective, the emergence of widespread interest in PTSD by the medical and behavioral sciences as well as in legal arenas of litigation is quite understandable and, perhaps, expectable when examined by a retrospective look at some major events of the twentieth century: two World Wars; the atomic bombing of Hiroshima; scores of nationalistic and colonial wars; widespread civil violence; mass genocide. . . . When it is considered that hundreds of millions of human lives have been adversely affected by such traumatic events, it only stands to reason that sooner or later scientific inquiry would accumulate enough momentum to began examining the multifaceted aspects of what traumatization means, and the potential long-term impact to human lives of such events.[40]

Moreover, PTSD has by now been thoroughly documented as resulting from a variety of traumatic experiences both natural and humanmade, and the central symptoms of which—particularly intrusive memory and debilitating depression—have been documented across an impressive variety of cultures around the world, from studies among Armenians surviving the massive earthquake of 1988 (6.9 on the Richter scale, 25,000 dead); Vietnamese and Cambodian refugees in the United States and Norway; and Sri Lankan, Israeli, Russian, and Indian survivors of disaster. The work continues, particularly on nuancing cultural variations in symptoms and expression of symptoms.

---

39. A few examples: Daniel Brom and Eliezer Witztum, "When Political Reality Enters Therapy: Ethical Considerations in the Treatment of Posttraumatic Stress Disorder," in *Beyond Trauma: Cultural and Societal Dynamics*, ed. R. Kleber, C. Figley, and B. Gersons (New York: Plenum, 1995) 237–48; D. Lukoff, F. Lu, and R. Turner, "Toward a More Culturally Sensitive DSM-IV," *Journal of Nervous and Mental Disease* 180, no. 11 (1992) 673–82; Derek Summerfield, "Addressing Human Response to War and Atrocity: Major Challenges in Research and Practices and the Limitations of Western Psychiatric Models," in *Beyond Trauma*, ed. Kleber, Figley, and Gersons, 17–30; and John P. Wilson, "The Historical Evolution of PTSD Diagnostic Criteria: From Freud to DSM-IV," *Journal of Traumatic Stress* 7, no. 4 (1994) 681–98.

40. Wilson, "Historical Evolution," 682.

A sampling from recent literature on PTSD is suggestive. As B. Gersons and I. Carlier point out, PTSD has its origins as a new diagnosis in response to the unique psychic consequences of war in the twentieth century, particularly in Viet Nam.[41] War continues to provide significant sources of research, even up to the Gulf War, for example, the impact of missiles fired at Tel Aviv neighborhoods,[42] and a very high instance of PTSD symptoms (over 50 percent) among military personnel who worked on identifying the dead (one worker reported crying out the name of the first identified body in his sleep).[43] One thinks of Ezekiel's vision of the valley of bones in ch. 37; note particularly that many modern scholars suggest that the vision is intended to depict a battlefield strewn with dead.[44] John Murray further notes that the literature suggests: "Combat exposure, its duration, witnessing the death of comrades, and participating in atrocities were the most frequent factors associated with PTSD."[45]

Participation in Viet Nam atrocities and the associated guilt appears to be a prominent feature among those generations who experienced that conflict.[46] J. Davidson and E. Foa concur: "of the event characteristics . . . physical injury, bereavement, participation in atrocities, exposure to grotesque death, and witnessing or hearing about death were more often associated with the development of PTSD."[47] Note here the suggestions about Ezekiel's hearing of the fall of Jerusalem, with the accompanying news of his wife's death.

What has been particularly important in PTSD research is that symptoms can persist, or even turn up, years after the events that triggered them.[48] Disaster workers reported symptoms three years following the sinking of the *Herald of Free Enterprise* ferry in the English Channel in 1987.[49] Further research turns up specific factors when dealing with children, such as prolonged exposure to violence in poor,

---

41. Cf. B. Gersons and I. Carlier, "Post-traumatic Stress Disorder: The History of a Recent Concept," *British Journal of Psychiatry* 161 (1992) 742–48.

42. Borkan et al., "Stories."

43. Sutker et al., "Psychological Symptoms."

44. Daniel Block hints at this in *The Book of Ezekiel: Chapters 25–48*, NICOT (Grand Rapids: Eerdmans, 1998) 374; and others have been more direct, e.g., Lawrence Boadt C.S.P., "Ezekiel," in *The New Jerome Biblical Commentary*, ed. R. E. Brown, J. A. Fitzmyer, and R. E. Murphy (Englewood Cliffs, N.J.: Prentice-Hall, 1990) 325.

45. Murray, "Posttraumatic Stress Disorder," 316.

46. Ibid., 317.

47. Davidson and Foa, "Diagnostic," 347. Cf. Ursano et al., "Longitudinal," 41.

48. Murray, "Posttraumatic Stress Disorder," 324.

49. Dixon, Rehling, and Shiwach, "Peripheral."

urban neighborhoods,[50] but also specifically with women, particularly in cases of rape.[51] Notable for our study of Ezekiel, Murray reports: "The interval between rape and presenting for treatment was about eight years for a woman who had lost her ability to speak in the meantime."[52] Ezekiel is struck mute for the duration of most of his symbolic actions and can speak only with the news of the fall of Jerusalem and the death of his wife. Furthermore, research indicates that PTSD symptoms are also found in those reacting to natural disasters.[53]

Research on specific symptoms is also intriguing. For example, C. Classen, C. Koopman, and D. Spiegal report of the symptoms of feeling detached, as if one is an observer of one's own mental or bodily processes: "Rape victims often speak of feeling as though they are floating above their own body, feeling sorry for the woman suffering the sexual assault. A car accident survivor said her experience, 'was as though I was separate from myself and watching, like in a dream when you are watching yourself.' . . . A Vietnam combat veteran said, 'I felt myself separating from myself and looking down at the person who was in combat, and feeling sorry for him.'"[54] Such specifics give us pause when thinking of Ezekiel's famous vision of being miraculously and bodily transported back to Jerusalem to witness the horrifying heresies of the temple in chs. 8–11.

Application of PTSD symptomology and literature to historical cases is also not new. Parry-Jones and Parry-Jones apply PTSD terminology to an eighteenth-century avalanche disaster and draw conclusions from the witnesses and surviving participants about the occurrences of PTSD symptoms.[55]

Of particular interest to us, of course, is the amount of PTSD research conducted with refugees. Psychologists and medical scholars have been interested in cross-cultural differences in exhibiting PTSD symptoms, and the length of time that symptoms are reported or persist among, for example, various refugee populations.[56] Indeed, scholars are moving

50. Kevin Fitzpatrick and Janet Boldizar, "The Prevalence and Consequences of Exposure to Violence among African-American Youth," *Journal of American Academy of Child Adolescent Psychiatry* 32:2 (1993) 424–30.

51. See Bownes, O'Gorman, and Sayers, "Assault Characteristics."

52. Murray, "Posttraumatic," 327.

53. Ibid., 326.

54. Classen, Koopman, and Spiegal, "Assault," 181.

55. B. Parry-Jones and W. Parry-Jones, "Post-Traumatic Stress Disorder: Supportive Evidence from an Eighteenth-Century Natural Disaster," *Psychological Medicine* 24 (1994) 15–27.

56. Carlson and Rosser-Hogan, "Cross-Cultural"; cf. Hauff and Vaglum, "Vietnamese Boat Refugees"; Mattson, "Mental Health."

toward a profound recognition that PTSD is allowing for a much greater depth in our understanding of the psychological and even spiritual impact of warfare and refugee life. The loss of one's way of life, one's entire world, may itself trigger such symptoms. According to D. Lukoff, F. Lu, and R. Turner, "cultural bereavement may exemplify a psychospiritual problem occurring within a non-Western ethnic group."[57] When this loss is connected to violent loss, as in refugee status from warfare or state-sponsored terrorism, then we begin to hear new tones in the voice of Ezekiel.

It seems only to be expected, then, that sociologists would soon begin to understand that state-sponsored terrorism against whole peoples and cultures would have its psychological as well as spiritual impact. Frantz Fanon, the noted Martinique-born psychiatrist who worked with the Algerian resistance from 1953 until his untimely death in 1961, needs to be remembered as much for his pioneering exploration of the psychological impact of colonization on the colonized and the sociopolitical context of psychological illness as for his political philosophy.

According to Hussein Bulhan, "to lock up a person in a cell, left to his fantasies and hurts, is simply to sanction and intensify the very 'pathology' to be cured. It is also to reenact, in the name of science and care, the very sadomasochism, rejection, and violence prevalent in his social life. Moreover, it is not enough to search for a 'cure' by conjuring up imaginary roles and concocting artificial groups when real aspects of the person and his social milieu can be engaged, confronted, and changed in the real society."[58]

Attention to the social, economic, and traumatic context at work in circumstances of subordination, disaster, warfare, or political oppression (either individually or a group) has also led in recent years to increased attention to PTSD as a means of understanding cultural groups who suffer as entire peoples. Eduardo and Bonnie Duran's brilliant work, *Native American Postcolonial Psychology*, is an excellent move in this direction and has obvious relevance to a fuller reading of Ezekiel and the book of Lamentations. They note the specific social impact of the First Contact Period, the Invasive War Period, and Subjugation and Reservation Period, the Boarding School Period, and finally the Forced Relocation and Termination Period. They refer to the research pointing out the cross-generational passing of PTSD symptomology, as noted in children

---

57. Lukoff, Lu, and Turner, "Toward," 676.
58. Hussein Bulhan, *Frantz Fanon and the Psychology of Oppression* (New York: Plenum, 1985), 275.

of Holocaust survivors, and discuss dreams in Native culture and practice as locations of pain and a groping for understanding.[59]

Finally, studies of dream analysis in populations of stress or refugee populations also provide an interesting source of insights for reading Ezekiel, who apparently dealt with many disturbing visions in his career as a priest/prophet of the exile. Raija-Leena Punamaki, a psychologist from the University of Helsinki, has done a number of significant studies on the dream culture of Palestinians in both occupied territories and in refugee camp settings.[60] Her work tends to focus on dreams as "compensation" for daily realities faced in violent circumstances and dreams of "mastery" as a response. It would seem that Ezekiel's "visions," such as the transport to Jerusalem, and the valley of dry bones particularly, would be interesting subjects of a study comparing the content of these visions with dream analysis in violent circumstances.

Another direction for this analysis, however, would be in citing "supernatural" phenomena in the context of oppressive working or living conditions. Investigating the occurrences of "spirit possession" among sewing sweatshops throughout Asia, Aihwa Ong has noted that factory women "untutored in ideologies" are capable of making alternative interpretations based on their own visceral experiences and cultural traditions, notably spirit possession: "Their vivid imagery defined the factory premises as a spiritually polluted place."[61] To read the vision of the valley of dry bones as the renewal of Israel from the strewn bodies of postdestruction Jerusalem is a powerful connection between contemporary analysis of visionary and dream content with studies of the book of Ezekiel.

59. Eduardo and Bonnie Duran, *Native American Postcolonial Psychology* (Albany: State Univ. of New York Press, 1995).

60. See "The Role of Dreams in Protecting Psychological Well-Being in Traumatic Conditions," *International Journal of Behavioural Development* 22, no. 3 (1998) 559–88; "Correspondence Between Waking-Time Coping and Dream Content," *Journal of Mental Imagery* 22:3–4 (1998) 147–64; "Determinants and Mental Health Effects of Dream Recall among Children Living in Traumatic Conditions," *Dreaming* 7:4 (1997) 235–61.

61. Aihwa Ong, "The Gender and Labor Politics of Postmodernity," in *The Politics of Culture in the Shadow of Capital*, ed. Lisa Lowe and David Lloyd (Durham, N.C.: Duke Univ. Press 1997) 83. But see also, from her own references, Ong, "The Production of Possession," *American Ethnologist* 15 (1988) 28–42; Soon Hua Sun, "Women, Work, and Theology in Korea," *Journal of Feminist Studies in Religion* 3 (1987) 124–34.

The Sign-Actions of Ezekiel: Reading Ezekiel with Lamentations

For the study of Ezekiel, the reading of refugee studies and the literature of PTSD forces us to ask serious questions about the adequacy of any textual assessment of Ezekiel apart from a full appreciation of the historical and social implications of the siege of Jerusalem, the deportations, and executions by the Babylonian armies and the exile. Furthermore, PTSD literature emphasizes that there is secondary trauma for which symptoms are widely documented. One need not be present at the death of a loved one—merely the news can be sufficiently traumatic. Furthermore, proximity to the time of the disasters or traumas is clearly an interesting aspect of PTSD studies, some of which document symptoms twenty to forty years after the events themselves.

Has the psychological exegesis of Ezekiel tended toward blaming the victim? A synoptic reading of the exile through Ezekiel and the book of Lamentations forces us to take a fresh look at the actions and behavior of Ezekiel. Lamentations, of course, consists of poetic memories of the fall of Jerusalem. To read Ezekiel with an eye to Lamentations suggests that many of Ezekiel's "bizarre" actions can be seen as modeling the trauma of the fall of Jerusalem, whether Ezekiel is acting on personal knowledge, or knowledge brought to him by recent refugees, or whether the texts have been redacted to reflect these realities. Let us consider some of the famous sign-actions in this way:

- Ezek 3:22-27—Ezekiel sits confined in his home, with his hands tied by cords. Compare the language of chains in Lam 3:7: "He has walled me about so that I cannot escape; he has put heavy chains on me."
- Ezek 4:1-3—The siege of Jerusalem that forces some people to eat impure foods, or foods prepared in an impure manner. Compare Lam 1:11; 2:12; 4:4, 9-10 about hunger leading to suggestions of cannibalism (cf. Jer 37:2; 52:6, 24; 2 Kgs 25:3?). Lamentations echoes the concern with the ability to feed oneself and family properly (Lam 1:11): "All her people groan as they search for bread; they trade their treasures for food to revive their strength. Look, O Lord, and see how worthless I have become." Compare also Lam 4:4-10:

> The tongue of the infant sticks to the roof of its mouth for thirst; the children beg for food, but no one gives them anything. Those who feasted on delicacies perish in the streets; those who were brought up in purple cling to ash heaps. For the chastisement of my people has been greater than the punishment of Sodom, which was overthrown in a moment, though no hand was laid on it. Her princes

> were purer than snow, whiter than milk; their bodies were more
> ruddy than coral, their hair like sapphire. Now their visage is blacker
> than soot; they are not recognized in the streets. Their skin has
> shriveled on their bones; it has become as dry as wood. Happier
> were those pierced by the sword than those pierced by hunger,
> whose life drains away, deprived of the produce of the field. The
> hands of compassionate women have boiled their own children;
> they became their food in the destruction of my people.

- Ezek 5:1-17—Ezekiel acts out the trifold punishment of Jerusalem: a
  third burnt in the city, a third dying by the sword, and a third exiled
  ("scattered to the wind"). Compare Lam 1:1 and 2:21: "The young and
  the old are lying on the ground in the streets; my young women and
  my young men have fallen by the sword; in the day of your anger you
  have killed them, slaughtering without mercy."
- Ezekiel 12—Ezekiel prepares "an exile's bag" and is led through a hole
  in a wall to exemplify being taken as a prisoner of war. He is reliving
  the events, both his own and his image of events to come. Compare
  Lam 1:3, 18, "Led into exile"; and 2:8: "The Lord determined to lay in
  ruins the wall of daughter Zion; he stretched the line; he did not with-
  hold his hand from destroying; he caused rampart and wall to lament;
  they languish together."
- Ezekiel 21—Babylonian forces are modeled by a sword. Compare Lam
  2:21, and notably 5:9, where the "sword" refers, again, to foreign rule:
  "We get our bread at the peril of our lives, because of the sword in the
  wilderness."

How do we read such synoptic accounts of exilic tragedies? On the one
hand, they can be psychologized away—the mental illness of a raving
lunatic that history preserves as the sayings of Ezekiel. Or, they are merely
the stereotypical language of lament, and thus with questionable historical value. Clearly, to quote Lamentations to elucidate Ezekiel raises the
question, what about Lamentations? So, in order to assess the impact of
our argument about refugee studies on these texts, we must make observations about Lamentations.

The Language of Lament: Does Literary Stereotype Mean Historical Nonexistence?

The issues raised in any reading of Lamentations always and inevitably
relate to the significance of the so-called treaty curses of Deuteronomy 28.
Indeed, as is frequently the case, the conclusions that one draws for

Deuteronomy 28 relate directly to the assessments of Lamentations, so let us focus briefly on Deuteronomy 28.

Deuteronomy 28 contains a series of descriptions of calamitous events, especially focusing on the horrors of siege warfare. It has often been suggested that Deuteronomy 28, or at least some parts of it, may have been written after the destruction of Jerusalem by the Neo-Babylonian Empire in 587/586 BCE. There have always been some dissenting views to this argument of a description based on the events of 587, of course, among whom were Peter Craigie and J. G. McConville, both of whom point out the striking similarities of many of the curses threatened in Deuteronomy 28 with the plagues "visited" upon Egypt in the story of the exodus.[62] This line of interpretation suggests that the threats in Deuteronomy 28 were really intended to threaten a reenslavement if the conditions of the covenant were not observed. The idea has some merit, of course, especially in the language of 1 Samuel 8, which implies that the appointment of a king is tantamount to choosing a native pharaoh to rule over them, under which they will once again find themselves "crying out" to God (1 Sam 8:18 compared to Exod 3:7, "I have heard their cry").

By far the majority view of Deuteronomy 28, however, is that these descriptions of suffering are among the "curses" that Israel is threatened with if they choose to disobey the laws that have immediately preceded them, and that these curses take the expected form of traditional curses that follow the literary pattern of an international treaty in the ancient Near East. It is precisely these curses that are often compared to the descriptions of suffering of the book of Lamentations.

In the 1950s George Mendenhall began to publish his observations about the striking similarities between the general form of the book of Deuteronomy and the Hittite suzerainty treaties.[63] These insights have

---

62. J. G. McConville, *Law and Theology in Deuteronomy*, JSOTSup 22 (Sheffield: Sheffield Academic, 1984), and Peter C. Craigie, *Deuteronomy*, NIC (Grand Rapids: Eerdmans, 1976).

63. For example, Mendenhall, *Law and Covenant in Israel and the Ancient Near East* (Pittsburgh: Biblical Colloquium, 1955). On this subject, cf. Ze'ev Weisman, "The Place of the People in the Making of Law and Judgment," in *Pomegranates and Golden Bells: Studies in Biblical, Jewish, and Near Eastern Ritual, Law and Literature in Honor of Jacob Milgrom*, ed. D. P. Wright, D. N. Freedman, and A. Hurvitz (Winona Lake, Ind.: Eisenbrauns, 1995) 407–20; Dale Patrick, "The Rhetoric of Collective Responsibility in Deuteronomy Law," in ibid., 421–36; Yair Hoffman, "The Deuteronomist and the Exile," in ibid., 659–75; J. G. McConville, *Law and Theology in Deuteronomy*, JSOTSup 22 (Sheffield: Sheffield Academic, 1984); Shemaryahu Talmon, "The Internal Diversification of Judaism in the Early Second Temple Period," in *Jewish Civilization in the Hellenistic-Roman Period*, ed. Talmon, JSPSup 10 (Sheffield: Sheffield Academic, 1991) 16–43; Moshe Weinfeld, *Deuteronomy and the Deuteronomic School* (Oxford: Clarendon, 1972); D. J. McCarthy, *Treaty and Covenant*, Analecta

created an extensive literature, and this general idea of the comparison (even if the specific Hittite associations are now rejected) between the two forms of literature—biblical and political treaty forms—certainly remains among the many enduring contributions made by Mendenhall. Scholars differ, however, as to which treaty traditions offer the more precise parallels to Deuteronomy. Similarities have now been noted among many treaty forms from the Assyrian Empire, the Aramaic texts of Sefire, as well as the earlier Hittite forms.[64] Collectively, these comparisons parallel the appearance of the blessings and curses in Deuteronomy 27–28. It seems beyond question that the writers of Deuteronomy have taken on the practice of placing blessings and curses at the end of treaties as an encouragement to obey, and a discouragement against disobeying, the terms of the treaty in question. But what has been the result of this now widely noted comparison? It is instructive to survey the development of views that followed Mendenhall's initial observations.

Adam Welch had observed in 1932, well before Mendenhall's thesis was published: "There is a note of pain and horror which can leave little doubt that the writer had lived through the conditions he described or had learned them from men who knew them at first hand."[65] It is precisely this openness to history that literary analysis can sometimes close off.

In his commentary on Deuteronomy, Gerhard von Rad's brief observations on ch. 28 summarize a common notion in the mid-twentieth century. Von Rad notes that the large amount of curses, compared with the brevity of the blessings, in vv. 15-68 lends support to his supposition that

Biblica 21 (Rome: Pontifical Biblical Institute, 1963); D. R. Hillers, *Treaty-Curses and the Old Testament Prophets*, BibOr 16 (Rome: Pontifical Biblical Institute, 1964); D. J. Wiseman, "Vassal-Treaties of Esarhaddon," *Iraq* 20 (1958): 1–100; Joel Kaminsky, *Corporate Responsi bility in the Hebrew Bible*, JSOTSup 196 (Sheffield: Sheffield Academic, 1995); Mark A. O'Brien, *The Deuteronomistic History: A Reassessment* (Freiburg: Universitätsverlag; Göttingen:Vandenhoeck & Ruprecht, 1989); J. G. McConville and J. G. Millar, *Time and Place in Deuteronomy*, JSOTSup 179 (Sheffield: Sheffield Academic, 1994); Horst Dietrich Preuss, *Deuteronomium*, Erträge der Forschung 164 (Darmstadt: Wissenschaftliche Buchgesellschaft, 1982); Ferdinand Deist, "The Dangers of Deuteronomy: A Page from Reception History of the Book," in *Studies in Deuteronomy: In Honour of C. J. Labuschagne on the Occasion of His Sixty-Fifth Birthday*, ed. F. García Martínez et al., VTSup 53 (Leiden: Brill, 1994) 13–29; A. R. Welch, *Deuteronomy: The Framework to the Code* (London: Oxford Univ. Press, 1932); Robert Carroll, "Madonna of Silences: Clio and the Bible," in *Can a History of Israel Be Written?* ed. L. L. Grabbe, European Seminar in Historical Methodology 1, JSOTSup 245 (Sheffield: Sheffield Academic, 1997) 84–103; G. von Rad, *Deuteronomy*, trans. D. Barton, OTL (Philadelphia: Westminster, 1966).

64. In addition to Hillers and Mendenhall, see Joseph Fitzmyer, *The Aramaic Inscriptions of Sefire*, BibOr 19 (Rome: Pontifical Biblical Institute, 1967).

65. Hillers, *Treaty-Curses*, 32, and Welch, *Deuteronomy*, 135.

it "is precisely the section of curses which has attracted gradual amplifica-
tions. . . . [This] is easy to understand, when we recall the catastrophe of
the exile of 587, regarded by many as the direct fulfillment of the threatened disaster."[66] He then finishes this section with the following observation: "We may suppose that in this section actual experiences are
reproduced which the population of Judah and Jerusalem had endured
during the invasion of the neo-Babylonian army in 587 (2 Kings 25.1ff.). It
must, however, be recalled that the eating of one's own children belongs
to the traditional accounts of the horrors conjured up when describing
the siege of towns (Lev. 26.29; 2 Kings 6.26; Jer. 19.9; Lam. 2.20; 4.10; Ezek.
5.10)."[67]

Von Rad's study is thus already showing the signs of a development in
the interpretation of Deuteronomy 28 and many other descriptions of
suffering, including most notably the book of Lamentations, that I wish
to highlight. Where once there was some confidence about some recollec-
tion of historical realities behind the narrative of Deuteronomy 28, now
there emerges considerable doubt as a result of the awareness of tradi-
tionalized, stereotypical accounts of suffering.

One scholar whose work has been heavily influential in this line of
interpretation is Delbert Hillers, whose extensive treatment of the vassal
treaties led him to compare them to the curses of Deuteronomy, but also
to a good deal of the threatening language of the prophets as well, and
these observations are featured in his Anchor Bible commentary on
Lamentations. In 1964 Hillers objected to the notion of historical recol-
lection in Deuteronomy 28 by observing: "The existence of a tradition of
curses over a thousand years old renders any attempt to relate individual
curses to particular historical periods highly suspect."[68]

A similar ambiguity about the historical significance of Deuteronomy 28 was raised about the same time in Dennis J. McCarthy's classic
text, *Treaty and Covenant*: "the element of military disaster and its consequences, hunger, slavery, exile . . . is common in the curse literature.
Hence we cannot reject out of hand any reference to exile as a secondary
addition. Why must Deuteronomy be denied the right to use it as a
threat as did the composer of Esarhaddon's treaty and of the Sfire text,
cases where there is no question of *vaticinium ex eventu*, but only
knowledge of the probable result of ancient warfare? Hence, a simple
reference to exile like that of 28:36-37 is hardly a sign that the passage is

66. Von Rad, *Deuteronomy*, 173.
67. Ibid., 176.
68. Hillers, *Treaty-Curses*, 35.

a later addition."[69] But McCarthy still felt compelled to speak of a difference in tone in the verses following 45, although he considered v. 48 to be
more likely a different voice:

> The problem of vv. 48 ff. is indeed more difficult. The common idea
> is that they reflect too explicitly the conditions of siege and exile to
> have been written before these events. The conclusion hardly imposes
> itself for these reasons. The D[euteronomic] writer was a stylist capa-
> ble of developing at length upon a familiar theme. There is, however,
> a problem with the change in the point of view on the curses which
> can be seen from v. 45 on. Up to that point the whole is commanded
> by vv. 1 and 15 which make the blessing and curses alternative possi-
> bilities facing Israel. With v. 45 there is a significant change. It is now
> a question of fact: the curses will come upon Israel because it has not
> obeyed. The difference is important and it does truly mark the con-
> cluding verses of c. 28 ff. off from what has gone before.[70]

This remaining openness to historical memory in Deuteronomy 28,
however, would soon fall out of fashion. Moshe Weinfeld includes his
own analysis of the Vassal Treaties of Esarhaddon as part of his classic
work, *Deuteronomy and the Deuteronomic School*. He makes special note
of parallels between Deuteronomy 28 and the Vassal Treaties of Esarhaddon that also, significantly, even follow in the same general order:

DEUTERONOMY		VASSAL TREATIES
28:23	brass sky, iron ground	(lines) 528-31
28:27	leprosy, skin disease	19-20
28:28-29	confusion, blindness, robbery	422-24
28:26	birds feed on corpses	425-27
28:30a	betrothed ravaged by others	428-29
28:30b	sons and daughters won't inherit	429-30a
28:33a	other nations take your goods	430b[71]

As for the supposed changes at v. 45, Weinfeld argues that these further
elaborations of the conditions of siege are not later reflections of actual
memories of the siege and destruction of Jerusalem and the devastation
of Judah in 587–586 BCE. However, he cites only lines 448-50 of the Vassal
Treaties of Esarhaddon, which speak of cannibalism, as evidence that
there are thematic parallels to the material following v. 45.

---

69. McCarthy, *Treaty*, 124
70. Ibid.
71. Weinfeld, *Deuteronomic School*, 116–38.

Thus Weinfeld had already taken the next step in the direction of denying historical bases for the treaty curses when he suggests that the curses in Deuteronomy 28 may well be part of the common metaphors of international language with regard to suffering the political consequences of breaking treaties, and therefore: "this fact implies that maledictions of this type do not necessarily reflect a real situation but belong rather to the typology of the political documents current in the eighth and seventh centuries BC."[72]

In this connection, I will cite only one further reference, turning now to related discussions of the descriptions of tragedy in the book of Lamentations. In the introduction to his commentary, Iain Provan provides important literary observations, including a discussion of stereotypical language: "[On the one hand] the events which the poems describe are cloaked in non-literal language . . . which renders the reality which lies behind them elusive. It is, on the other, demonstrably hyperbolic."[73] The result of Provan's line of literary analysis, however, suggests that a necessary caution in dealing with descriptions of suffering has begun to give way to open skepticism: "If it is true . . . that accounts of suffering in the Ancient Near East were to some extent, at least, written up in a stereotypical manner, without thought of the immediate 'facts,' our first difficulty is to know when it is right to look for concrete historical reality behind the text at all."[74]

Now, it may well be the case here that we cannot make presumptions about the historicity of details that fit a clearly established pattern of images. And it seems beyond doubt that we are dealing with patterns in the descriptions of suffering, but it is also difficult to avoid the impression of a classic slippery slope in these arguments.

Before taking up this concern, however, I think that it is important to mention that the literary approach that suggested the presence of layers in Deuteronomy 28 continues. For example, in his 1982 survey of Deuteronomy scholarship, H. D. Preuss spoke of a general sense of the early date for the short, stylistic blessings and curses of 28:3-6 and 16-19, and later dates for much of the curses. While there is a general consensus that v. 44 ends a section that is clearly related to, if not influenced by, parallels to vassal treaties and other Near Eastern treaty forms, some scholars have persisted that Deuteronomy 28 is not to be entirely dismissed as a source of some historical reflection on the tragedy of 587/586.[75]

72. Ibid., 127.
73. Iain Provan, *Lamentations*, NCBC (Grand Rapids: Eerdmans, 1991) 6.
74. Ibid., 12.
75. Preuss, *Deuteronomium*, 154.

The proposed later additions to Deuteronomy 28, of course, have important parallels in Deut 4:25-31; 30:1-10; and Solomon's prayer in 1 Kgs 8:46-53. But Preuss contends that Weinfeld's (and other scholars') objections based on treaty parallels do not overcome the literary-critical arguments that at least some of the material of Deuteronomy 28 does not merely reflect stereotypical language, or remove the impression of a developed tradition that was later expanded. Preuss notes that vv. 58-68 already presume a reader of a book, an advance on the parallel material in vv. 47-57.[76] For Preuss, notwithstanding the frequent appeals to treaty parallels, the detail with which a siege and resulting exile are discussed in this and comparable passages (and not neglecting Ezekiel) suggests that we are dealing with recollections, if not communal traditions, about the actual destruction of Jerusalem and Judah.

In light of the occasional caution of scholars like Preuss, however, I am more concerned to take issue with the general drift that the treaty-parallel line of textual and literary analysis has taken with regard to the question of studying the exile. I think it is demonstrably the case that scholars are moving from proper caution in dealing with literary forms of language (e.g., stereotypical language) to open skepticism that such language has any historical referent at all. In recent work, scholars seem to have doubts about the very impact of the exile. In other words, where the references like Deuteronomy 28, certain lines in Lamentations, and other passages that describe the results of siege and military conquest were formerly considered at least partially stereotypical in form, there is a tendency now to speak of these stereotypical references as historically *fraudulent*. Is it legitimate to move from the conclusion that certain literary forms of narrative employ stereotypical language, to a conclusion that stereotypical suffering is therefore not suffering at all? For instance, Robert Carroll begins his analysis of the exile with strong words about the historical reality of the crisis of 587/586: "to use the term 'exile' in a book title is to connive at, conspire or collaborate with the biblical text in furthering the myth represented by the ideological shaping of biblical history."[77] Furthermore, "any concatenation of such problems must render any and all historiographic approaches to reading the Bible highly suspect as attempts at historical reconstructions of an imagined past."[78]

---

76. Ibid., 154-55.
77. Carroll, "Exile! What Exile? Deportation and the Discourse of Diaspora," in *Leading Captivity Captive*, ed. L. L. Grabbe, JSOTSup 278 (Sheffield: Sheffield Academic, 1998) 66-67.
78. Ibid., 70.

I believe, however, that Carroll can be misread in this context. As I read Carroll's work, he is not arguing against the historical realities of 587/586, but rather protesting that the literary and theological assessment of the significance of those events ought not to be dictated by one particular theological tradition—certainly not only those of the central temple elite from Jerusalem. This is, I think, a helpful caution, and I furthermore quite agree that there are many reactions to the catastrophe of 587/586 in the varied texts of the Hebrew Bible. But I still think that the event itself was an actual catastrophe.

Preliminary Conclusions

Reading Deuteronomy 28, Lamentations, and Ezekiel in the context of PTSD and the literature of refugee experience and exile, our assessments of the stereotypical language of the Bible with regard to suffering suggest a disturbing modern analogy. While living in the Middle East between 1986 and 1988, I became troubled by a clear Western media bias when reporting on local disasters in Israel and the West Bank. Many news reports in the West featured the demonstrations of great emotional outbursts of both Arab men and women in the face of disaster or death. Such emotional displays were often met in Western reporters' eyes with a certain kind of disgust. Albert Memmi, in his classic work on the colonial situation, reflects on precisely this aspect of what some writers have since referred to as the "colonial gaze": "Even a native mother weeping over the death of her son or a native woman weeping over the death of her husband reminds [the colonizer] only vaguely of the grief of a mother or a wife."[79] The point hardly needs to be labored. Stereotypical language may suggest literary creativity in the absence of an actual event, or alternatively, it may be the culturally acceptable way to express precisely the emotional reactions to an actual catastrophic event. That language is demonstrably stereotypical—in either the Bible or the modern Mediterranean cultures—is not the same thing as saying that a language is demonstrably fraudulent—or that it is language that is not reacting to real trauma. In short, while some critical scholars seem intent on blaming a "Sunday school" bias (cf. Barstad) for the view that an actual crisis took place in 587, I would suggest that they would hardly do well to replace this with an equally objectionable and culturally insensitive Western bias that seems disappointed that Mediterranean peoples do not mourn "as we do" or refer to events "as we do."

---

79. Memmi, *The Colonizer and the Colonized* (Boston: Beacon, 1965) 86.

I do not want to make light of the implications of this. If we are able to read stereotypical language of the Bible in reference to suffering—and particularly the suffering involved in siege warfare—as a measure not so much of the historical details of the disaster or catastrophe, but rather as a measure of the emotional, social, and obviously therefore spiritual impact of the disaster (after all, this is religious literature), then our analysis of a good deal of biblical literature in relation to the exile would need to be rethought. Stereotypical literature of suffering is not literature that can somehow be "decoded" to mean that the exiles actually lived in Babylonian comfort.

What is important here is simply that a reading of refugee studies, disaster studies, and the assumption of trauma transforms our image of Ezekiel from merely a neurotic psychopath (Halperin) or a merely creative writer (Zimmerli) to one whose imagery and prose can be taken as indications of the experience of exile. To read Lamentations in this light, albeit in stereotypical language, is once again to recover Lamentations as a measure of the psychological and spiritual crisis of the exile. To read these texts without some sense of the trauma of exile is tantamount to blaming the victims at the very least, and perhaps grossly misunderstanding much of the power of the text in its social context.

To summarize, that "exile" becomes a central myth in biblical literature is clear, but what I believe must also be clear is that there is not necessarily a fictional, contrived, or exaggerated event behind the use of such influential literary motifs. Along these lines, Halperin's exclusively internal reading of Ezekiel the prophet as struggling almost entirely with issues of sexuality, when read from the perspective of refugee studies, PTSD, and attention to social realities of the exile, has the unfortunate result of blaming the victim. Similarly in reading Lamentations, the results of literary analysis can render chains and fetters, swords and suffering into sanitized metaphors that insulate the modern reader from the trauma of the historical exile as an event in the life of the Hebrews. Exclusively literary approaches seem similar to questioning the sanity of Ezekiel or the reality of experience in Lamentations and thus can thereby question how seriously we must consider such material matters in doing theology. When Halperin confidently asserts, at the end of his engaging study, that a focused psychoanalysis of Ezekiel himself allows us to "at last . . . hear Ezekiel," I maintain that we do not "hear" Ezekiel clearly unless we also "hear" the imperial voice of Nebuchadnezzar the conqueror.

4.

SHAME AND TRANSFORMATION:
On Prayer and History
in the Diaspora

O NE OF THE CLEAREST RESULTS OF THE STUDY OF BIBLICAL TEXTS
related to the experience of exile is the obvious interest in history.
Two major historical works emerge from the experience of exile and continued existence in the Diaspora—the Deuteronomistic History (even
though its origins may have been rooted in texts that began prior to 597
BCE), and the Chronicler's History. I have noted in the survey of refugee
studies that an interest in history is typically rehearsed as a matter deeply
related to identity formation. But biblical scholars have recently made
similar observations. Judith Newman, for example, observes that "the
combination of scripture and remembrance of tradition was the regener-
ative force in which community self-understanding was reinforced
through worship."[1] History is thus also part of a response to the disruptive
dilemmas of exilic life. According to the Palestinian-American Edward
Said: "Exile is fundamentally a discontinuous state of being. Exiles are cut
off from their roots, their land, their past. They generally do not have enemies, or states, though they are often in search of these institutions. This
search can lead exiles to reconstitute their broken lives in narrative form,
usually by choosing to see themselves as part of a triumphant ideology or
a restored people. Such a story is designed to reassemble an exile's broken
history into a new whole."[2]

---

1. Judith Newman, *Praying by the Book: The Scripturalization of Prayer in Second Temple
Judaism,* Early Judaism and Its Literature 14 (Atlanta: Scholars, 1999) 219.
2. Edward Said, "The Mind of Winter," *Harpers* (September 1984) 51.

Said speaks of the powerlessness of exiles. This theme of responding to powerlessness is also an important aspect of the two classical contributors to the origins of postcolonial theory, Albert Memmi and Frantz Fanon. As Fanon states it: "The claim to a national culture in the past does not only rehabilitate that nation and serve as a justification for the hope of a future national culture. In the sphere of psycho-affective equilibrium it is responsible for an important change in the native."[3] Sometimes, however, this "historical reconstructive therapy" cannot be openly practiced. Anticipating some of James Scott's important insights, Fanon further recognized that: "A national culture under colonial domination is a contested culture whose destruction is sought in systematic fashion. It very quickly becomes a culture condemned to secrecy. . . . This new vigor in this sector of cultural life very often passes unseen; and yet its contribution to the national effort is of capital importance. By carving figures and faces which are full of life, and by taking as his theme a group fixed on the same pedestal, the artist invites participation in an organized movement."[4]

In a fascinating analysis of narrative as a social process of "repairing identities," Hilde Nelson has presented the construction of alternative narratives as a creative move to counter the dominant narrative. She maintains that "counterstories redefine a past that has been, until now, characterized incorrectly. They take a story that has (for the moment at least) been determined, undo it, and reconfigure it with a new significance."[5] Very much in the tradition of Memmi's early analysis of how colonialist presumptions can be taken up in colonized cultures even as they try to resist those dominant cultures, Nelson points to the ambiguities of this "narrative construction":

> Rather than invoking master narratives as a means of moral justification, counterstories resist these narratives by attempting to uproot them and replace them with a better alternative. They operate on the supposition that the norms of the community are to be found not only in its foundational narratives, but also in stories that offer other vantage points from which to assess a community's social practices. The teller of a counterstory is bound to draw on the moral concepts found in the master narratives of her tradition, since these played a key role in her moral formation regardless of how problematic her

3. Fanon, *The Wretched of the Earth* (New York: Grove, 1963) 210–11. Cf. Albert Memmi, *The Colonizer and the Colonized* (Boston: Beacon, 1965).
4. Fanon, *Wretched*, 237, 242.
5. Hilde Lindemann Nelson, *Damaged Identities, Narrative Repair* (Ithaca, N.Y.: Cornell Univ. Press, 2001) 18.

place within that tradition has been, but she isn't restricted to just these concepts. To the extent that her experiences of life and considered judgments make them available, she can also help herself to alternative understandings of lying, heroism, fairness, or propriety, testing her conceptions of these things for adequacy against conceptions offered by people within both her found communities and her communities of choice.[6]

Nelson also points out that the most successful counterstories redefine a group in the minds of the dominant culture as well as the minority. But there can obviously be circumstances where the "narrative repair" is effective for the group in question, whether the dominant society accepts it or not. Among the reasons that such narrative repair can be effective, Nelson notes, are that the new formulation helps to make sense of the world and redefines elements of the master narrative.[7] Finally, Nelson makes fascinating observations about how counterstories can themselves "go bad" and become as destructive as the master narrative they were designed to resist. If a group builds itself up by scapegoating yet another group, to try and deflect criticism onto another group, this is clearly not a positive development. Furthermore, if the story establishes a rigid identity that does not allow further development or creativity within the group, this can clearly set up a new dominant minority within the group. Finally, a story can "throw out the baby with the bathwater." (For example, Nelson identifies attempts to redefine physical handicaps as "normal" as well-meaning, but they can also be used to defeat attempts to increase healthcare spending.[8])

Nelson's analysis is applied to contemporary issues, of course, and has its limitations when applied to historical texts. But her analysis is also quite suggestive within these limitations. For example, one can cite Ezra's concern with mixed marriage as creating such a rigid internal definition of social solidarity that it caused as many problems for postexilic social reconstruction as it attempted to prevent in assimilation. Theologies of "God's punishment," an interesting feature of the Deuteronomistic History, could lead to a destructive self-image and a sense of hopelessness in renewing or reviving a people's social and religious identity or existence.

It is precisely this aspect of the Deuteronomistic historical work that is the object of analysis for this section. While some would consider the Deuteronomistic Historian's moralism with regard to Israel's past to

6. Ibid., 67.
7. Ibid., 157–64.
8. Ibid., 176–83.

verge on being destructive, I would argue that it serves a crucial purpose in redefining identity.

A Sociology of Deuteronomistic History?

Although not entirely absent, social elements have rarely been a feature of the torrent of literature that emerged after Martin Noth's magisterial work, *The Deuteronomistic History,* was first published in 1943. Some modern scholars suggest that the composition of the Deuteronomistic historical books went through a long and complex development rather than Noth's notion of a single author.[9] Noth's original arguments focused on the book of Deuteronomy itself, and then the historical works, but interest in identifying "Deuteronomic influence" has lately expanded to include many other biblical books (including, in some views, even wisdom material). Moshe Weinfeld's widely cited study of Deuteronomy and the "Deuteronomic School" added to Noth's study and set out some of the standard theological motifs usually associated with Deuteronomic theology, including the struggle against idolatry, the centralization of the cult, the importance of exodus and the covenant, and an emergent monotheism.[10] But some of these themes may not be unique to Deuteronomy, and the fact that one finds them elsewhere may not necessarily allow a conclusion that other work was "influenced" by Deuteronomic theology. A recent Sheffield compendium with a characteristically puckish title, *Those Elusive Deuteronomists,* contains a number of papers that question a phenomenon they refer to as "Pan-Deuteronomism," by which they mean an apparent overextension of Deuteronomic influence throughout the Hebrew biblical texts.

Out of the discussions, however, I would hazard an observation that there remains some important points of general consensus. First, King Josiah (640–609 BCE) based his famous reform movements—briefly described in 2 Kings 22–23—on a document that closely resembles the legal portions of the book of Deuteronomy as we now have it (especially chs. 12–26). Second, part of the continued influence of this reform led to the composition of an impressive historical work that, since Noth, has

9. See the summaries in Mark Boda, *Praying the Tradition: The Origin and Use of Tradition in Nehemiah 9,* BZAW 277 (Berlin: de Gruyter, 1999); and Linda Shearing and Steven L. McKenzie, eds., *Those Elusive Deuteronomists: The Phenomenon of Pan-Deuteronomism,* JSOTSup 268 (Sheffield: Sheffield Academic, 1999).

10. Moshe Weinfeld, *Deuteronomy and the Deuteronomic School* (Oxford: Clarendon, 1972). A helpful summary is in James Richard Linville, *Israel in the Book of Kings: The Past as a Project of Social Identity,* JSOTSup 272 (Sheffield: Sheffield Academic, 1998) 62–63.

been called the Deuteronomistic History. Third, this historical work has been supplemented in the exilic period, and perhaps many times, even if some of it originated in the final years of the Judean monarchy. William Schniedewind suggests the strong possibility that some of the literature has origins already in the time of Hezekiah[11] but certainly also includes a major period of writing after the time of Josiah.

Debate continues about how much of the material of the Deuteronomistic History is "preexilic." Some modern scholars write as if the question is settled—the entire work is a late fictional composition.[12] But the issue, as I have discussed, must not be left exclusively to literary analysis with no thought to the social and economic realities of empire.

An eye toward these realities of empire (for example, as surveyed in chapter two) would suggest that the debate whether a document may have been written during the events after the (apparently momentous) death of Josiah at Megiddo in 609, rather than after the final destruction of Jerusalem by the Neo-Babylonian armies in 587/586, may not be terribly significant. Too much can be made of the difference between "preexilic" and "postexilic" in this entire period (as Thomas Thompson quipped, "There was exile . . . often!"[13]). Considering Josiah's possible alliances with the Neo-Babylonian Empire and Jehoiakim's clear allegiances to Egypt, one wonders if the actual destructive events of 587/586 are not better seen as a tragic finale to the deconstruction of the Southern Kingdom *throughout* this period in the face of growing Mesopotamian ambitions toward Egyptian territories. Certainly the actual destruction of Jerusalem and especially the temple are not to be underrated as a religiously significant watershed, but one is permitted to wonder if major political, economic, and social differences were not already part of day-to-day life under Babylonian and/or Egyptian political dominance. In other words, even if "preexilic" (in the sense of the period 640–587), the Deuteronomistic History is clearly the product of a seriously declining political independence and a growing awareness that the people of Israel are becoming pawns in the conflicting interests of large-scale Near Eastern empires.

Clearly, one wants to construct a history that serves a purpose under these conditions. In the case of the exile(s), one of the primary questions

11. This is argued by William M. Schniedewind, *Society and the Promise to David. The Reception History of 2 Samuel 7:1-17* (New York: Oxford Univ. Press, 1999).

12. See Jan-Wim Wesselius, "Towards a New History of Israel," *Journal of Hebrew Scriptures* 3 (2000): article 2 [http://www.arts.ualberta.ca/JHS].

13. Thomas L. Thompson, "The Exile in History and Myth: A Response to Hans Barstad," in *Leading Captivity Captive*, ed. L. L. Grabbe, JSOTSup 278 (Sheffield: Sheffield Academic, 1998) 101–19.

that the construction of history attempts to respond to is: What led us here? Even more important, What can we hope for in our future? In an important study, subtitled *The Past as a Project of Social Identity*, James Linville contends that the books of Kings reflect this need to rethink identity in the context of exile: "Identity, regardless of how multiple or chang ing, results from people locating themselves or being located within a set of emplotted stories. They describe ontological narratives as stories that social actors need to make sense of their lives. They are necessary for self-identity and action. . . . People will fit stories to their own identities and will tailor reality in accordance with their stories."[14]

How is an interest in history a reaction to the exile? It is a truism that the Deuteronomistic Historian writes history with a clear moral agenda; among those items in the theological agenda is the judgment passed on most members of the monarchy for its support of Canaanite religious actions. This can be examined readily by simply following the career of the term *high places*, the religious shrines rejected by the writer as a sign of pagan influence:

> The people were sacrificing at the high places, however, because no house had yet been built for the name of the LORD. Solomon loved the LORD, walking in the statutes of his father David; only, he sacri-ficed and offered incense at the high places. (1 Kgs 3:2-3)

> He walked in all the way of his father Asa; he did not turn aside from it, doing what was right in the sight of the LORD; yet the high places were not taken away, and the people still sacrificed and offered incense on the high places. (1 Kgs 22:43)

> He sacrificed and made offerings on the high places, on the hills, and under every green tree. (2 Kgs 16:4)

Furthermore, we can see the moral tone of Deuteronomy in a character-istic construction using *rāq* in the sense of "however," or "only," and at times with the sense of "nevertheless." Often this follows a positive com-mand or statement and has the force of pointing out an exception, a cause for concern or attention: "You did not encroach, *however*, on the land of the Ammonites, avoiding the whole upper region of the Wadi Jabbok as well as the towns of the hill country, just as the LORD our God had charged" (Deut 2:37). Similarly, Deut 4:9; 12:16; 15:5; 17:16; 20:16, and so on. This construction becomes even more important in Kings, where it has the interesting impact of passing judgment on the royal lives of selected

14. Linville, *Israel*, 81.

kings, almost as if the reader expects positive comments on royal history, only to have his/her attention drawn to the notable mistakes:

> Solomon loved the LORD, walking in the statutes of his father David; *only*, he sacrificed and offered incense at the high places. (1 Kgs 3:3)

> Because David did what was right in the sight of the LORD, and did not turn aside from anything that he commanded him all the days of his life, *except (raq)* in the matter of Uriah the Hittite. (1 Kgs 15:5; cf. 1 Kgs 15:4; 21:25; 2 Kgs 3:2)

Note how the criticism becomes more common as the narrative continues into 2 Kings, that is, further into the divided monarchy:

> *Nevertheless* he clung to the sin of Jeroboam son of Nebat, which he caused Israel to commit; he did not depart from it. (2 Kgs 3:3; cf. 2 Kgs 10:29; 12:3; 14:3, 4; 15:4; 15:35; 17:2)

What might be the social function of the critical tone of the Deuteronomistic History? There is one further example of this critical tone that I think is particularly instructive: the tradition of prayer beginning with 1 Kings 8, Solomon's great prayer of dedication, and this final example may shed light on at least some aspects of the exilic history writing.

Penitential Prayer in the Postexilic Period

Even if there is some doubt about the exact chronological parameters of the Deuteronomistic History, there is one genre of literature that is clearly a product of the crises of the sixth century and continues to be utilized in subsequent literatures of later periods: the rise of a postexilic prayer form known as "Penitential Prayers" or "Postexilic Lament Prayers." If we wish to understand the meaning of history for the postexilic community, especially in relation to a theology of exile, few places are better suited for such an analysis than these postexilic prayers, because such prayers would not only be the documents of a literate elite, but would likely have been the public pronouncements around which large-scale identity would be constructed.

Indeed, many of the prayers are set in a context of a listening public. This is the case even if Mark Boda is correct that these prayers may well have also included individual use.[15] But finally, we are justified in examining the

---

15. Boda, *Praying the Tradition*, 40.

penitential prayer tradition as an element of exilic thinking about history because, as we shall see, history is a major element of these prayers, and the tradition of these prayers has a long life in pre-Christian Hebrew/ Jewish literature (some of which, of course, comes to us in Greek).

There is general agreement that we have a series of such penitential prayers, and that many ideas and idioms, and occasionally precise phrases, are shared in common. The parade examples of these postexilic prayers begin with 1 Kings 8 but are also identified in Nehemiah 9, Ezra 9, Daniel 9, and Baruch 1–2. There has been a great deal of recent interest in these prayers, and often other examples are included from later literature, such as 4Q504, "The Words of the Luminaries," and Judith 9.[16] But in order to examine this tradition, let us begin with what is normally taken as the earliest full example, Solomon's prayer in 1 Kings 8.

1 Kings 8—The Transitional Prayer?

Study of the dedicatory prayer of Solomon in 1 Kings 8 has tended to run in different directions, reflecting differing approaches. Literary approaches to the prayer have attempted to use the analysis of chiastic structures to establish not only the unity of the prayer itself,[17] but its place in larger literary units. For example, Amos Frisch writes about the literary unity of the entire account of Solomon's reign in 1 Kings and suggests an arrangement as follows:

(1) 1:1—2:26
    (2) 3:1-15
        (3) 3:16—5:14
            (4) 5:15-32
                (5) 6:1—9:9
            (4') 9:10-25
        (3') 9:26—10:29
    (2') 11:1-13
(1') 11:14—12:24[18]

16. See F. García Martínez, *The Dead Sea Scrolls Translated: The Qumran Texts in English*, 2d ed. (Grand Rapids: Eerdmans, 1996) 414–18. Both of these texts, as well as 3 Macc 2:2-20, were included in Newman, *Praying by the Book*. As her interest was the use of scripture, her work does not deal with what are otherwise more exclusively considered to be penitential prayers. 4Q504 certainly fits as a penitential prayer, but I would argue that Judith 9 and 3 Maccabees 2 do not, even if there are obvious similarities.

17. Gary N. Knoppers, "Prayer and Propaganda: Solomon's Dedication of the Temple and the Deuteronomist's Program," *CBQ* 57 (1995) 229–54.

18. Amos Frisch, "Structure and Its Significance: The Narrative of Solomon's Reign (1 Kings 1—12.24)," *JSOT* 51 (1991) 3–14.

This arrangement allows Frisch to make a number of interesting observations, if he is correct in his structural approach. First, it makes the dedicatory prayer a fulcrum of the entire account of Solomon's reign. Second, it allows Frisch to observe that the accounts up to the dedicatory prayer are more positive, while afterward the account moves into a more negative assessment of Solomon's behavior after reaching a kind of "apex" at the dedication of the temple. In other words, it reads as a "rise and fall" of Solomon. Thus the prayer serves a similar literary function to the characteristic Deuteronomic style of presenting a positive, and then turning on a "nevertheless." Rodney Werline argues along similar lines: "1 Kings 8 reflects a crucial transitional moment in Deuteronomic thought because it recasts Deuteronomy's idea of repentance into a theory for penitential prayer. According to 1 Kings 8, the nation can bring an end to the ultimate covenantal curse—foreign domination and exile—by confessing its sins in prayer."[19]

But is this prayer an early postexilic form? It is fair to say that Newman's assessment represents a general consensus about the date of 1 Kings 8: "The multi-layered prayer in 1 Kings 8 bespeaks a complex process of transmission and editing, but likely became a part of the text in final form during the exilic period."[20] Eep Talstra's analysis attempts to delineate in more detail the "complexity" of this prayer,[21] and Tomes has tried to be more precise about the actual composition—suggesting the period between 597 and 586, for example.[22] Gary Knoppers, however, maintains that the substance of the prayer is preexilic. Even the references to exile are not convincing for Knoppers, who sees these references as too general (perhaps based on such stereotypical curses as those already found in Deut 28–29) and out of place for a text that so emphasizes the temple: "If an exilic Deuteronomist wished to downplay the temple's importance, why would this writer stress that the temple was the focal point of Israelite life and insist that people use the temple in all sorts of predicaments to supplicate Yhwh 'at this house,' or 'toward this place'?"[23] Perhaps the central issue upon which Knoppers argues for the entire prayer

---

19. Rodney Alan Werline, *Penitential Prayer in Second Temple Judaism: The Development of a Religious Institution*, Early Judaism and Its Literature 13 (Atlanta: Scholars, 1998) 7.

20. Newman, *Praying by the Book*, 20.

21. Eep Talstra, *Solomon's Prayer: Synchrony and Diachrony in the Composition of 1 Kings 8,14–61*, Contributions to Biblical Exegesis and Theology (Kampen: Kok Pharos, 1993).

22. Roger Tomes, "'Our Holy and Beautiful House': When and Why Was 1 Kings 6–8 Written?" *JSOT* 70 (1996) 33–50. Tomes argues for a date between the two main deportations, e.g., in the reign of Zedekiah 597–587 BCE.

23. Knoppers, "Prayer," 231.

as preexilic, although probably close to the events that would lead to the exile, is precisely the role of the temple in the prayers. "Why would an exilic writer extend and expand the function of a temple that had been destroyed? . . . Moreover, why would an exilic author list in such detail the various circumstances—purgatory oaths, famine, drought, blight, pestilence, military defeat—in which the temple could be a channel of blessing and justice to people in the land?"[24]

Linville, I think, may offer some intriguing responses to some of Knoppers's questions: the temple as structure is not what is important—rather it becomes the designated place of identity and the "direction" of prayer among the Diaspora communities. As Linville points out, not only is the temple, oddly, described as inadequate for God precisely at the moment of its dedication, but the emphasis seems not on the cultic practice that takes place there at all. "It is, therefore, the dedication of a sacred site which, however geographically defined, finds its true sacrality in the past, not the present. With such a focal point, both spatially and temporally, the whole of the world is given a sacred orientation. Wherever Israel may be scattered, there is a line of communion with the god of the sacred land, and sacred past."[25]

Seen in this way, the role of the temple did not decrease after its destruction. Further, the temple and its reconstruction became emblematic of reconstruction for the priesthood and is reflected in the elaborate descriptions of Ezekiel 40–48 and the forceful words of Haggai and Zechariah in the aftermath of early Persian period return of some exiles. That physical structures can become symbols of cultural identity is clear to anyone who knows something of the history of Hagia Sophia in Istanbul; or the emotion surrounding the rebuilding of Beirut for modern Lebanese around the world; or the symbolic destruction of holy sites in the Hindu and Islamic struggles in India and the former Yugoslavia, to say nothing of Buddhist sites in Tibet as nationalist issues in the face of Chinese occupation. There is, in short, an imaginary architecture of exile.

Jon D. Levenson has been among those who have suggested that the exilic circumstances point to a transformation in the meaning of the temple: a move from a place of sacrifice to a place of prayer. For Levenson, this change is the foundation for the development of the later synagogue as a "house of prayer."[26] But as an exilic construct, it is clear that the temple is

24. Ibid., 247.
25. Linville, *Israel,* 296.
26. Jon D. Levenson, "From Temple to Synagogue: 1 Kings 8," in *Traditions in Transformation: Turning Points in Biblical Faith,* ed. B. Halpern and J. Levenson (Winona Lake, Ind.: Eisenbrauns, 1981) 143–66.

part of the architecture of exilic identity and is part of the postexilic theology of recovery and identity. But one could argue that in 1 Kings 8 the temple has been transformed into a concept that is functional for the Diaspora—it is a place toward which prayers can be directed. As Linville concludes about the Deuteronomistic Historian's views of institutions like the temple: "the past imagined in Kings . . . does not so much offer unqualified legitimization for particular institutions as it does show their relative inadequacy or imply their impermanence."[27]

But the temple, and the prayers associated with it after the exile, also become a focus for the recitation of postexilic history. This brings us to an analysis of the comparative features of postexilic prayer forms.

The Petitions

Among the unique elements of 1 Kings 8 that are frequently noted are the famous "petitions" included in the prayer—petitions that are not a typical element of the later prayers. These petitions have puzzled scholars for some time, particularly when one notes an apparent lack of thematic unity. But is there a common thread between these petitions of 1 Kings 8? This appears to be an important question, if only for the fact that this is one of the most unusual aspects of this prayer when compared to other penitential prayers that are otherwise so similar in later biblical texts (on this, see below).

Consider, for example, 8:31, which appears to involve a legal case: "If someone sins against a neighbor. . . ." Solomon, of course, was the proverbial wise judge. Kings portrays the famous case of Solomon deciding between the two "harlots" who "stood before the king" (3:16-28; cf. swearing "before your altar" in 8:31) and claimed the same child. It is said, related to this incident, that Solomon was famous throughout Israel (3:32). Yet in the prayer God is called to make a judgment between two "neighbors" in the case of an oath, to determine guilt and innocence. Where is the famous king? The prayer appears to presume a circumstance where the only viable authority is the spiritual presence of God. Talstra notes comparative cases of swearing oaths before judges (e.g., Exod 22:8; Deut 25:1; Prov 17:15),[28] but these cases all presume human involvement in the decision (judges, elders, etc.) *and* the sentence. In 1 Kgs 8:31-32 God determines guilt and innocence, *and* miraculously carries out the punishment. Where are the authorities? Is this a case of "internal law" apart from the official powers of occupation, either Babylonian or Persian? In other words, do these petitions apply to the Diaspora community, where no

27. Linville, *Israel*, 300.
28. Talstra, *Solomon's Prayer*, 111–13.

Israelite king can enact the judicial system and thus God is appealed to directly?

Once this reading is provisionally accepted—that this petition presumes a loss of political jurisdiction and authority—then the other petitions can certainly be read to presume similar situations of diaspora and exile: defeat in battle (vv. 33-34), inability to pay in-kind agricultural taxes because of drought or other weather conditions (vv. 35-37a), conditions of siege (v. 37b), the presence of foreigners (did they come as individuals to Jerusalem by free choice? Or are they occupation forces? vv. 41-43), and fighting as conscripted soldiers who pray "toward" Jerusalem (vv. 44-45). The final petition about the circumstances of exile also presumes that Jerusalem is far away, and God is asked to "hear in heaven" precisely as in the first petition: "if they repent with all their heart and soul in the land of their enemies, who took them captive, and pray to you toward their land, which you gave to their ancestors, the city that you have chosen, and the house that I have built for your name. . . ." Finally, again as frequently noted, the results of these prayers are not liberation and freedom, but rather a lighter circumstance—a better condition of exile.

Once we assert that 1 Kings 8 and the penitential prayers are diaspora prayers par excellence, then our analysis of the common elements of all the prayers can proceed. For the purpose of this survey, I will suggest a rough chronological outline. In the first instance, we will examine the most important section of 1 Kings 8 in relation to a discussion of "diaspora situations." Note also the additional material in 8:56-61, which emphasizes obedience to the commandments and teachings as mediated by Moses. I wish to call attention to four aspects of these two texts that remain constant in the penitential prayer tradition that follows. This is best noted by choosing relevant passages from Ezra 9 and Nehemiah 9, which may well represent a midpoint (ca. 450–400?) in the tradition. For example, in his exhaustive study of Nehemiah 9, Boda concludes: "Neh. 9 in particular, and Penitential Prayer in general are indebted to D[euteronomistic] and Ezekielian/Priestly theology. Here is evidence of the ongoing legacy of these tradition circles even to the point of producing a new Gattung . . . which would become a dominant expression for many of those facing the pain of the exilic crisis."[29]

Then will follow some extracts from Daniel 9 and Baruch, both typically dated to the second century BCE, if not later. One should note, however, that the prayer in Daniel 9 may be older than the Baruch tradition. Daniel 9 is certainly an excellent example of the postexilic penitential prayer form. This particular prayer includes a standardized form of

29. Boda, *Praying the Tradition*, 195.

prayer or confession and request for deliverance, which can be compared to other texts with very similar emphases and contents. Was the prayer therefore an earlier form and added in the second century to the section Daniel 7–12? Norman Porteous and André Lacocque note that v. 21 follows v. 2 quite comfortably, and vv. 3 and 20 look like "seams" written in to accommodate the addition of the prayer in vv. 4-19.[30] Lacocque suggests that vv. 1-3 and 21-27 were written in 166–164 BCE, before the rededication of the temple by Judas Maccabeus. Furthermore, John Goldingay and John Collins note that the Hebrew of the prayer is much more regular and free of Aramaic influences than the surrounding material.[31] But these conclusions, if correct, would only further confirm the significance of a line of tradition represented by these prayers.

The specific sections of these prayers that I draw attention to are: statements of shame, the sins of the ancestors, exile or slavery as conditions the people were warned about, and the importance of Moses' ethics.[32]

Statements of Shame
Ezra 9 / Nehemiah 9

> *EZRA 9:6* O my God, I am too ashamed and embarrassed to lift my face to you, my God, for our iniquities have risen higher than our heads, and our guilt has mounted up to the heavens.

> *NEH 9:26* Nevertheless they were disobedient and rebelled against you and cast your law behind their backs and killed your prophets, who had warned them in order to turn them back to you, and they committed great blasphemies. (Cf. 9:29 and also 1:6.)

Daniel 9 / Baruch 1

> *DAN 9:5-7* We have sinned and done wrong, acted wickedly and rebelled, turning aside from your commandments and ordinances. We have not listened to your servants the prophets, who spoke in your name to our kings, our princes, and our ancestors, and to all the people of the land. Righteousness is on your side, O Lord, but open shame, as at this day, falls on us, the people of Judah, the inhabitants of Jerusalem, and all Israel, those who are near and those who are far away, in all the lands to which you have driven them, because of the treachery that they have committed against you.

---

30. Porteous, *Daniel*, 135; Lacocque, *Daniel*, 178.

31. John E. Goldingay, *Daniel*, WBC 30 (Waco, Tex.: Word, 1989) 236–37; John J. Collins, *Daniel*, Hermeneia (Minneapolis: Fortress Press, 1993) 347.

32. I have intentionally abbreviated other presentations of the prayer tradition that note many more similarities. See, e.g., Boda, *Praying the Tradition*, 25–29.

BAR 1:15-17 And you shall say: The Lord our God is in the right, but there is open shame on us today, on the people of Judah, on the inhabitants of Jerusalem, and on our kings, our rulers, our priests, our prophets, and our ancestors, because we have sinned before the Lord.

Sins of the Ancestors
Ezra 9 / Nehemiah 9

EZRA 9:7 From the days of our ancestors to this day we have been deep in guilt,

NEH 9:16-17 But they and our ancestors acted presumptuously and stiffened their necks and did not obey your commandments; they refused to obey, and were not mindful of the wonders that you performed among them; but they stiffened their necks and determined to return to their slavery in Egypt. (Cf. 9:34.)

Daniel 9 / Baruch 1

DAN 9:8 Open shame, O LORD, falls on us, our kings, our officials, and our ancestors, because we have sinned against you.

BAR 1:16-17 and on our kings, our rulers, our priests, our prophets, and our ancestors, because we have sinned before the Lord.

Exile or Slavery as Conditions the People Were Warned About
Ezra 9 / Nehemiah 9

EZRA 9:7 And for our iniquities we, our kings, and our priests have been handed over to the kings of the lands, to the sword, to captivity, to plundering, and to utter shame, as is now the case.

NEH 9:36 Here we are, slaves to this day—slaves in the land that you gave to our ancestors to enjoy its fruit and its good gifts. (Cf. 1:8.)

Daniel 9 / Baruch 2, 3

DAN 9:12-13 He has confirmed his words, which he spoke against us and against our rulers, by bringing upon us a calamity so great that what has been done against Jerusalem has never before been done under the whole heaven. Just as it is written in the law of Moses, all this calamity has come upon us.

BAR 2:1-4 So the Lord carried out the threat he spoke against us: against our judges who ruled Israel, and against our kings and our rulers and the people of Israel and Judah . . . in accordance with the threats that were written in the law of Moses. . . . He made them subject to all the kingdoms around us, to be an object of scorn and a desolation among all the surrounding peoples, where the Lord has scattered them. (Cf. 2:24.)

BAR 3:8 See, we are today in our exile where you have scattered us, to be reproached and cursed and punished for all the iniquities of our ancestors, who forsook the Lord our God.

Importance of Moses' Ethics
Ezra 9 / Nehemiah 9

EZRA 9:10-11 And now, our God, what shall we say after this? For we have forsaken your commandments, which you commanded by your servants the prophets.

NEH 9:13-14 You came down also upon Mount Sinai, and spoke with them from heaven, and gave them right ordinances and true laws, good statutes and commandments, and you made known your holy sabbath to them and gave them commandments and statutes and a law through your servant Moses.

NEH 9:29 And you warned them in order to turn them back to your law. Yet they acted presumptuously and did not obey your commandments, but sinned against your ordinances, by the observance of which a person shall live. They turned a stubborn shoulder and stiffened their neck and would not obey.

CF. NEH 1:7-8 We have offended you deeply, failing to keep the commandments, the statutes, and the ordinances that you commanded your servant Moses. Remember the word that you commanded your servant Moses.

Daniel 9 / Baruch 1

DAN 9:4B-5 Ah, Lord, great and awesome God, keeping covenant and steadfast love with those who love you and keep your commandments, we have sinned and done wrong, acted wickedly and rebelled, turning aside from your commandments and ordinances.

BAR 1:18 We have disobeyed him, and have not heeded the voice of the Lord our God, to walk in the statutes of the Lord that he set before us.

The Exilic Theology of Penitential Prayers

Why this long tradition of penitential prayer? Why keep praying a standardized prayer for help and deliverance for five hundred years when the requested deliverance seems not to be happening? The issue, perhaps, is not in focusing on the *answer* (or lack thereof) to these prayers, but the meaning of praying such a confession with the themes I have noted. The prayers are historical statements as much as they are entreaties, and they most certainly reflect a theology of judgment on Israelite history.

A Social Function of Shame?

The central theme of these prayers is arguably the expressions of shame. Statements of shame serve an important function, though not in the contemporary sense of "spiritually cleansing," nor are they associated with some psychological view of necessary penitence. To miss the social significance of a litany of shame is to miss much of the integrative and transformative function of these prayers. In these prayers, "our shame" is associated with *too closely identifying with a past that was destructive*. Recent work on the function of shame in society emphasizes its societal and integrative aspects, especially biblical discussions of "shame and honor" as social elements of Mediterranean society, and thus themes that may shed light on biblical literature.[33]

Recent psychological literature has taken a somewhat more complex line of analysis. Shame seems to be a complicated emotion (interestingly also called "an under-studied aspect of psychology").[34] Shame is notably combined with other emotional states that can change what we mean when we use a term as deceptively simple as *shame*. Shame can be, for example, a form of embarrassment, of humiliation, or of regret; or it can be connected to great sadness as in circumstances of shame brought about by trauma. K. C. Hanson has captured some elements of this complexity in his call to be more precise in the translation of terms dealing with honor and shame in both Old and New Testament contexts.[35]

How might this affect our reading of the constant call of the penitential prayers to have a sense of shame? These prophetic calls to shame in the context of history are not calls to a paralyzing personal guilt or humiliation. It is a call to recognize the constant failures of living according to alternative ideals and values—universally identified in the penitential prayers as the Mosaic laws. Shame, therefore, is not a psychology, it is a

33. See the special issue, *Honor and Shame*, *Semeia* 68 (1996), ed. Victor Matthews and Don Benjamin, particularly K. C. Hanson, "How Honorable! How Shameful! A Cultural Analysis of Matthew's Makarisms and Reproaches," 81–112. See also J. G. Peristiany, ed., *Honor and Shame: The Values of Mediterranean Society* (Chicago: Univ. of Chicago Press, 1966); and Paul Gilbert and Bernice Andrews, eds., *Shame: Interpersonal Behaviour, Psychopathology, and Culture* (Oxford: Oxford Univ. Press, 1998), esp. Nancy Lindisfarne, "Gender, Shame, and Culture: An Anthropological Perspective," 246–60.
34. See Gilbert and Andrews, eds., *Shame: Interpersonal Behaviour*.
35. Hanson, "How Honorable!"

politics. The penitential prayers are "narrative repair," to use Nelson's term noted at the outset of this chapter. They are the recitation of alternative values and a critical reading of history. Associating shame with history is, indeed, the ancient Hebrew equivalent of doing "critical historiography"—lessons on how "*not* to do it." Consider the role of shame in Jer 6:15: "They acted shamefully, they committed abomination; yet they were not ashamed, they did not know how to blush. Therefore they shall fall among those who fall; at the time that I punish them, they shall be overthrown, says the LORD." In his commentary on Jeremiah, William Holladay wants to substitute "how to be humiliated" for "how to blush."[36] To take another example: Ezekiel's call—which sounds so different to modern ears—to "loathe yourself!" must be read in the context of his clarification that God "has no pleasure in the death of the wicked" (Ezek 33:7-10). A positive is implied in the negative. The issue is not "feelings" but behavior and identity.

An important key is the notion of the shame *of the ancestors*. In short, it is not "our" shame that is the central issue (although this element is not absent). To recall shame on the ancestors is to recall history—to recall mistakes. Who are these ancestors? From the frequency of the references to the kings and events "since Egypt" (Neh 9:34; Dan 9:6; Bar 1:16) and the fact that 1 Kings 8, already supposedly in the monarchy, does not refer to "ancestors" but rather to contemporary events (the only reference to "ancestors" in 1 Kings 8 is a positive reference to the wilderness, not a negative judgment), then we can conclude that it is precisely the period of the monarchy and the central period of prophecy. As exile ended that period, and this is the theme of the Deuteronomistic Historian's work, this is also the central period of blame—the model of social existence being rejected in the penitential prayer. The penitential prayer calls for nonconformity with the mistakes of the ancestors and a recommitment to what they rejected—the ethics of Moses.

Radical nonconformity for the exilic communities means the creation of a radically different identity from that exemplified by the period of the monarchy, and this requires a heightened sense of the shame of acting in other ways. It is even more powerful if one's own ancestors serve as the negative example, because the threat is clear: it is to say that "we have, in fact, tried this before." In the prayers, shame comes from disobedience to the Mosaic ideals, from the mistreatment of the poor and the weak; and it is the proper mind-set for calling on God's miraculous assistance.

Thus one can argue that shame is a form of modesty—it is a vigilance over one's own tendencies. There can certainly be misplaced shame, as

---

36. William L. Holladay, *Jeremiah 1,* Hermeneia (Philadelphia: Fortress Press, 1986) 217.

Freud has clearly shown, but there can be a political avoidance of appropriate shame that can have even more destructive results. We have seen in the twentieth century the horrific results of the refusal to embrace shame, especially in regard to the "sins of the ancestors." An intransigent Turkish foreign policy continues to refuse or acknowledge the massacre of Armenian ancestors. A sector of American policy making grows weary of accepting appropriate shame from the treatment of Native Americans, Asian laborers, and African American slaves. Michael Sells notes with distressing clarity how the Serbian Orthodox Church continues to refuse to acknowledge the savagery with which Serbs carried out genocidal and brutal policies.[37] The list is depressingly long.

In the end, shame is a mark of honesty—it is an admission that allows transformation because it offers hope that the new way will not repeat the acknowledged mistakes of the old way. The persistent refusal to acknowledge history and feel shame, for example, in the twentieth century, leaves a legacy of mistrust in contemporary social relations. To confess that a society was wrong in the past is to declare that a new identity is necessary, and perhaps even emergent: "We are not them." To call on God in the face of resisting dominance is a form of reidentification as a resistant people. The penitential prayers are a call to break with the past, to be an alternative people of God. How can we see this in a reading of 1 Kings 8 and thus in the entire tradition of these prayers?

A politics of penitence accepts that a status of apparent "national" weakness is neither ineffective nor temporary. To remind oneself constantly of the failure of power (in the ancestors and kings) is to advocate an alternative mode of living, not simply to pine for a change of status. The way many scholars read penitential ideology, it is as if the praying community is rejecting their circumstances and waiting for a return to power. But it is the experiment with power that is carefully blamed and rejected in every prayer! The prayer does not allow the fantasy of power to go unchallenged.

In a courageous essay, the modern Turkish social historian Taner Akcam analyzes the continued Turkish official silence about the Armenian genocide. Among the more notable comments: "A society, a state does not like to confront an imagery that is at variance with its self-imagery, and, as such, is likely to destroy its world of fantasies. Herein lies the reason for our sharp reaction to those who call our attention to that reality."[38]

---

37. See Michael Sells, "Kosovo Mythology and the Bosnian Genocide," in *In God's Name: Genocide and Religion in the Twentieth Century*, ed. O. Bartov and P. Mack (New York: Berghahn, 2001) 180–207.

38. Taner Akcam, "The Genocide of the Armenians and the Silence of the Turks," in *Studies in Comparative Genocide*, ed. L. Chorbajian and G. Shirinian (New York: St. Martins, 1999) 125–46.

Similarly, in his analysis of American academic cynicism about modern study of the "counterhistories" of minority groups, Lawrence Levine speaks with appropriate criticism of those historians who never tire of attacking what they call an "obsession with guilt" under whose driving force American history supposedly becomes "primarily a history of oppression" that is then cynically called "oppression studies."[39] Presumably, there is connected to this a call for a return to the study of history of power and privilege—the history of the victors, the "foundations of Western culture and tradition." Is this what archaeologist William Dever refers to when he writes that he "abhors revisionism in all forms"?[40] When Dever lumps together postmodernist challenges in biblical studies with New Left political activism, multiculturalism, communitarianism, universalism, feminism, and environmentalism,[41] is this a call to reject the challenges of counterhistories in the West? Is this yet another weary call to return to the dominant narratives of power and privilege? Such a perspective is clearly annoyed with the biblical tradition of critical history and theological shame in the face of their own experiments with power and privilege.

The refusal of shame, and thus the refusal to condemn agendas of power and denial, have clear biblical analogies—as even a cursory reading of the Maccabean literature reveals. With its constant references to the Davidic imagery of restoration and the total absence of the penitential prayer form, 1 Maccabees reveals the presence of the countertradition to the penitential prayer ethos. Whatever change is being specifically requested by the penitential prayer tradition, it is always requested in the context of remaining a penitent people for whom a call to revive Mosaic ideals is, at the same time, to be mindful of the shame of our ancestors. The Mosaic ideals appear to offer hope for a new and different social formation for exiles— to become the people of God in a manner that avoids the sins of the ancestors.

---

39. *The Opening of the American Mind: Canons, Culture, and History* (Boston: Beacon, 1996) 148.

40. William G. Dever, *What Did the Biblical Writers Know and When Did They Know It?* (Grand Rapids: Eerdmans, 2001) 291.

41. Ibid., 291, 292. Dever is citing David Gress, *From Plato to NATO*, for this list, but then proceeds to say that, in reference to Gress's line of argument, "I could not agree more wholeheartedly." While I am sympathetic to some of Dever's criticism of certain scholarly trends toward hypercritical readings of biblical history, I think the arguments of his final chapter are unfortunate in that they overstate the association between such critical views of the Bible and a host of important theoretical and political concerns. I would argue that one can well be feminist, communitarian, multicultural, as well as critical of major elements of Western tradition, and still hold to the central importance of the Bible.

5.
ISRAELITE MISSION AND
HUMAN TRANSFORMATION

IT HARDLY COMES AS A SURPRISE THAT THE BIBLICAL LITERATURE OF the exilic and postexilic periods includes a serious discussion with regard to interaction between non-Hebrews and the Israelites/Hebrews, who were a new minority, thrown in with conquered peoples from around the Babylonian Empire. One could argue that there was always some discussion of this (e.g., laws for "foreigners" in the Covenant Code, e.g., Exod 22:20), but given the struggles for autonomy and religious developments connected to premonarchical discussions, the interaction was typically hostile, most notably toward the "Canaanites." The preexilic prophetic literature may often have considered foreign armies to be the punishing "arm" of the Lord, but such a perspective would hardly be expected to encourage some kind of dialogue of creative interaction when exiles are thrown into an entirely new situation. Yet the fact remains that in the context of the exilic events and thereafter, hostility is occasionally mitigated by new openness to the possibility that positive change may not always mean defeat or destruction of non-Hebrews. The hoped-for developments may involve a transformation of the non-Hebrew into a nonthreatening presence in the worst case and potential comrades in the best case. Debates surrounding these alleged changes have tended to focus on whether there was a new Hebrew sense of "universalism" in the postexilic literature. These discussions almost inevitably focus on Second Isaiah but often include Jonah and Ruth.

The Universalism of Late Isaiah Texts

There are a number of interesting problems with regard to the alleged universalism in postexilic sections of Isaiah. In his article reviewing the problems of universalism in Second Isaiah in the light of recent research,

Joseph Blenkinsopp points out that more positive readings of foreigners need to be balanced with the fact that there are certainly negative portrayals of foreign nations—being punished, being humbled, indeed humiliated—in addition to more positive-sounding images.[1] Related to this, Blenkinsopp suggests that the long-presumed literary divisions in the book of Isaiah ought to be questioned. He contends (with other recent work on early "servant" language in chs. 40–48[2]) that Cyrus is the subject of chs. 40–48 and something else is the subject of chs. 49–55.

What does this mean for his reading of universalism in Isaiah? Take the classic passage of "light to the nations" in Isa 49:6: God says, "It is too light a thing that you should be my servant to raise up the tribes of Jacob and to restore the survivors of Israel; I will give you as a light to the nations, that my salvation may reach to the end of the earth." Blenkinsopp[3] maintains that the traditional division of this passage (as one of the so-called Servant Songs) has meant that it has been falsely separated from the images that follow this passage in Isaiah, images that portray the foreign nations "licking the dust" at the feet of the redeemed and empowered Israelites, such as 49:23-25: "With their faces to the ground they shall bow down to you, and lick the dust of your feet. Then you will know that I am the LORD; those who wait for me shall not be put to shame. Can the prey be taken from the mighty, or the captives of a tyrant be rescued? But thus says the LORD: Even the captives of the mighty shall be taken, and the prey of the tyrant be rescued; for I will contend with those who contend with you, and I will save your children."

Compare this with Isa 60:14: "The descendants of those who oppressed you shall come bending low to you, and all who despised you shall bow down at your feet; they shall call you the City of the LORD, the Zion of the Holy One of Israel." Certainly the image of bowing or licking dust, or having one's face in the dust, is an image otherwise found in reference to low status, and/or the humbling of foreign rulers. The psalmist expresses the same sentiment, and Micah portrays "licking dust" as the proper fate of

---

1. J. Blenkinsopp, "Second Isaiah—Prophet of Universalism," *JSOT* 41 (1988) 83–103. On the problem of universalism more generally, see my "Between Ezra and Isaiah: Exclusion, Transformation, and Inclusion of the 'Foreigner' in Post-exilic Biblical Theology," in *Ethnicity and the Bible*, ed. M. Brett (Leiden: Brill, 1996) 117–42, and the literature cited therein, though the literature on the question of universalism in the Hebrew Scriptures is growing.

2. Lisbeth S. Fried, "Cyrus, the Messiah? The Historical Background to Isaiah 45:1," presented at the SBL annual meeting, Nashville, 2000. Dr. Fried's paper, at the time of this writing, is forthcoming in print. I am grateful to Dr. Fried for providing me with a draft of this work.

3. Blenkinsopp, "Second Isaiah," 91–94.

Nineveh because of Assyrian oppression: "May his foes bow down before him, and his enemies lick the dust" (Ps 72:9); "they shall lick the dust like a serpent, like the crawling things of the earth; they shall come trembling out of their strongholds, they shall turn in dread to the LORD our God, and they shall fear because of thee" (Mic 7:17).

Furthermore, such reversal of fortune motifs are similar to the invective evident in Esther and Daniel 6. Take Isaiah's notion that being crushed in the dust was Israel's fate at the exile: "Thus says your Sovereign, the LORD, your God who pleads the cause of his people: See, I have taken from your hand the cup of staggering; you shall drink no more from the bowl of my wrath. And I will put it into the hand of your tormentors, who have said to you, 'Bow down, that we may walk on you'; and you have made your back like the ground and like the street for them to walk on" (Isa 51:22-23).

While it is true that such reversal motifs may well mirror Israel's own fate, it is also true that even among the Israelites themselves, the poor are also often portrayed as being "crushed into the dust" (the famous image in Amos 2:7 where the heads of the poor are trampled into the dust) or those who are raised up from low status: "He raises up the poor from the dust; he lifts the needy from the ash heap, to make them sit with princes and inherit a seat of honor. For the pillars of the earth are the LORD's, and on them he has set the world" (1 Sam 2:8); "he raises the poor from the dust, and lifts the needy from the ash heap" (Ps 113:7).

But there are indications that we must read apparently obvious images carefully. There are decidedly mixed images in relation to foreigners, for example, the famous "Peaceable Kingdom" scene: "The wolf and the lamb shall feed together, the lion shall eat straw like the ox; and dust shall be the serpent's food. They shall not hurt or destroy in all my holy mountain, says the LORD" (Isa 65:25). Here too there is the unlikely picture of fellowship between otherwise bitter enemies, the wolf and the lamb. But there is an interesting sense of the humbling of the especially threatening animals, too, symbolized by the lions and serpents. The lions are portrayed as eating straw rather than as brutal carnivores. The serpent, humbled, eats dust. But it would be an inconsistent picture to presume that the serpent, of all animals, is suffering a humiliating punishment, while the others are portrayed as content with their new circumstances. Does this kind of humbling always imply defeat and humiliation? In some cases it seems so (e.g., Isa 49:26 stands out), but in others it is not so clear.

For example, the famous "swords into plowshares" passage has all nations destroying their weapons and "learning war no more." There is nothing here of domination by Israel, but there is the disarmament of all nations (and no hint that Israel's weapons are exempted, incidentally). Similarly, although the prose additions to ch. 20 start with a hint of vindictiveness in v. 16, this passage rapidly turns into a profound vision of foreign peoples sharing a blessing from God—a God who punishes, but after striking, heals, resulting in a new "day": "In that day there will be a highway from Egypt to Assyria, and the Assyrian will come into Egypt, and the Egyptian into Assyria, and the Egyptians will worship with the Assyrians. In that day Israel will be the third with Egypt and Assyria, a blessing in the midst of the earth, whom the LORD of hosts has blessed, saying, 'Blessed be Egypt my people, and Assyria the work of my hands, and Israel my heritage'" (Isa 19:24-25).[4]

Are we to understand that punishment of a few ("striking and healing," 20:22) allows for the rest of the nations to live in peace? Consider the more positive images of foreign kings and queens approaching Israel in what seems to be a positive (even joyful?) image of a procession of holding children on shoulders. Ironically, this image appears just before the "licking dust" episode: "Thus says the Lord GOD: I will soon lift up my hand to the nations, and raise my signal to the peoples; and they shall bring your sons in their bosom, and your daughters shall be carried on their shoulders. Kings shall be your foster fathers, and their queens your nursing mothers" (49:22-23a). Compare 60:4: "Lift up your eyes and look around; they all gather together, they come to you; your sons shall come from far away, and your daughters shall be carried on their nurses' arms."

Other passages, while clearly imagining a humbling of foreign peoples, certainly do not present them in an entirely negative light, even if some "reversal of fortune" bitterness is evident in ideas like, "they will build *your* walls" (cf. 61:5: aliens shall stand and feed your flocks, foreigners shall be your plowmen and vinedressers): "Foreigners shall build up your walls, and their kings shall minister to you; for in my wrath I struck you down, but in my favor I have had mercy on you. Your gates shall always be open; day and night they shall not be shut, so that nations shall bring you their wealth, with their kings led in procession" (60:10-11). That gates are to be left open in an era so familiar with the ravages of siege warfare is a clear signal of peace.

As we have seen and as Blenkinsopp has shown, the images are definitely mixed.[5] But we cannot overlook the strikingly "universalist" nature of many of these passages. Yes, there is the difficulty the writer(s) has with

---

4. On this see J. F. A. Sawyer, "'Blessed be my people Egypt' (Isaiah 19.25): The Context and Meaning of a Remarkable Passage," in *A Word in Season: Essays in Honour of William McKane*, ed. J. D. Martin and P. R. Davies, JSOTSup 42 (Sheffield: JSOT Press, 1986) 57–72.

5. Blenkinsopp, "Second Isaiah," 91.

an unmitigated forgiveness, or a totally positive view of foreigners. The former empires will be humbled, often at their own initiative (e.g., the Ninevites in Jonah). But the positive movement is unmistakable—a kind of universalism is definitely at work in the Isaiah corpus, proven by the overt statement about the acceptability of foreigners among the people of God: "And the foreigners who join themselves to the LORD, to minister to him, to love the name of the LORD, and to be his servants, every one who keeps the sabbath, and does not profane it, and holds fast my covenant— these I will bring to my holy mountain, and make them joyful in my house of prayer; their burnt offerings and their sacrifices will be accepted on my altar; for my house shall be called a house of prayer for all peoples. Thus says the Lord GOD, who gathers the outcasts of Israel, I will gather yet others to him besides those already gathered" (56:6-8).

Compare this with the even more striking suggestion (if it does, indeed, refer to the foreigners themselves, and not to the returned Judeans) that some of the foreigners who bring the Israelites home shall be made priests and Levites: "They shall bring all your kindred from all the nations as an offering to the LORD, on horses, and in chariots, and in litters, and on mules, and on dromedaries, to my holy mountain Jerusalem, says the LORD, just as the Israelites bring a grain offering in a clean vessel to the house of the LORD. And I will also take some of them as priests and as Levites, says the LORD" (66:20-21). Here we have, once again, the image of being brought home by foreigners put in a positive light. Some punished or humbled, as we have seen above, but others praised and even welcomed among the people of God.

Is the "humbling of the enemy" to be contrasted with the positive imagery, or is it an integral part of the new reality of a transformed relationship? Let us take up the image of "lick the dust," considered by Blenkinsopp to be clearly a contrasting image to the more positive view of being a "light to the nations."

In his commentary on Second Isaiah, Klaus Baltzer suggests a different reading of the Isaiah procession theme, including the finale in humbled bowing (the "proskynesis"). Baltzer portrays the entire episode as a joyful, even playful, image: "A procession of this kind, ending with the people falling on their faces in the prokynesis, must have been good fun."[6] He cites Persian precedent for this rather surprising interpretation of humbled bowing before superiors. But such an alternative view does have support in Persian historical analysis: "It would seem that for Achaeminids even proskynesis did not signify the abject humility before a god, but

6. Klaus Baltzer, *Deutero-Isaiah*, trans. M. Kohl, Hermeneia (Minneapolis: Fortress Press, 2001) 330.

rather a sign of respect towards royalty . . . even, in the case of supplication or requests, full prostration on the ground."[7]

If the images are more positive (Baltzer) or only moderately positive (Blenkinsopp), Blenkinsopp clearly believes that the key to this transformation, however complicated it is by a struggle in thought (different writers?), is that Israel has become a confessional community, and as such, has begun to consider itself open to "converts."[8] He concludes: "Perhaps the most we can say, therefore, is that Second Isaiah laid the foundations for later developments by making it possible to think of a role for Israel in the salvation of humankind."[9] What begins in Isaiah, however, takes even further root in Jonah.

Universalism in Jonah

This notion of transformation by humbling finds even greater expression in Jonah. It is almost universally held among biblical scholars that the book of Jonah comes from a late period in the history of the Hebrew people, and most certainly after the fateful destruction of Jerusalem by the Babylonian armies under Nebuchadnezzar in 587 BCE. Thus, the book most likely derives from the long period of political and economic occupation of those Hebrews who lived in the land and the period of diaspora existence for those who did not.[10] Hans Walter Wolff notes that Sirach already lists "twelve" prophets; there is late Persian-period terminology like "God of Heaven" (cf. 2 Chr 36:23; Ezra 1:2; 5:11; Dan 2:18-19, 37; etc.); there is a familiarity with Deuteronomic theology of repentance; and there is familiarity with the liturgical utterance of Yahweh's mercy that was typical of postexilic psalms.[11] Does the setting of Jonah, however fictional, support this?

7. Richard Frye, *The Heritage of Persia* (London: Weidenfeld and Nicolson, 1962).

8. Blenkinsopp, "Second Isaiah," 86.

9. Ibid., 94.

10. M. Burrows, "The Literary Category of the Book of Jonah," in *Translating and Understanding the Old Testament,* FS Herbert May, ed. H. T. Frank and W. L. Reed (Nashville: Abingdon, 1970) 80–107; Terence E. Fretheim, *The Message of Jonah* (Minneapolis: Augsburg, 1977); A. Lacocque and P.-E. Lacocque, *The Jonah Complex* (Atlanta: John Knox, 1981); J. Magonet, *Form and Meaning: Studies in Literary Techniques in the Book of Jonah* (Sheffield: Almond, 1983); H. W. Wolff, *Obadiah and Jonah,* trans. M. Kohl, Continental Commentaries (Minneapolis: Fortress Press, 1991); J. M. Sasson, *Jonah,* AB 24B (New York: Doubleday, 1990); John Day, "Problems in the Interpretation of the Book of Jonah," *Oudtestamentische Studiën* 26 (1990) 32–47.

11. Wolff, *Jonah,* 75–83.

Nineveh, to which Jonah is "called," was for a time a central city of the Neo-Assyrian Empire. So it seems clear that the tale intends to suggest that Jonah is called to deliver his prophetic message to the massive capital city of one of the most feared regimes that the Hebrews ever faced—even if the story is told long after the demise of the Assyrian Empire, it was obviously well remembered as the regime that not only devastated the northern state of Israel, but tried to conquer Jerusalem as well at the time of Hezekiah and the prophet Isaiah (ca. 705 BCE). Furthermore, however, "Assyria" is used symbolically of other rulers long after the time of the Neo-Assyrian Empire (e.g., 3 Macc 13:9 reads "Assyria" for Babylon; the late tale of Tobit clearly thought a location in Nineveh was significant for Hellenistic era readers; Ezra 6:22 even uses the term in reference, apparently, to the Persians).

Thus, if Jonah is a postexilic tale of interaction with foreigners, what kind of interaction is presumed? Is Jonah a further development of late Isaianic universalism in Diaspora thinking?

Etan Levine has argued that the typical exegesis of Jonah that sees it as a book about "forgiving enemies" has no basis.[12] But forgiving enemies is not the point—*God's transformation* of a former enemy is the point. Levine resists this interpretation, suggesting that Nineveh is not a symbol of the Assyrian Empire, and that Jonah 3:8 and 10 refer to personal sins of violence, not the political violence of the empire. The city is full of personal evil, suggests Levine, and Jonah has no "political" message about Assyrian oppression.

This argument can be countered in a number of ways. First, the use of Nineveh. We have already noted its widespread use as a euphemism for imperial power. Was this a reference for the Assyrian Empire itself? Note that the prophet Nahum earlier delivers a blistering prophetic oracle of judgment against Nineveh as precisely a symbol of the Assyrian Empire. Furthermore, the terms used for sin in Jonah 3:8 and 10 most certainly can refer in biblical literature to what might be called "political" violence. Evil *(ra'a)* and violence *(ḥms)*, for example, can be seen in the following contexts of warfare, and thus one might argue, "political" sin. Nahum himself cites the "evil" of the city using *ra'a:* "There is no assuaging your hurt, your wound is grievous. All who hear the news of you clap their hands over you. For upon whom has not come your unceasing *evil?*" (Nah 3:19). Jeremiah uses the same term in reference to Babylonian oppression, first in announcing the coming of the Babylonians, and then their

---

12. See Etan Levine, "Reopening the Case of Jonah v. God," in *Heaven and Earth, Law and Love: Studies in Biblical Thought,* BZAW 303 (Berlin: de Gruyter, 2000) 67–96.

punishment: "Then the LORD said to me, 'Out of the north *evil* shall break forth upon all the inhabitants of the land'" (Jer 1:14); "'I will requite Babylon and all the inhabitants of Chaldea before your very eyes for all *the evil* that they have done in Zion,' says the LORD" (Jer 51:24).

The "violence" *(ḥms)* of the Nineveh peoples is also similar to other political uses of *ra'a* to refer to warfare and conquest, particularly notable again in late Isaiah but not exclusive to Isaiah: "*Violence* shall no more be heard in your land, devastation or destruction within your borders; you shall call your walls Salvation, and your gates Praise" (Isa 60:18); "'the *violence* done to me and to my kinsmen be upon Babylon,' let the inhabitant of Zion say. 'My blood be upon the inhabitants of Chaldea,' let Jerusalem say" (Jer 51:35); "Let not your heart faint, and be not fearful at the report heard in the land, when a report comes in one year and afterward a report in another year, and *violence* is in the land, and ruler is against ruler" (Jer 51:46); "Egypt shall become a desolation and Edom a desolate wilderness, for the *violence* done to the people of Judah, because they have shed innocent blood in their land" (Joel 3:19).

Yet Nineveh is forgiven. Again, contra Levine (who maintains that the forgiveness of Nineveh is an unprecedented violation of God's own justice), this divine mercy has precedent. Consider God's own violation of the Covenant Code in sparing David despite his adultery, or sparing Cain despite his murder of Abel. Indeed, a prophet's message of condemnation can often be taken as the basis of a hope that God will "change his mind": "It may be that the house of Judah will hear all the evil which I intend to do to them, so that every one may turn from his evil way, and that I may forgive their iniquity and their sin" (Jer 36:3).

The key to Jonah is the repentance and transformation of the enemy— the humbling of the Ninevites meant forswearing the "violence of their hands." The power of the tale of Jonah, however, goes deeper, and I agree with Friedemann Golka's assessment that "the book of Jonah is an astonishing theological development."[13] Related to this, the allegorical interpretation of Jonah as a symbol of the Israelite people themselves in exile has much to commend it.[14] Jonah, like Israel, is called on a "mission." Jonah, like Israel, rejects God's call (according to the entire Deuteronomistic tradition, and most of the classical prophets of the exilic era, the exile was a direct result of Israel's own sins). Jonah, like Israel, goes into darkness (the exile itself). But when Jonah is released, his mission is to the foreign city of Nineveh; in other words, Jonah is called to be an example of Isaiah's

13. Friedemann Golka, with G. A. F. Knight, *Song of Songs/Jonah*, ITC (Grand Rapids: Eerdmans, 1988).

14. Once again raised by J. Rogerson, "Jonah," in *Prophets and Poets: A Companion to the Prophetic Books of the Old Testament*, ed. G. Emmerson (Nashville: Abingdon, 1994) 238–43.

"light to the nations." Thus, one might argue that the story of Jonah is a kind of midrash on Isa 49:6 and other universalist inclinations of Second Isaiah. Such a symbolic interpretation of Jonah is clearly anticipated by passages such as Jer 51:34: "Nebuchadrezzar the king of Babylon has devoured me, he has crushed me; he has made me an empty vessel, he has swallowed me like a monster; he has filled his belly with my delicacies, he has rinsed me out."

But the psalm in Jonah 2 also contains a number of images reminiscent of images of exile. The references to missing the temple (v. 4) and being away from the land, and the allusions to "prison" (note the mention of bars, v. 6) all suggest that this is a psalm from the period of the exile— when the people in Diaspora lamented their fate as exiles from the home-land (cf. Ps 137). On other occasions the exilic period is compared to living "in prison" (see Isa. 42:7 below; but also Ps 107:10-16; Lam 3:34).

Other images in Jonah 2 also have exilic associations: "The warriors of Babylon have ceased fighting, they remain in their strongholds; their strength has failed, they have become women; her dwellings are on fire, her bars are broken" (Jer 51:30); "to open the eyes that are blind, to bring out the prisoners from the dungeon, from the prison those who sit in darkness" (Isa 42:7); "Israel is a hunted sheep driven away by lions. First the king of Assyria devoured it, and now at the end King Nebuchadrezzar of Babylon has gnawed its bones" (Jer 50:17); "For thus says the Lord GOD: When I make you a city laid waste, like cities that are not inhabited, when I bring up the deep over you, and the great waters cover you" (Ezek 26:19). If this is the case, then surely part of the point of the tale is the reluctance of Jonah to be an agent of forgiveness rather than judgment. As we have seen, Levine wants to maintain that Jonah has the force of Mosaic law on his side—punishment must be exacted or the law is worthless.[15] But, as noted above, God's mercy is a common theme in the Hebrew Bible—a mercy that can abrogate death in favor of life as noted especially in Jeremiah (36:3) and Ezekiel: "Have I any pleasure in the death of the wicked, says the Lord GOD, and not rather that they should turn from their ways and live?" (Ezek 18:23). Again, Blenkinsopp's explanation for such changes of mood seem to be rooted in the changed circumstances of the exilic community—from nation to confessional community—in our terms, from nation to diaspora.[16]

15. Levine, "Reopening," 90.
16. On this idea generally, see the characteristically provocative thoughts of Sze-Kar Wan, "Does Diaspora Identity Imply Some Sort of Universality? An Asian-American Reading of Galatians," in *Interpreting Beyond Borders: The Bible and Postcolonialism*, ed. F. F. Segovia, Bible and Postcolonialism 3 (Sheffield: Sheffield Academic, 2000) 107–31.

I have traced the development of ideas some have called "universalist." But I have also noted that there appear to be contradictions in this. One might assert, however, that the "contradictions" are exaggerated by those who look for a sentimental, syrupy universalism that denies the very realities of evil in the world. Certainly universalism—the idea that non-Israelites may well be part of the future plans of God in constructing a people again after the exilic crisis—does not depend on an avoidance of the reality of evil in the world. God is called upon to do justice, but God's mercy is equally apparent.

To summarize, Baltzer has moved in a different direction in the interpretation of the images of Isaiah by suggesting that the humbling of foreign nations is not the humiliation of these peoples. The key is the meaning of bowing. In the Persian context, such bowing can be acts of obeisance that do not imply defeat or humiliation, but rather that humbling acceptance of transformation—it is reflected in the lion eating straw and the serpent crawling in the dust. Why does humble bowing mean defeat and humiliation when it is used in reference to enemies, but something entirely different when used in reference to Israelites themselves? The Israelites, after all, also bow before God, using precisely the same term as that used for foreign nations: "But I, through the abundance of your steadfast love, will enter your house, I will bow down toward your holy temple in awe of you" (Ps 5:8 [Eng. 7]); "O come, let us worship and bow down, let us kneel before the LORD, our Maker" (95:6); "I bow down toward your holy temple and give thanks to your name for your steadfast love and your faithfulness; for you have exalted your name and your word above everything" (138:2). Furthermore, the psalmist, too, speaks of the transformation of nations: "All the nations you have made shall come and bow down before you, O Lord, and shall glorify your name" (86:9). Even more significant, Psalm 72 seems to move from "bowing" and "licking dust" before the Ruler of Israel, to these same kingdoms being blessed through the agency of the Ruler of Israel. Such praises are transferred to God as well.

It would seem important to note that when, in the imagery of Isaiah, the animals live in peace, the "lions" and "serpents" are not wiped off the face of the earth in some apocalyptic application of the ban. The true contrast is not between peacefulness or forgiveness on the one hand, and repentance and humbling of former enemies on the other. They are integrally related. Strong negative reactions to scholarly interest in universalism often presume that those who read a development of this universalist ethos are promoting an irresponsible (and overly modern) liberal attitude that minimizes the reality and consequences of evil. But the humbling of the empires is the direct recognition of evil—evil is recognized, rejected, repented of, and *then* dismissed. Where is the basis for the frequent assertion that these foreign nations are being forced to bow before their unjustly brutalized former captives? They have paraded the Hebrew children to Zion (Isa 49), they have gathered at the lecture halls of peace, having destroyed their weapons (Isa 2)—they are, in short, transformed enemies. Punishment is held out for those who clearly refuse the realization of their sin and brutality (e.g., those who are *not* bowing), but this only magnifies the significance of the transformation of the others.

To embody a "Jonah" message in the postexilic community is to suggest that the Israelite communities recognize that they are tools of God's transformative justice and mission. But just as the Israelite people are penitent for their own sin, so are the "nations" to be penitent for their sin. Such language is a radical change from the notions that guided preexilic bravado toward the nations, including even prophetic rhetoric of punishment. It is a change, and one that is particularly intelligible in a diasporic context.

6.

"PURITY" AS NONCONFORMITY:
Communal Solidarity as
Diaspora Ethics

A S ALREADY NOTED, WE HAVE PRECIOUS LITTLE DIRECT INFORMATION
about ancient Jewish life in the Babylonian Diaspora. I have also had
occasion to note the recently translated cuneiform tablets from Babylonia
dated from early in the Achaemenid period (ca. 532, 530/520, and 498 BCE)
that refer to the "villages of the Jews" accompanied by Hebrew names.[1]
Other studies of the Jewish names found in various documents, including
the later Murashu Archive and the Elephantine Papyri,[2] combine with
studies of brief indications in the books of Ezekiel and Jeremiah (references to settlements and perhaps even walled towns in Ezekiel, letters to
these settlements in Jer 29, etc.) to give us glimpses of Hebrew identity in
Diaspora life. What we do seem to have, therefore, is clear evidence of the
maintenance of identity as Judeans, if not also information on the communal associations in the Diaspora that facilitated that maintenance.

Despite the difficulties of overconfidence with such minimal evidence, two aspects of the Hebrew Diaspora communities can be clearly

1. F. Joannes and A. Lemaire, "Trois tablettes cunéiformes a onomastique ouest-
sémitique (collection Sh. Moussaieff) (Pls. I-II)," *Transeu* 17 (1999) 26–27.

2. See Matthew Stolper, *Entrepreneurs and Empire: The Murašû Archive, the Murašû
Firm, and Persian Rule in Babylonia*, Uitgaven van het Nederlands Historisch-Archaeologisch
Instituut te Istanbul 54 (Leiden: Brill, 1985); Bezalel Porten and Ada Yardeni, *Textbook of Ara-
maic Documents from Ancient Egypt: Texts and Studies for Students*, vol. 1: *Letters*, Hebrew
University Department of the History of the Jewish People, Texts and Studies for Students
(Winona Lake, Ind.: Eisenbrauns, 1986); and Bezalel Porten, "The Jews in Egypt," in *Cam-
bridge History of Judaism*, vol. 1, *Introduction; The Persian Period*, ed. W. D. Davies and L.
Finkelstein (Cambridge: Cambridge Univ. Press, 1984) 372–400.

indicated: (1) a strong sense of identity that is separate from those traditions and cultures that surround them, and (2) the necessity to "maintain their social boundaries," that is, to protect this unique identity through a strong emphasis on internal solidarity and consistency. In this chapter, I want to briefly outline some textual elements of this boundary maintenance in the postexilic communities.

The Exile and Theologies of "Community"

How did preexilic Israel think of themselves? Paul Hanson, who has written the most systematic study of biblical concepts of community in the Hebrew Bible suggests that the early Mosaic notion of a "covenant relationship" between God and a people is already the central notion of community in the Hebrew Bible: "The birth of what we can identify as a distinctly Israelite notion of community occurs in intimate relation to one foundational event, the experience of escape from Egyptian bondage interpreted as deliverance by the God Yahweh."[3] George Mendenhall had earlier summarized similar thoughts, but with a stronger emphasis on the resulting communal structure: "What happened at Sinai was the formation of a new unity where none had existed before, a 'peace of God' among a 'mixed multitude,' and tribally affiliated families who had in common only the deliverance from an intolerable monopoly of force."[4] Here, however, how preexilic Israel thought of itself as a people or nation cannot be the central issue. But we can certainly ask whether we can discern any changes in how that relationship was conceived based on tracking the uses of certain terms to refer, simply, to fellow Hebrews. It is important to note in the following that I presume that the legal discussions of Exodus represent an older form of law than that represented in the Deuteronomic legislative texts.[5]

Who Is "We"? Some Observations on the Biblical Vocabulary of Community

"Neighbor," "Friend," and "Brother"

Let us first examine the use of the simple term typically translated "friend," "compatriot," "neighbor." It is often used to express the common

3. Paul D. Hanson, *The People Called: The Growth of Community in the Bible* (San Francisco: Harper & Row, 1986) 86.

4. George E. Mendenhall, *The Tenth Generation* (Baltimore: Johns Hopkins Univ. Press, 1973) 21.

5. See Bernard Levinson, *Deuteronomy and the Hermeneutics of Legal Innovation* (New York: Oxford Univ. Press, 1997).

notion of the "other" to whom one speaks, literally one speaks as "a man to his compatriot/neighbor/friend" (Gen 11:3; cf. 11:7; Exod 33:11, where too much can be been made of the term, incidentally, in traditional translations; Judg 10:18; 1 Sam 10:11; Ps 12:2; Isa 41:6; Jer 31:34; 46:16; Jonah 1:7; Zech 8:16; Mal 3:16). In the legal discussions of the Covenant Code, the references to the legally relevant "other person" is typically expressed using this term. Note the following examples: "When individuals quarrel and one strikes *the other* with a stone or fist so that the injured party, though not dead, is confined to bed" (Exod 21:18); "When someone delivers *to a neighbor* money or goods for safekeeping, and they are stolen from the neighbor's house, then the thief, if caught, shall pay double" (22:7). It is important to note, however, that on many occasions (although not consistently), the later Deuteronomic Code (ca. 640–609 BCE) replaces the simple "neighbor" with the term used for "brother." Compare the two following cases, Exodus using "neighbor," and Deuteronomy using "brother":

> If someone's ox hurts the ox *of another (rēa')*, so that it dies, then they shall sell the live ox and divide the price of it; and the dead animal they shall also divide. (Exod 21:35)
>
> When someone delivers *to another (rēa')*, a donkey, ox, sheep, or any other animal for safekeeping, and it dies or is injured or is carried off, without anyone seeing it. . . . (Exod 22:9 [Eng. 10])
>
> You shall not watch *your neighbor's* (lit. "your brother's," '*āḥ*) ox or sheep straying away and ignore them; you shall take them back to their owner. (Deut 22:1; literally, "back to your brother")

That this use of "brother" tends to be chronologically late is clear from the late addition made in Exodus 32, which highlights the importance of the Levites in a rather gruesome episode of mass punishment. In this late passage, the term for "brother" is used in parallel to other terms and thus closer to the use in the spirit of Deuteronomy: "He said to them, 'Thus says the LORD, the God of Israel, "Put your sword on your side, each of you! Go back and forth from gate to gate throughout the camp, and each of you kill your brother *('aḥ)*, your friend *(rēa')*, and your neighbor *('îš 'et qarôbo)*" ' " (Exod 32:27).[6]

6. The influence from older tradition is especially evident when an established legal phrase, a technical term, such as "neighbor's wife," is used. Note the comparison of the Deuteronomy passage with occasions in the even later (post–587 BCE) Priestly influenced material, even down to Ezekiel: "You shall bring both of them to the gate of that town and stone them to death, the young woman because she did not cry for help in the town and the man because he violated his neighbor's wife. So you shall purge the evil from your midst" (Deut 22:24); "If a man commits adultery with the wife of his neighbor, both the adulterer and the adulteress shall be put to death" (Lev 20:10; cf. Ezek 18:6, "defile his neighbor's wife"; cf. 18:11, 15; 22:11; 33:26; cf. Jer 5:8; 7:5; Prov 6:29).

Is there any significance to a late and often Deuteronomic change to "brother"? Is it simply a matter of stylistic change in the use of common language? The older, pre-Deuteronomic term may later have come to mean something more than merely a fellow Israelite. In the later (i.e., postexilic) wisdom tradition, for example, the older term seems to make more sense in a setting where the "other" (as opposed to a "brother") is most likely a *foreign* "neighbor/other."[7] There are references to other people with whom one must interact morally and uprightly, but we get little sense of "others" who occupy a special status as comrades or coreligionists in contrast to others of different status. Wisdom, famously, moves in a highly individualistic milieu. Take the following ethical maxims, typical of the wisdom tradition:

One who secretly slanders a neighbor *(rēaʿ)* I will destroy. A haughty look and an arrogant heart I will not tolerate. (Ps 101:5)

With their mouths the godless would destroy their neighbors *(rēaʿ)*, but by knowledge the righteous are delivered. (Prov 11:9)

The violent entice their neighbors *(rēaʿ)*, and lead them in a way that is not good. (Prov 16:29)

It is senseless to give a pledge, to become surety for a neighbor *(rēaʿ)*. (Prov 17:18; cf. Prov 18:17; 21:10; 27:4)

Suspicion arises about the late nature of these wisdom aphorisms, given that many of them virtually contradict the moral instruction of the Mosaic laws. For example, as I note in chapter seven below, giving a pledge is outright discouraged in Prov 17:18 yet appears quite acceptable in Deut 24:10-15 under appropriate conditions of generosity. Prov 20:16 further discourages (and clarifies) about giving pledges to "foreigners" and "strangers." Deut 15:3 and 23:20 allow interest for loans to foreigners—but certainly do not discourage loaning to foreigners.

The following, and final, example is particularly interesting, suggesting that a foreign monarch, rather than an Israelite one, is the subject of the advice. Given the popularity of the "Jewish adviser to the foreign king" motif in postexilic literature (Daniel, Mordecai and Esther, Nehemiah, Zerubbabel, Ezra, etc.), it would seem that we can posit a postexilic setting

---

7. If foreigners are implied in this use of the older term in the wisdom tradition, this increases the sense of the advice that essentially asks the reader not to annoy people, e.g., foreigners, and likely foreigners from the ranks of the privileged culture of dominance—those who have the power to make life difficult. Such practical advice is a theme that many minorities are all too familiar with and provides insights into the social context of wisdom literature.

for advice such as the following: "Those who love a pure heart and are gracious in speech will have the king as a friend (rēaʿ)" (Prov 22:11).

In summary, it would seem that the language of relationships within a defined group (e.g., the Israelites) evolved toward the language of kinship—"brother"—in Deuteronomy, precisely at a time when there was growing interaction with, and awareness of, regular contact with non-Israelite "others" in the postexilic period. In other words, a stronger sense of "community identity" arises under circumstances of minority, stateless existence. Is there a corresponding change in the conception of the community that uses such terminology? Ronald Clements, for one, thinks so: "In spite of the clear recognition that Israel is a nation, living on the land given to it by God, the image that is presented of the nation is more that of a family, or clan, than of a nation with all its mixed and varied elements. In consequence, all Israelites are encouraged to think of themselves as 'brothers' (Deut 14:7; 15:2, 3)."[8]

If this proposed change in the nomenclature for "associates" is accurate, especially from older materials to more recent Deuteronomic materials, does this also reflect changes in social consciousness? Bernhard Lang argued that Deuteronomy reflected tighter communal language because the Deuteronomists themselves were a minority within late monarchical society: "The exclusivists, those who were loyal to YHWH alone, were an embattled minority embarked on a mission to convert their compatriots to their 'radical' views."[9] Richard Nelson's analysis of the sociology of Deuteronomy also concludes that there was a carefully defined "in-group" implied in the ethics of the famous Deuteronomic codes: "Deuteronomy insists on benevolence and consideration for resident aliens and other needy and marginalized groups, but does so only on the basis of a recognition of some level of community membership and of obligations created by shared experience."[10]

Even if I am going beyond the available evidence to conjecture a tighter sense of communal identity and membership, however, the language of kinship (e.g., "brother," but also using terms like bet 'abot for a new social construction[11]) certainly expanded in the postexilic period

8. R. E. Clements, *Deuteronomy*, Old Testament Guides (Sheffield: JSOT Press, 1989), 56.

9. Bernhard Lang, *Monotheism and the Prophetic Minority: An Essay in Biblical History and Sociology*, Social World of Biblical Antiquity Series 1 (Sheffield: Almond, 1983) 2, 55.

10. "*Ḥerem* and the Deuteronomic Social Conscience," in *Deuteronomy and Deuteronomic Literature*, FS C. Brekelmans, ed. M. Vervenne and J. Lust, BETL 133 (Leuven: Leuven Univ. Press, 1997) 49.

11. On this the classic study is still Joel Weinberg, "The *Bet 'Abot* in the Sixth to Fourth Centuries BCE," in *The Citizen-Temple Community*, trans. D. L. Smith-Christopher, JSOTSup 151 (Sheffield: JSOT Press, 1992) 49–61.

even further to express decidedly nonkin relationships. It would seem that this vocabulary may express changes in the nature of community reflected in the use of familial language that implies a tighter-knit social consciousness of the community,[12] Are there other terms that may reflect this? We turn to communal group terminology.

Vocabulary of Groups
There is a similar shift in vocabulary discernible in the biblical language used for the group. As opposed to speaking of the assembly, or "all Israel," a move seems discernible in the late Priestly writing toward the language of Israel as "the congregation." Note the relationship of the terms "gathering/assembly" and "congregation":

> If the *whole congregation (kol ʿedat)* of Israel errs unintentionally and the matter escapes the notice of the *assembly (qāhal)*, and they do any one of the things that by the LORD's commandments ought not to be done and incur guilt . . . (Lev 4:13)

> He shall carry the bull outside the camp, and burn it as he burned the first bull; it is the sin offering for *the assembly (qāhal)*. (Lev 4:21)

> Assemble *the whole congregation (kol haʿedah)* at the entrance of the tent of meeting. (Lev 8:3)

> As for *the assembly (qāhal)*, there shall be for both you and the resident alien a single statute, a perpetual statute throughout your generations; you and the alien shall be alike before the LORD. (Num 15:15)

> But the LORD said to Moses and Aaron, "Because you did not trust in me, to show my holiness before the eyes of the Israelites, therefore you shall not bring this assembly into the land that I have given them." (Num 20:12)

In the Deuteronomistic literature, the term translated "assembly" refers to the act of bringing people together (Deut 4:10; cf. 31:12; Judg 21:8; 1 Sam 17:47) or to an actual time when people were gathered, presumably for a ceremony of some sort. The later (postexilic) Chronicler picks up on this use of "assembly," but in this late Persian period narrative, the term can also be a euphemism for all Israelites.

This later concept is suggested in Ezra-Nehemiah, where the "assembly" seems to imply the entire community, whether able to assemble in one place or not. Note Ezra 2:64: "The whole assembly *(kol haqahal)* together

---

12. See Smith, *The Religion of the Landless* (Bloomington, Ind.: Meyer-Stone, 1989) 93–126.

was forty-two thousand three hundred sixty" (cf. Ezra 10:12, 14; Neh 5:13; 7:66; 8:2, 17).

In sum, the late tradition conceived of the people of Israel as "the people gathered for worship," and thus always a "congregation," which is implied in the change in Priestly language, from the earlier "assembly" *(qahal)* to the frequent use of "congregation" *('edah)*. This apparent change in the conception of the community was famously summarized by Antonin Causse, who suggested that "it was not in any way a question of restoring a political past, with its social organization and national life, which had deteriorated from the time of the judges and first kings to the eventual fall of the two kingdoms. It was, rather, a question of a new sociological formation that would be neither a federation of clans nor a nation but a religious community whose destiny would not necessarily be tied to the conditions of an ethnic group or to a state."[13]

"Those Around You"—The Others in Exilic Terminology

Exilic texts of the Bible reveal a strong awareness of the "nations that are around you" (built on the root *sābab*). Although Joel 3:11 and Obadiah 16 refer to the surrounding nations in terms of judgment, interaction other than warfare is implied beginning already in the Deuteronomic literature. The sense of the social differences between the Hebrews and the nations that surround the Israelites suggests a new awareness of interaction and involvement: "When you have come into the land that the LORD your God is giving you, and have taken possession of it and settled in it, and you say, 'I will set a king over me, like all the nations that are around me'" (Deut 17:14). This develops in important ways already in Ezekiel, from the earlier period of exile: "But she has rebelled against my ordinances and my statutes, becoming more wicked than the nations and the countries all around her, rejecting my ordinances and not following my statutes. Therefore thus says the Lord GOD: Because you are more turbulent than the nations that are all around you, and have not followed my statutes or kept my ordinances, but have acted according to the ordinances of the nations that are all around you" (Ezek 5:6-7; cf. 11:12; 36:7, 36).

A reference in Elephantine documents reveals that, despite the quite different circumstances for Jewish presence at the military base there, an awareness of cultural and ethnic differences was not only clear, but may have played a major part on the anti-Jewish violence that led to the

---

13. Antonin Causse, "From an Ethnic Group to a Religious Community: The Sociological Problem of Judaism," in *Community, Identity, and Ideology: Social Science Approaches to the Hebrew Bible*, ed. C. E. Carter, Sources for Biblical and Theological Study 6 (Winona Lake, Ind.: Eisenbrauns, 1996) 102.

destruction of the famous "YHW temple" there,[14] in the Aramaic document dated November, 407 BCE. Bezalel Porten also observed that ethnic indicators are a prominent and constant feature of the Aramaic documentation from this period in Egypt.[15]

This awareness in the Hebrew biblical texts of the differences between the Hebrews and these "nations surrounding you" merges into a diaspora awareness of the differences between the Hebrews and other peoples in the later Persian material and remains a feature even in Palestine-based Hellenistic material. The theme is arguably a seamless trajectory of increasingly significant self-awareness. Note, for example, Esth 3:8: "Then Haman said to King Ahasuerus, 'There is a certain people scattered and separated among the peoples in all the provinces of your kingdom; their laws are different from those of every other people, and they do not keep the king's laws, so that it is not appropriate for the king to tolerate them.'" The Greek additions go further toward the notion of a "hostile" people, suggesting that as time has passed, the differences have become issues of frequent dispute. Note Esth 13:4 from the Greek addition: "There is scattered a certain hostile people, who have laws contrary to those of every nation and continually disregard the ordinances of kings, so that the unifying of the kingdom that we honorably intend cannot be brought about." In the later Maccabean literature, these sentiments are also common: "Instead they gossiped about the differences in worship and foods, alleging that these people were loyal neither to the king nor to his authorities, but were hostile and greatly opposed to his government" (3 Macc 3:7). What are some of the features of this increasing "self-consciousness"?

Issues of Community Formation after the Exile

If these lexical changes reflect actual sociological changes, then what is the context for such changes in thinking about the nature of the "community"? I maintain that the answer is tied to the social and political circumstances of the move from the monarchy to the period of exile. In exile the Hebrews become a stateless minority in the context of a massive empire, first under the Persians, then under Hellenistic rule after Alexander, and finally under the Romans into the Common Era with Christianity. In later biblical thought, consciousness of being "a certain people scattered and

---

14. The letter is numbered differently according to the edition (e.g., "Cowley 30"). I consulted B19 in Bezalel Porten, *The Elephantine Papyri in English: Three Millennia of Cross-Cultural Continuity and Change* (Leiden: Brill, 1996) 141.

15. Porten, *Papyri*, 125.

separated among the peoples" is also evident in metaphors for Israel as the "righteous remnant" (*še'ar*, a term used heavily in Jeremiah and Ezekiel, as well as in postexilic prophets like Haggai and Zechariah) that suggest a minority consciousness that was an important aspect of post-exilic Israelite communal existence.[16]

Even more profound is the related argument of William Schniedewind in regard to the older promise of a Davidic messiah to carry on the monarchy. In his important recent work, Schniedewind traces the history of the interpretation (within the Bible) of the original promise made to David in 2 Sam 7:1-17. The crisis of exile ended the Davidic rule and thus apparently violated the promise. But Schniedewind argues that the monarchical promise was radically democratized in the circumstances of exile and thus applied to the community as a whole: "The crisis brought on by the end of the Davidic monarchy and the destruction of the Jerusalem temple necessitated a creative, innovative reading of the promise to David. No longer could it be understood to give divine sanction to a simple reading of the Promise to David. . . . The end of the monarchy ironically forced the democratization of Israel. Monarchy is an autocratic form of government. The end of the monarchy brought with it a dramatic restructuring of the political and social institutions of ancient Israel. . . . The Promise to David receives a radical new understanding as applying to all Israel."[17]

This argument is even more convincing, however, when one considers that changes in communal consciousness parallel the rise of "boundary awareness" in Jewish literature of the postexilic period. In other words, I have briefly summarized "in-group" language. We must now consider "out-group" language.

The Priestly Theology of Policing the Boundaries: Purity and Social Solidarity

The strong communal sense of "boundaries" or identity-maintenance mechanisms in the biblical literature has been labeled "xenophobic," "nationalist," or "ethnocentric." The evidence associated with these terms

---

16. 2 Kgs 19:31; Ezra 9:8, 13, 14, 15; esp. Isa 10; 28:5; Jer 6:9; etc. The classic study of this concept is Gerhard F. Hasel, *The Remnant: The History and Theology of the Remnant Idea from Genesis to Isaiah*, Andrews University Monographs 5 (Berrien Springs, Mich.: Andrews Univ. Press, 1972).

17. William M. Schniedewind, *Society and the Promise to David: The Reception History of 2 Samuel 7:1-17* (New York: Oxford Univ. Press, 1999) 117–18.

usually consists of three kinds of material: (1) the increased language of purity in postexilic texts, which is particularly reflected in (2) the concern for the threat of mixed marriages, and (3) an increased sense of threat from differences with non-Jewish populations. Any biblical theology of diasporic existence must include a review of the social and theological function of these socioreligious processes. What appears to be common to all these processes is the language and themes of the priesthood. In short, it appears that the language of purity, in Priestly terms, was the "code" that expressed the most effective issues of social and religious identity and thus also the language used to refer to those outside this identity.

One must say, however, that the Priestly influence in the postexilic community has rarely been read with either theological or sociological sympathy, most notably in the case of "reading" Ezra. If proof is needed that the interests of the scholarly reader can influence his/her reading of the biblical text, surely we need look no further than the mixed-marriage crisis in Ezra 9–10 to find emotionally charged comments such as Hugh Williamson's view that "the treatment described in these two chapters of how Ezra tackled the problem of mixed marriages is among the least attractive parts of Ezra-Nehemiah, if not the whole Old Testament."[18] Similarly, David Clines is "appalled by the personal misery brought into so many families by the compulsory divorce of foreign wives [and] outraged at Ezra's insistence on racial purity, so uncongenial to modern liberal thoughts."[19] Certainly, the behavior of the postexilic community has frequently been described as "xenophobic."[20] But Ezra's policies must be placed within two wider circles in order to make sense both sociologically and theologically (even if one still has moral objections). First, Ezra is a priest, and thus is representative of the Priestly traditions that include Leviticus and Ezekiel. The second, and wider, circle within which Ezra must be read is not only other biblical examples of Priestly attitudes and ideologies, but also in the context of minority and refugee behaviors in circumstances of subordination. Let us consider groups of texts that illustrate these issues of communal solidarity.

18. H. G. M. Williamson, *Ezra, Nehemiah*, WBC 16 (Waco: Word, 1985) 159.

19. D. J. A. Clines, *Ezra and Nehemiah*, NCBC (Grand Rapids: Eerdmans, 1984) 116.

20. Lester L. Grabbe, "Triumph of the Pious or Failure of the Xenophobes? The Ezra-Nehemiah Reforms and Their Nachgeschichte," in *Jewish Local Patriotism and Self-Identification in the Greco-Roman Period*, ed. S. Jones and S. Pearce, JSPSup 31 (Sheffield: Sheffield Academic, 1998) 50–65.

The Background to Daniel's Resolution to Be "Undefiled" by the Emperor's Food

In the first tale of Daniel (in the Hebrew, as opposed to the expanded Greek text), Daniel refuses the king's food and wine with a request that he not be forced to "defile himself" *(gā'al)*. The term in question, "to defile," is an interesting one that may well imply more than simply a priestly influenced desire to "eat kosher." For example, although arguing that the king's food and wine seems not to raise questions of pentateuchal law, John Collins maintains that "there can be no doubt that the defilement in question is primarily ritual."[21] He notes, for example, that the same root, used in the sense of defilement, can be found in connection with blood (Isa 59:3; Lam 4:14) but also with disqualification from the priesthood in Ezra-Nehemiah (Ezra 2:62; Neh 7:64). These parallel cases, however, suggest the possibility of further analysis that would expand on Collins's observations.

The defiling blood in Isa 59:3 and Lam 4:14 is connected with sinful behavior that led to the defilement—the blood was symbolic of that behavior and thus paralleled "iniquity": "For your hands are defiled with blood, and your fingers with iniquity; your lips have spoken lies, your tongue mutters wickedness" (Isa 59:3). Similarly, in Lamentations, it was the sin of killing the "righteous" that led to the defilement: "It was for the sins of her prophets and the iniquities of her priests, who shed the blood of the righteous in the midst of her. Blindly they wandered through the streets, so defiled with blood that no one was able to touch their garments" (Lam 4:13-14). Compare also the use of "defiled city" in Zephaniah: "Ah, soiled, defiled, oppressing city! It has listened to no voice; it has accepted no correction. It has not trusted in the LORD; it has not drawn near to its God" (Zeph 3:1-2). Just as significantly, in the so-called Golah List accounts in Ezra-Nehemiah (supposedly a list of the Judean community back in the land, but this is highly disputed), the defilement was a matter of exclusion from a particular social group, for example, the priesthood: "These looked for their entries in the genealogical records, but they were not found there, and so they were excluded from the priesthood as unclean" (Ezra 2:62).

These texts suggest that "defilement" can have as significant a social implication as a ritual one. In other words, defilement has to do with inclusion or membership as much as individual status. This is more dramatically confirmed in the use noted in Neh 13:29-30, where clarifying membership is a matter of "purification" from everything foreign:

---

21. John J. Collins, *Daniel,* Hermeneia (Minneapolis: Fortress Press, 1993) 142.

"Remember them, O my God, because they have defiled the priesthood, the covenant of the priests and the Levites. Thus I cleansed them from everything foreign." The final phrase here is a key to understanding the social significance of diasporic categories of "purity."

In a widely read work, anthropologist Mary Douglas proposed a "symbolic anthropological" reading of the purity regulations of Leviticus, suggesting that the language of purity has as much to do with regulating social boundaries of groups as worries about maintenance of ritual status. K. C. Hanson's recent summary of Douglas's main argument seems helpful here: "Purity rites are instituted in order to define social boundaries and sustain the structures of society."[22] Indeed, in his magnificent commentary on Leviticus 1–16, Jacob Milgrom also notes the essentially communal nature of the Priestly theology of sin. Collective guilt is symbolized in the need to purify the temple.[23]

An excellent example of this is the legal material of Leviticus, which according to most commentators has undergone a redactional stereotypical "framing" for each of the legal precepts. This frame places each legal discussion in the context of the Sinaitic laws of Moses, and thus Leviticus 11 is similarly arranged. But each of the legal discussions have themselves undergone additional comments and interpretation as well. For example, Rolf Rendtorff isolated 11:2b-3 as the *Urform* of ch. 11—that is, the positive command regarding animals that can be eaten. This law is "framed" by the second-person permission "you may eat. . . ."[24] Verse 4, then, begins a restrictive clause and is considered a second, later elaboration in the negative. In v. 9 we have another short positive command followed again by detailed elaboration.

Because of the similarity of Deut 14:1-2 to Lev 11:2-23, however, Karl Elliger already supposed an independent source for these legal materials; thus the laws and the elaboration must have existed in some pre-Deuteronomic cultic practice.[25] What is significant, however, is that only Leviticus continues the section with the material found in vv. 24-47, with its detailed elaboration of laws and regulations regarding the

---

22. K. C. Hanson, "Sin, Purification, and Group Process," in *Problems in Biblical Theology*, FS Rolf Knierim, ed. H. T. C. Sun et al. (Grand Rapids: Eerdmans, 1997) 175.

23. Jacob Milgrom, *Leviticus 1–16: A New Translation with Introduction*, AB (New York, Doubleday, 1991) 49–50.

24. R. Rendtorff, *Die Gesetze in der Priesterschrift*, 2d ed., FRLANT 62 (Göttingen: Vandenhoeck & Ruprecht, 1963) 39, n.44.

25. Karl Elliger, *Leviticus*, Handbuch zum Alten Testament 1 (Tubingen: Mohr/Siebeck, 1966) 145–46.

transfer of pollution and the means by which this pollution is removed. I have previously argued that the first section of Leviticus 11 (i.e., vv. 2-23) is concerned with the inherent status of certain animals, whereas the issue changes to the transfer of pollution in the second section, especially the section unique to Leviticus 11 and thus probably later than either Deuteronomy 14 or the first section of Leviticus 11. The difference between the two sections is significant and reveals a change of emphasis.[26]

The final redactional element in the second section of ch. 11 is the conclusion, vv. 46-47. Here a summary is provided of the concerns of the entire section. (As Rendtorff suggests, each legal precept consists of a basic law much older than P, its elaboration, and then finally an introduction placing it in the frame of Sinai, and a summary at the end.) These verses provide an essential key to understanding the exilic significance of Levitical legislation about the pure and impure: "This is the law pertaining to land animal and bird and every living creature that moves through the waters and every creature that swarms upon the earth, to make a *distinction* between the unclean and the clean, and between the living creature that may be eaten and the living creature that may not be eaten." The key term is *bādal* ("to distinguish or separate"). The term appears also in Lev 19:19, where the context is preventing the "mixing of species," and in 20:22, where there appears a warning that the land will "vomit out the unclean inhabitants" in association with the call to maintain "separation." Note especially 18:24-30, where the pollution caused by strangers is the key concept.

The Hebrew term for "to separate/divide" *(bādal)* is generally used in late biblical material. Although not in itself an especially technical term, the vast majority of instances appear in cultic contexts. Sometimes the sense is merely a "selection" or "setting apart" to perform a duty, such as David's selection of the Gadites (1 Chr 12:9; 25:1 [Eng. 8]), the setting apart of the cities of refuge (Deut 4:41; 19:2, 7), Ezra's selection of elders to rule in the community (Ezra 10:16), or finally the choosing of people to bury the dead (Ezek 39:14). However, even in some of these cases, notably the cities of refuge and people who must handle the dead, there are overtones of maintaining purity.

These examples are virtually the only possible exceptions to an otherwise quite impressively consistent context for the use of the term "to separate"—the context of maintaining pure and impure people in juxtaposition with other people. Consider the thematic use of separations in

---

26. See my *Religion of the Landless,* 139–51.

Lev 20:24-26: "But I have said to you: You shall inherit their land, and I will give it to you to possess, a land flowing with milk and honey. I am the LORD your God; I have *separated* you from the peoples. You shall therefore make a *distinction* between the clean animal and the unclean, and between the unclean bird and the clean; you shall not bring abomination on yourselves by animal or by bird or by anything with which the ground teems, which I have *set apart* for you to hold unclean. You shall be holy to me; for I the LORD am holy, and I have *separated* you from the other peoples to be mine."

The term becomes more significant, however, in the mid-Persian period texts, Ezra-Nehemiah: those who separated themselves from the "aliens of the land" (Ezra 6:21); those not separated from the "people of the land" (9:1); those who separated from their foreign wives (10:11); those separated from the Golah (10:8); separate the holy seed from all the "sons of foreigners" (Neh 9:2); those who separated from the "peoples of the land" (10:29); those who separated themselves from those of foreign descent (13:3). What emerges from this summary is an interesting late biblical use of purity language to indicate characteristics of social groups with a concomitant emphasis on the separation of Israelites from foreigners. This use is particularly evident in the use of the term in Ezra-Nehemiah to describe the separation of the pure Israel from foreigners, especially foreign wives.

One passage that particularly deserves comment is Isa 56:3, the apparent reassurance to converts that the exilic boundaries will not necessarily (or perhaps should not, in the writer's view) mean that these foreigners are to be rejected. Was this a protest on the part of certain members of the community—those with clear sympathies to the traditional tales of Ruth and Jonah—that the Priestly concern for boundaries must not become obsessive? Before commenting, however, I need to recall one famous case of separation, the mixed-marriage crisis as presented in Ezra-Nehemiah.

Social Separation: The "Mixed-Marriage Crisis" in Ezra-Nehemiah

Although there is some debate about whether Neh 13:3 deals with the mixed-marriage issue, it is dealt with at great length in Ezra 9–10 and again in Neh 13:23-31. Commentators have usually approached this issue as two examples of the same problem with the postexilic community.

Many of these discussions of the dissolution of mixed marriages have tended to focus on two main points: (1) the Deuteronomic legal basis for the action taken by Ezra in Ezra 9–10 and Nehemiah in Nehemiah 13, and the Deuteronomic laws being stretched to justify this action;[27] and (2) the social meaning of this action in the context of the postexilic community, and its attempt to preserve its "purity" and/or maintain its economic holdings without threat of foreigners "inheriting" land.[28] Tamara Eskenazi has argued in support of the view that inheritance was a major issue of concern in the postexilic community, particularly noting that women could inherit land, as shown in the Elephantine Papyri.[29]

That land tenure was a significant factor in all marriages in ancient Israel can hardly be doubted, although as Carol Meyers points out in her analysis of exogamy and endogamy in ancient Israel, the cultural influences of "foreign" women must also be considered.[30] If we follow the land tenure issue—or more broadly the economic issue—then modern analysis of mixed marriages raise some interesting questions that apply to a historical analysis of Ezra and Nehemiah's cases.[31]

The Sociology of Mixed Marriage
What are the "relevant" considerations that defined the marriage "crisis"? Ezra, for one, defines the terms both ethnically (by citing the

---

27. See William Horbury, "Extirpation and Excommunication," *VT* 35 (1985) 13–38, who argues that an interpretation that combines laws regarding admission to the temple congregation and penalties for breach of covenant (Deut 17, 18, 19, and 20 as well as Deut 7) could result in such a justification; and Gerald Blidstein, "Atimia: A Greek Parallel to Ezra x 8 and to Post-Biblical Exclusion from the Community," *VT* 24 (1974) 357–60, who argues that Ezra may well have been given just such an authority to exile offenders in Artaxerxes' letter in Ezra 8. At least since Batten's commentary, scholars have noted that the Torah does not really authorize Ezra's action. See L. Batten, *Ezra and Nehemiah,* ICC (Edinburgh: T. & T. Clark, 1913) 331; Wilhelm Rudolph, *Esra und Nehemia* Handbuch zum Alten Testament (Tübingen: Mohr/Siebeck, 1949) 87–97; J. Blenkinsopp, *Ezra-Nehemiah,* OTL (Philadelphia: Westminster, 1988) 176; Williamson, *Ezra, Nehemiah,* 130–32. Also now see Milgrom, *Leviticus,* 359–60, for interesting observations on the cultic context of Ezra's language.

28. Note Fensham (and others): "The reason for this attitude had nothing to do with racism, but with a concern for the purity of the religion of the Lord . . . in the end it was a question of the preservation of their identity" (*Books of Ezra and Nehemiah,* NICOT [Grand Rapids: Eerdmans, 1982] 124); cf. Batten, *Ezra,* 331; Blenkinsopp, *Ezra-Nehemiah,* 176. The economic issues have also been noted by Blenkinsopp and by J. Weinberg, "Die Agrarverhältnisse in der Berger-Tempel-Gemeinde der Achämenidenzeit," *Acta Antiqua* 22 (1974) 473–85.

29. Tamara Eskenazi, "Out from the Shadows: Biblical Women in the Post-Exilic Era," *JSOT* 54 (1992) 25–43. See also J. Blenkinsopp, "The Social Context of the 'Outsider Woman' in Proverbs 1–9," *Bib* 74 (1991) 457–73.

30. See Carol L. Meyers, *Discovering Eve: Ancient Israelite Women in Context* (Oxford: Oxford Univ. Press, 1988) 180–88.

31. Robert K. Merton, "Intermarriage and the Social Structure: Fact and Theory," *Psychiatry* 9 (1941) 362.

national/ethnic categories of Canaanite, Hivite, Perizzite, etc.) and religiously (by citing such terms as "the holy seed"). In this case Ezra is wor-
ried about marrying outside a religious and ethnically defined group (e.g.,
"endogamy"). It is clear that Ezra conceived of the approved group as
consisting only of former exiles (9:4). But even if this was a rigid definition for the writers of Ezra, the possibility remains that these "mixed marriages" were considered "mixed" only by Ezra and his supporters and not
in the first case by the married persons themselves. The issue is made
more precise by Robert Merton's widely noted sociological definition of
endogamy: "Endogamy is a device which serves to maintain social pre-
rogatives and immunities within a social group. It helps prevent the dif-
fusion of power, authority and preferred status to persons who are not
affiliated with a dominant group. It serves further to accentuate and symbolize the 'reality' of the group by setting it off against other discriminable
social units."[32] Furthermore, in a comment that virtually defines Ezra's
attitude as it appears in the biblical texts, Merton suggests that public out-
cries against mixed marriage "stabilize the existing organization of interpersonal relations and groups."[33]

There has been a considerable discussion of mixed marriage in sociological and anthropological literature, often in dialogue with Merton's
programmatic article where he outlined his functionalist perspective to
guide further study.[34] In his discussion, two significant parts of his theoretical formulation are "exchange theory" and the related "hypergamy"
theory. Other social scientists emphasize group identity as the main fac-

32. Ibid., 368.
33. Ibid., 369.
34. Among the more helpful articles consulted for this book, see Christopher Bagley,
"Patterns of Inter-Ethnic Marriage in England," *Phylon* 29 (1968) 347–50; Susan Benson,
"Interracial Families in London," in *Ambiguous Ethnicity* (Cambridge: Cambridge Univ.
Press, 1981) 146–49; Noel Gist, "Cultural Versus Social Marginality: The Anglo-Indian Case"
Phylon 28 (1967) 361–75; Joseph Gold, "Patterns of Negro-White Intermarriage," *American
Sociology Review* 19 (1954) 144–47; George A. Kourvetaris, "Patterns of Generational Subcul-
ture and Intermarriage of Greeks in the United States," *International Journal of Sociology of
the Family* 1 (1971) 34–48; Barbara Lobodzinska, "A Cross-Cultural Study of Mixed Mar-
riages in Poland and the United States," *International Journal of Sociology of the Family* 15,
nos. 1–2 (1985) 94–117; Simon Marcson, "Theory of Intermarriage and Assimilation," *Social
Forces* 29 (1950) 75–78; John Mayer, "Jewish-Gentile Intermarriage Patterns: A Hypothesis,"
Sociology and Social Research 45, no. 2 (1961) 188–95; Thomas P. Monahan, "Interracial
Marriage in the United States: Some Data on Upstate New York," *International Journal of
Sociology of the Family* 1 (1971) 94–105; Ernest Porterfield, "Perspectives on Black-White
Intermixture," *Black and White Mixed Marriages* (Chicago: Nelson-Hall, 1978) 1–184; Gary
D. Sandefur, "American Indian Intermarriage," *Social Science Research*, 15, no. 4 (1986)
347–71.

tor in protecting "boundaries."[35] On a secondary level, it is also important
to mention romantic/democratic "violations" of ethnic boundaries and
the argument that violations of group identity in mixed marriages result
from deviance or alienation from the strictures of a specific ethnic or cultural group.[36] I will comment on many of these and their relevance to the
Ezra-Nehemiah texts in turn.

Hypergamy Theory
In his analysis of black-white intermarriages, Ernest Porterfield works
with Levi-Strauss's idea that marriages are an effective control of human
commodities, and that they are "exchanged" in order to gain certain
advantages. This "exchange" basis for the analysis of mixed marriages has
led to the so-called hypergamy theory. When applied to black-white marriages in the United States, for example, this theory suggests that typically
the black male "exchanges" educational/financial success for the white
female's racial status.[37] The advocates of the hypergamy theory contend
that success- or status-minded males from low status groups will attempt
to "marry up" among females of the majority or higher status groups.
Males from the majority, higher status groups usually do not need to
legitimate mixed liaisons with formal marriage but have tended to keep
mistresses instead. But this point may be open to question. The data
about Asian women shows that the issue is not gender, but which of the
two genders in a particular context has a sense of freedom to pursue

35. Many studies cite social deviance as a major factor in mixed marriages. This approach
seems less promising as a guide to biblical research but is important to mention. In discussing
Arab-Jewish marriages in Israel, Erik Cohen states that in nearly every case he found, "the
Jewish women had in some respect been marginal in Jewish society" ("Mixed Marriage in an
Israeli Town," *Jewish Journal of Sociology* 11 [1969] 49). Similarly, Kuo and Wong point to couples who share a certain disregard of social norms in Singapore, and mixed couples of Malay
and Chinese and occasionally Indians, occur (Eddie C. Y. Kuo, "Population Ratio, Intermarriage and Mother Tongue Retention," *Anthropological Linguistics* 20, no. 2 [1978] 85–93; Kuo
and Aline K. Wong, "Ethnic Intermarriage in a Multiethnic Society," in *The Contemporary
Family in Singapore* [Singapore: Singapore Univ. Press, 1979] 168–88).
    There is very little in the Bible, however, that would support the supposition that those
who engaged in mixed marriages were social outcasts or marginal to the society in question.
In the one possible example, Ruth, her poverty and compassion make her exceptionally positive rather than negative; i.e., her alienation from Moabite society is not a negative factor.
She is certainly a case of alienation from her native traditions, however, and is honored in
the Bible. Indeed, the shock of mixed marriage in Ezra 9–10 is precisely to be attributed to
Ezra's horror that it is the leaders who are involved, most especially the priests.
    36. Kuo, "Population Ratio," 86.
    37. Delores P. Aldridge, "Interracial Marriages" *Journal of Black Studies* 8, no. 1 (1977)
361–68.

"mixed" associations. In the Asian context it is the women who seek to "marry up" in greater number. This theory of intermarriage as the attempt to "marry up" in status is supported by studies in India, where "the predominant pattern of intercaste marriage involved a low caste husband and a high caste wife . . . between the professional male of low caste group and the non-professional female of high caste group."[38] Most intermarriages in India between caste and outcaste people mirrored the pairings for American blacks and Jews—that is, subordinate group males and dominant group females—although none of the observers of this phenomenon have come up with a convincing rationale for this situation.[39]

Within the United States, the same pattern has been noted for the Asian upper classes, who marry advantaged members of the majority population.[40] John Mayer's work on Jewish-Gentile marriages in times of anti-Semitism concluded that there was a rise in Jewish male–gentile female mixed marriages in the data from Europe between 1876 and 1933.[41] To read the text from the perspective of exchange theory asks the biblical reader to consider what "upward" advantages were perceived by those men of the exilic community who "married out"[42] and raises interesting questions about the relative advantages of the postexilic community vis-à-vis the surrounding communities. I shall return to these questions, but the second main theoretical approach to mixed marriages is also helpful for my analysis.

Group Boundary Maintenance
Some sociologists prefer to see prohibitions against mixed marriage as a sociopsychological indicator of worries by a group for their own identity and cultural survival. E. L. Cerroni-Long observes: "When a human group finds itself uprooted and isolated and faced by a strong pressure to conform to alien standards it instinctively falls back on the primary ties of the kinship network both to reaffirm its individuality in the face of threats of

38. Das M. Singh, "An Exploratory Study of Touchable-Untouchable Intercaste Marriage in India," *Indian Journal of Sociology* 1/2 (1970) 130–38.
39. Paul R. Spickard, *Mixed Blood: Intermarriage and Ethnic Identity in Twentieth-Century America* (Madison: Univ. of Wisconsin Press, 1989) 350.
40. Larry Hagime Shinagawa and Gin Young Pang, "Intraethnic, Interethnic, and Interracial Marriages among Asian Americans in California, 1980," *Berkeley Journal of Sociology* 33 (1988) 109.
41. John Mayer, "Jewish-Gentile Intermarriage Patterns: A Hypothesis," *Sociology and Social Research* 45, no. 2 (1961) 188–95.
42. See, e.g., E. L. Cerroni-Long, "Marrying Out: Socio-Cultural and Psychological Implications of Intermarriage," *Journal of Comparative Family Studies* 15, no. 1 (1984) 25–46.

extinction and to maintain some form of normal existence amidst unforeseeable and stressful contingencies."[43] This seems borne out by the fact that in cases where socialization skills have been radically disrupted, intermarriage can be high even in cases of high concentration, such as the high instances of Native American intermarriages (even in geographical locations where numbers are high), and the dramatic increase of Japanese and Filipino women marrying into the "victorious" white society of the occupation soldiers.[44] Glick notes that early immigrant men are often more willing to marry local women until the immigrant group can establish itself as a viable community.[45]

Once the pressure of being a disadvantaged group eases, endogamous marriage becomes more common. This approach to mixed-marriage analysis also raises interesting questions for understanding the biblical community, such as the possible breakdown of communal boundaries and socialization (until Ezra and Nehemiah attempted to reinforce them) that would otherwise have discouraged these relationships more effectively. Again, the patterns suggest a traumatized community, whose "socialization" is low. But did "romance" influence decisions about mixed marriages?

On Romance in the Bible

There is, however, a wild card in the study of the sociology of mixed marriage: the role and influence of ideas of romance. Sociologists take certain values seriously as factors that may mitigate the separation of social groups, such as romantic values or democratic idealism. Indeed, Merton already pointed out that romantic or democratic notions may lead to violations of group solidarity,[46] and Paul Glick noted that "romantic" attachments increased among minorities of generations following the immigrant generation.[47]

Certain societies will also tolerate mixed marriages as a democratic value, or as an expression of equality. It is clear that normative social sanctions against mixed marriages sometimes conflict with equally strong values of romantic idealism ("true love conquers all"), and the latter can

43. Ibid., 28.
44. See Bok-Lim C. Kim, "Casework with Japanese and Korean Wives of Americans" *Social Casework* (May 1972) 273–79.
45. Clarence E. Glick, "Intermarriage and Admixture in Hawaii," *Social Biology* 17, no. 4 (1970) 280.
46. Merton, "Intermarriage," 366–67.
47. Paul C. Glick, "Intermarriage among Ethnic Groups in the United States," *Social Biology* 17, no. 4 (1970) 297.

occasionally overcome the group boundaries for some, if not all, of the persons involved (obviously the couple themselves, and perhaps the immediate family, etc.).

It is therefore important to point out that a romantic basis of marriage is not at all a far-fetched notion in relation to the Bible references to some causes for mixed marriages. Notable examples are Moses and Zipporah (Exod 2:21), Joseph and Asenath (Gen 41:45), and Samson's marriage to a Philistine woman (Judg 14). Proverbs' famous warnings against the "foreign woman" (even though clearly an analogy) includes the assumption that the foreign woman will exert an exotic romantic attraction. Clearly not all of these "mixed marriages" are condemned, but it is interesting that "love" is almost always mentioned in cases of mixed marriage.

The same list of nationalities represented among the foreign women in Ezra 9–10 is also found in 1 Kgs 11:1-2, which mentions Solomon's wives, among whom were Ammonite, Moabite, Edomite, Sidonian, and Hittite.[48] Here, interestingly, we have another of the few references to romantic love in the entire Bible (note also Isaac's love for Rebekah in Gen 24:67; Jacob's love for Leah and Rachel in Gen 29:18, 30, 32; Amnon's love for Tamar in 1 Sam 13:1, 4) outside of Song of Songs, since the vast majority of cases deal with pious or religious "love" between God and the people. Furthermore, the only example of the phrase "I love you" between a man and woman is Judg 16:4 and 15, which also deal with a "mixed marriage" between Samson and Delilah.[49]

Finally, the increasing concerns expressed in Proverbs 1–9 (but especially ch. 5) shows how love/romance can lead to assignations with the "alien" woman, the results of which may be that "your labors will go to the house of an alien." It appears to be the case, then, that romantic love is dealt with in the Bible with a certain circumspection, because it can lead to unwise marital ties with "foreigners"; Joseph Blenkinsopp has suggested that the warnings about Solomon's wives now found in the Deuteronomistic History may come from the postexilic era.[50]

The typical examples of romantic attachments in the Bible are dealt with in individual stories, but we are dealing with a group in Ezra 9–10 (in Neh 13 the situation is a bit more specific). Perhaps we can conclude from

---

48. There is a good discussion of this in Blenkinsopp, *Ezra-Nehemiah*, 174–79.

49. Although Delilah is never explicitly identified as Philistine, when one notes the parental concern over Samson's love for a Philistine woman in ch. 14, this appears to be a logical conclusion. See Edward Lipinski, "Love in the Bible," in *Encyclopedia Judaica* (Jerusalem: Keter, 1971) 11:523–27.

50. Blenkinsopp, *Ezra-Nehemiah*, 175.

this group interest in Ezra that the editors intentionally focus attention away from the "human" individual level of possible romantic relationships, but with an emphasis instead on the disobedience of "the people." This group focus in Ezra, especially when read in the context of the explicit mention of Solomon's wives in Nehemiah, suggests an unwillingness of postexilic editors to accept "romance" as an acceptable excuse for mixed marriages. The later texts, such as Proverbs, show an increasing suspicion toward mixed marriage in a romantic/erotic setting.

The Ezra and Nehemiah Accounts of Mixed Marriage: Different Issues?

In Ezra, reflecting an interest in Priestly terminology and concerns, the sins of the priests and Levites are prominent among the guilty (9:1, and note that the priests and Levites are listed first among the guilty). The foreign peoples are blamed for "abominations." Note the frequent cultic context of this term. Ezekiel uses it to describe the sins of the people, particularly their ritual/religious sins: Ezek 5:9, 11; 7:3, 8; 16:22; describing idols in 16:36 and 14:6. In Proverbs the term is used in reference to things that God "hates" (3:32; 6:16; 15:8, 9); but this includes justice issues, such as a false balance (financial cheating, 11:1, 20; 20:23; on the implications of this in Proverbs, see below). In ritual law, Lev. 18:24-30 associates foreign practices (of the "nations I am casting out before you," v. 24) with "abominations." The use of this term seems predominantly late, with over one-third of all instances found in Ezekiel alone.

Ezra's orientation reflects the Priestly writer's obsessions with "separations" (again, noting the use of the term *bdl*, "to separate") between the pure and impure. Such concerns with separation and identity maintenance in much of the Priestly legislation is consistent with a group under stress. Yet this sociological picture in the Ezra account of the breakup of mixed marriages is not at all compatible with a tendency among modern scholars to see the exiles as a privileged elite.[51] I contend that Ezra's action was an attempt at inward consolidation of a threatened minority.[52] The Ezra texts reveal a profound consciousness of "us" and "them," and describe a group intent on its internal affairs and survival. Terms such as "the holy seed" clearly indicate a group xenophobia.

But if Ezra is from a "Priestly" perspective, this raises troubling questions after one has considered the modern sociological material. Why are

---

51. Let one example stand for many others: Norman K. Gottwald, *The Hebrew Bible: A Socio-Literary Introduction* (Minneapolis: Fortress Press, 1985) 433.

52. Wilhelm T. in der Smitten, *Esra: Quellen, Überlieferung und Geschichte*, Studia Semitica Neerlandica 15 (Assen: Van Gorcum, 1973) 138–44.

the priests involved in this mixed-marriage problem in the first place? I have established that it is the Priestly writer of the exilic/postexilic period who is most passionately concerned with the maintenance of boundaries of separation. Ezekiel's concerns with purity are an excellent example of this. Are we to believe, then, that the mixed-marriage "crisis" of Ezra, where the priests are so heavily implicated, represents a mass dereliction of duty on the part of exilic priests who abandon one of their central defining concepts? Or do the priests involved simply disagree with Ezra as to what constitutes a marriage that is actually "mixed"? There are good grounds for seeing the presence of a disagreement between Jews. Essentially, the only basis for Ezra's objection is that the foreigners were simply Jews who were not in exile. This is supported by two categories of evidence: (1) the presence of texts clearly arguing for a more lenient attitude toward some of the people of foreign origin who affiliate with Israelites (Isa 60:1-5; Jonah; Ruth, etc.); and (2) the fact that the groups with which these "mixed" marriages are taking place are identified with old terms that almost surely have become stereotypically pejorative slurs referring to those ethnic groups long since either disappeared or assimilated, and condemned historically as those unclean peoples "justifiably" destroyed by Joshua in the legendary patriotic tales of the founding of the Davidic house. The Nehemiah texts point in a different direction. An internal struggle is not the issue with the Nehemiah material, where "the chief danger was perceived to come from outside Judah."[53]

Political considerations seem predominant in Nehemiah, giving the impression of treacherous power-grabbing in both temple and government through strategic marriages. With Nehemiah we are dealing with specific cases again, which is, as noted, the more typical biblical form for describing these cases of mixed marriage.

Tobiah ("the Ammonite") and Sanballat ("the Horonite"), for example, were leaders of the opposition to Nehemiah's work of rebuilding Jerusalem. It appears that they have local authority, although the precise nature of their authority is not clear. According to Williamson, "the context clearly presupposes that they were the leaders of those already in the land and not part of the group who returned with Ezra. Thus the suggestion that they were district governors . . . is attractive."[54]

Only Nehemiah names Tobiah and Sanballat, although the actual descent of Tobiah and Sanballat is in question. On onomastic grounds, it

53. Blenkinsopp, "Social Context," 460.
54. Williamson, Ezra, Nehemiah, 130.

is typically supposed that at least Tobiah must be a Yahweh worshiper.[55] But Williamson has objected, stating that "Ammonite" should be taken as an ethnic categorization. He believes that Sanballat is governor of Samaria, and Tobiah is a lesser official under him, although he rejects the idea that he is governor of Ammon. Sanballat himself is probably of Moabite origin (linking him with the Horonaim).[56] It is interesting to note, in this context, the explicit association of Jewish "nobles" *(ḥorim)* who "spoke well of Tobiah" to Nehemiah because of marital ties (Neh 6:17-19). When we meet Tobiah again in Nehemiah 13, it is in the context of Nehemiah ejecting him from temple accommodation (vv. 4-9), where we also find a breakup of foreign marriages (vv. 23-27) and another state- ment about intermarriage between the family of Sanballat and Eliashib the high priest (v. 28). The example that Nehemiah chooses to illustrate the problems of foreign marriage is one of political leadership: Solomon. From Nehemiah, much more clearly than from Ezra, we gain the strong impression that foreign marriages are primarily a political problem, involving the Jewish aristocracy and local governmental leadership. Blenkinsopp also considered the political and economic advantages of such marriages: "As sparse as our information is, it reveals a network of relationships cemented by *mariages de convenance* between the Sanbal- lats, Tobiads, and important elements of the lay and clerical aristocracy in Jerusalem."[57] What we are clearly dealing with in Nehemiah is the attempt to intermarry the leadership of the temple with the local political leader- ship, while in Ezra we have no such suggestion. Indeed, the example of Solomon is cited only in Nehemiah, which suggests an even more explic- itly political concern in the Nehemiah texts. The politics of associating with the descendants of Ammon and Moab is also much more explicitly a reference to local leadership than is the case with Ezra, where the ethnic categories in use seem more pejorative than informative.

This has led some commentators to speculate on the sociopolitical goals that may have been sought through these "alliances." Wilhelm Rudolph, for example, suggested that the community leaders, while aware of the negative implications of foreign wives, "had no desire to sacrifice good relations with neighbors, or financial ties, for the sake of a principle."[58]

55. See Peter R. Ackroyd, "Tobiah," in *Harper's Bible Dictionary,* ed. P. J. Achtemeier (New York: Harper & Row, 1985) 1080.

56. Williamson, *Ezra, Nehemiah,* 182–83.

57. Blenkinsopp, *Ezra-Nehemiah,* 365.

58. Rudolph, *Esra und Nehemia,* 87–89.

In the Nehemiah case, which is probably the case dealing with "foreign marriage," exchange theory would raise the issue of what advantages would have been gained in the postexilic community "marrying up" among those defined as "outsiders." The guilty are males who are presumably attempting to "marry up" to exchange their low status of "exiles" for participation in aristocratic society. This suggests that the exilic community perceived themselves in a disadvantaged position vis-à-vis the "peoples of the land." Once again, sociological inferences lead one to conclude that the mixed marriages are built on the presupposition that the exile community was the relatively disadvantaged one of the two (or more) groups involved in the marriages.

An examination of the Ezra and Nehemiah cases in relation to modern sociological studies of mixed marriage has strongly suggested that the postexilic community shows signs of disintegration and trauma, to which they responded with attempts to shore up boundaries and remove economic or political temptations by pointing to their dire consequences in Israel's past. The Nehemiah texts, however, raise a further possibility because of their specific attention to political, and foreign, leadership.

Finally, however, we must ask whether there is a conceptual link in the exilic/diasporic circumstances of ritual language and social implications. Is there a link, in other words, between Daniel's refusal to "pollute" himself with Babylonian food, the Levitical counsel to keep proper "separations" from the impure, Ezra-Nehemiah's use of the same term to imply separation from noncommunity members, and Proverbs' increasing use of ritual terms to speak of social and economic injustices? The conceptual link is precisely the increased consciousness of identity in a minority subculture thrown into extensive contact with other cultures. In such a social context, "purity" becomes the language of "nonconformity."

Purity and Nonconformity: Ezra as an Amish Elder

In Ezra 9:14 Ezra considers the intermarriage crisis to be a case of committing an "abomination" (tā'ab). The term has an interesting history in the postexilic period. In the legal material of both Leviticus and Deuteronomy, the term refers almost exclusively to improper sacrifice or idolatrous sacrifice. Not unexpectedly, given his priestly background, Ezekiel accounts for 41 of the 112 occurrences of the term in the entire Hebrew Bible. In Ezekiel, too, the term is almost entirely used for improper sacrifice or ritual acts. There are, however, interesting exceptions. Ezek 18:13 refers to "all these abominable things" as clearly including social and economic injustices. What is interesting to note is that in the wisdom literature, and particularly in Proverbs, the term turns up almost entirely with social and economic associations, for example (as we noted above), cheating with weights, 11:1 and 20:23; royal or juridical injustice, 17:15; and injustice 29:27. Clearly, what began as a term used almost exclusively in a ritual context developed toward a term with social and economic importance. To be "pure" of "abominations" was, at a later point also a matter of how one engaged one's life activities as well as conducted ritual actions of faith.

We are already familiar with tendencies among the later prophets to favor a behavioral value over ritual values: "Is such the fast that I choose, a day to humble oneself? Is it to bow down the head like a bulrush, and to lie in sackcloth and ashes? Will you call this a fast, a day acceptable to the LORD? Is not this the fast that I choose: to loose the bonds of injustice, to undo the thongs of the yoke, to let the oppressed go free, and to break every yoke?" (Isa 58:5-6; cf. Psalm 50; Jeremiah 7). Why would language from ritual evolve toward social behavior in the later postexilic period? Part of the reason, of course, may be the changed role of ritual in the diasporic context, where behavior largely replaced centralized religious ritual (thus, e.g., stories like Tobit raise up an example of a righteous life in the setting of "Nineveh" and the emphasis on behavior in Psalm 119).

I contend that there is a strong conceptual parallel to recent religious minority groups concerned about group integrity and identity. Here the language of faith has social expression as well. In religious traditions, such as the Anabaptists, Quakers, and other minority groups, this attention to purity, which also encompasses social "boundaries," has at times resulted in practices such as worries about "marrying in" versus "marrying out" of the accepted social group and a religious emphasis on what I am calling "policing the boundaries." Inappropriate as some of these actions may have been in their past (breeding intolerance, wrong emphasis on exclusion rather than faithfulness, etc.), the concern to maintain identity against the pressures of dominant cultures is essential to the survival of a minority witness.

In his analysis of the Amish, Marc Olshan points out that the widely noted categorization of the Amish as a "folk culture" seriously underestimates the careful thought and creativity evident in Amish life as they self-consciously manipulate the terms of their own social development. Seen in this way, their ability to critically engage wider social innovations is "a model for other modern societies."[59]

---

59. Marc A. Olshan, "Modernity, the Folk Society, and the Old Order Amish: An Alternative Interpretation," *Rural Sociology* 46, no. 2 (1981) 297–309. See Donald B. Kraybill and Marc A. Olshan, eds., *The Amish Struggle with Modernity* (Hanover, N.H.: Univ. Press of New England, 1994).

This model of "purity" as simply the religious manner chosen to speak of a selected form of social and ideological nonconformity can be further illustrated in the life and witness of the American Quaker pamphleteer and itinerant activist, John Woolman. Woolman had taken to wearing a very unfashionable undyed cloth and explained his action in his famous pamphlet, *A Plea for the Poor:* "Wealth is attended with power, by which bargains and proceedings contrary to universal righteousness are supported: and here oppression, carried on with worldly policy and order, clothes itself with the name of justice and becomes like a seed of discord in the soil. . . . May we look upon our treasures and the furniture of our houses and the garments in which we array ourselves and try whether the seeds of war have any nourishment in these our possessions or not."[60]

The concept of purity, as expressed in much Quaker and Anabaptist (e.g., Mennonite, Amish) theological tradition, is articulated by a faith-driven "nonconformity to the world." I already noted that purity language clearly related to the social consciousness of nonconformity in Daniel 1, as well as Daniel 6. Thus I have argued in this chapter that the diasporic Hebrew language of "purity" and "separation" needs to be read within the social context of minority existence in diaspora, and as such, takes on important social implications of definition and social identity. What is to be kept "pure," in short, is the social group itself. In other words, the language of purity can be read as the diasporic Hebrew means of emphasizing social identity and "nonconformity to the world." While one may agree with the dangers of isolationist stances in relation to the world, in the ancient Hebrew context such a separation was not an option. It is precisely because actual physical isolation is not an option that attention to identity and social integrity become essential to survival.

Whatever objections modern readers may have with Ezra's tactics, one must also recognize that attending to issues of nonconformity and identity were essential to survival in diaspora. The *concerns,* if not also the specific tactics, were genuine.

---

60. *The Journal and Major Essays of John Woolman,* ed. P. P. Moulton (New York: Oxford Univ. Press, 1971) 255.

7.

THE WISDOM WARRIOR:
Reading Wisdom and Daniel as
Diasporic Ethics

SCHOLARS AND STUDENTS WORKING ON LATE HEBREW LITERATURE ARE understandably fascinated with the development and flowering of unique forms of religious literature. Among the more interesting examples are the continued development of wisdom literature and the appearance of literary traditions of storytelling that have their location in diaspora settings, tales such as those of Daniel, Esther, and Tobit. As John J. Collins points out, previous to Gerhard von Rad's famous argument in his classic work *Wisdom in Israel*, scholars had suggested a relationship between these two genres, but it was von Rad's strong statement that apocalypticism actually derived from wisdom literature that defined the lines of the debate in Old Testament scholarship.[1] James Crenshaw does not give this claim much credence, as its "widening of the net threatens to distort the meaning of wisdom beyond repair," and Roland Murphy's introduction does not even discuss the matter.[2] While some have continued attempts to read a common movement or mind-set behind both the development of wisdom and the diaspora tales,[3] I want to suggest an approach to this issue

---

1. John J. Collins, "Wisdom, Apocalypticism, and Generic Compatibility," in *In Search of Wisdom: Essays in Memory of John G. Gammie*, ed. L. G. Perdue, B. B. Scott, and W. J. Wiseman (Louisville: Westminster John Knox, 1993) 166 n. 9.

2. James L. Crenshaw, *Old Testament Wisdom: An Introduction* (Atlanta: John Knox, 1981) 41; Roland E. Murphy, *The Tree of Life: An Exploration of Biblical Wisdom Literature*, 2d ed. (Grand Rapids: Eerdmans, 1996).

3. A helpful survey of the literature is provided by B. A. Mastin, "Wisdom and Daniel," in *Wisdom in Ancient Israel*, FS J. A. Emerton, ed. J. Day, R. Gordon, and H. G. M. Williamson (Cambridge: Cambridge Univ. Press, 1995) 161–69.

from the perspective of an exilic challenge to the authors, storytellers, and wise advisers that may be behind *both* of these forms of literature. A helpful entry to this issue is provided by reviewing Susan Niditch's ideas about "trickster tales."

On Tricksters and Wise Men

Susan Niditch's important work in comparing folklore motifs of "tricksters and underdogs" with certain biblical stories of clever heroes points to the significance of reading these biblical stories with an understanding of the nearly universal figure of the trickster. Often admired precisely for underhanded or deceptive ingenuity, the trickster (in all its various story forms across many cultures) "is a subtype of the underdog. A fascinating and universal folk hero, the trickster brings about change in a situation via trickery."[4] Niditch explains the talents and values appropriate to tricksters and wise men in relation to biblical figures that she wants to contrast, such as Joseph the wise over against Jacob the clever: "Joseph, an innocent youth with mantic talents, matures into a court wise man, winning a position of power in the establishment that he maintains until his death. Jacob, an anti-establishment trickster, matures into a more institutionalized figure who declines into senescence much as did his own father. Appropriate to roles of wise man and trickster are alternative views of authority and alternative settings."[5]

I wish to take up Niditch's last observation in this quotation, particularly in regard to the idea that wisdom and trickery are alternatives in biblical narrative. Are the ethics of the trickster, with its definite lack of respect for establishment ethics, so different from the ethics of wisdom? It is almost universally presumed that wisdom comes from the elite classes of Israel and has its roots in the privileged scribal class of the monarchy, even if much of the material is edited during the exilic/diaspora period. Thus, it is also assumed that wisdom ethics are establishment ethics par excellence. This has led to an interesting disagreement about the social context of wisdom literature in the Persian period. On the one hand, C. L. Seow's commentary on Ecclesiastes has been widely quoted, particularly his suggestion that during the Persian period there were many "entrepreneurial opportunities" for Judeans.[6] Christine Yoder finishes her interest-

---

4. Susan Niditch, *Underdogs and Tricksters: A Prelude to Biblical Folklore* (San Francisco: Harper & Row, 1987) xi.

5. Ibid., 124.

6. *Ecclesiastes*, AB 18c (New York: Doubleday, 1997). See esp. "Socioeconomic Context," pp. 21–36. Seow cites Matthew Stolper to buttress his argument that Ecclesiastes could be a well-off entrepreneur who had taken advantage of some of these "opportunities." However,

ing summary of Persian period Palestine by suggesting that Palestine "was not a distant, isolated corner of the Persian Empire. Rather, communication, people, and goods flowed in and out freely. Letters and documents traded hands. Travelers journeyed from place to place. Migrant workers set up shop and then moved on. Foreign merchants settled in the cities and gathered at the marketplaces to sell their wares. And imperial troops passed through or were stationed at regional outposts."[7]

But one can make too much of the evidence, which certainly suggests imperial priorities and troop movements, but seems (according to Matthew Stolper's work on the Murashu Archive)[8] decidedly oriented to the advantages of the central regime. Joseph Bryant's reading of Persian economics would tend to support a more limited view of "economic opportunities": "The Persian Great Kings were the very embodiment of unrestrained autocracy. As self-proclaimed earthly representatives of the creator god Ahura-Mazda, their every whim had the force of sanctioned command, and summary executions of subordinates who displeased were not uncommon. . . . There was the great pomp and circumstance that exalted the majesty of the royal person and symbolically projected his immense wealth and power: the banquets that fed thousands at a time; the imposing works of monumental architecture, suitably graced by the stern visage or imperious proclamations of the supreme ruler."[9]

This is surely the reality, then, that is reflected in Ezra's prayer about the "rich yield" of the lands of Palestine, going "to the kings whom you have set over us because of our sins" (Neh 9:37), a passage that certainly

too much can be made of this. I have quoted Stolper (above, p. 52) to the effect that the Persian economy did not have great opportunities for advancement. It seems Seow and I have read Stolper's work on the Murashu Archives differently. See Matthew Stolper, *Entrepreneurs and Empire: The Murašû Archive, the Murašû Firm, and Persian Rule in Babylonia*, Uitgaven van het Nederlands Historisch-Archaeologisch Instituut te Istanbul 54 (Leiden: Brill, 1985) esp. 154.

Seow's somewhat more sanguine reading of the Persian period economy has influenced subsequent commentaries and summaries, such as Richard Clifford, *The Wisdom Literature* (Nashville: Abingdon, 1998) 100–101; and Robert Brown, *Ecclesiastes*, Interpretation (Louisville: John Knox, 2000) 7–9. Contrast this with Leo Perdue's observation that in Yehud, "times were hard during Persian rule" ("Wisdom Theology and Social History in Proverbs 1–9," in *Wisdom, You Are My Sister*, FS R. E. Murphy, ed. Michael L. Barré, S.S., CBQMS 29 [Washington, D.C.: Catholic Biblical Association of America, 1997] 81). It seems that Seow wants to locate Ecclesiastes in a monied social setting, so he must establish that it was possible to be a wealthy Hebrew in the Persian period economy of the time.

7. Christine Roy Yoder, *Wisdom as a Woman of Substance: A Socioeconomic Reading of Proverbs 1–9 and 31:10-31*, BZAW 304 (Berlin: de Gruyter, 2001) 48.

8. Stolper, *Entrepreneurs and Empire*.

9. Joseph Bryant, *Moral Codes and Social Structure in Ancient Greece: A Sociology of Greek Ethics from Homer to the Epicureans and Stoics* (Albany: State Univ. of New York Press, 1966) 149.

does not sound like the land of opportunity in Persian period Yehud. I want to suggest that we may presume too much of economic opportunities in reading wisdom literature. Perhaps the "economics" involved were not of the nature of business but of the nature of occupied peoples attempting to insulate their communities from the reach of imperial control. In short, the archaeological and textual evidence can be interpreted in different ways. What difference would this make in reading wisdom literature? A great deal.

Reading Wisdom in Diaspora and Occupied Palestine

Reading the book of Proverbs from the same social perspective as the trickster tales of Jacob can present some interesting alternatives. Mark Brett is well aware of the potential for this, as intimated in his reading of Genesis as ultimately a Persian period document that frequently polemicizes against authority figures (he thinks that this would contrast with the attitude shown toward the Persian imperial powers in Ezra and Nehemiah). For example, Brett writes of Jacob's famously questionable integrity: "Folkloric texts often contain the theme of trickery, and, as many scholars have suggested, this theme appeals to an 'underdog' audience which has no other means of combating the dominant culture. Thus, we should not expect the representation of God in folkloric texts to cohere with the God who upholds ethical standards in some of the other Genesis traditions."[10]

This approach reminds one of James Scott's analysis of the "hidden transcripts" of the subordinated in their opposition to power, particularly when Scott points out that certain behaviors are seen as part and parcel of survival: "A second and vital aspect of the hidden transcript that has not been sufficiently emphasized is that it does not contain only speech acts but a whole range of practices. Thus, for many peasants activities such as poaching, pilfering, clandestine tax evasion, and intentionally shabby work for landlords are part and parcel of the hidden transcript. For dominant elites, hidden-transcript practices might include clandestine luxury and privilege, surreptitious use of hired thugs, bribery, and tampering with land titles."[11]

Especially for the subject of this work, significant illustrations of precisely these "subaltern" or "subcultural" ethics may be found in some work on the creation of refugee cultures in modern relief work. John

10. Mark G. Brett, *Genesis: Procreation and the Politics of Identity* (London: Routledge, 2000) 92.
11. James Scott, *Domination and the Arts of Resistance: Hidden Transcripts* (New Haven, Conn.: Yale Univ. Press, 1990) 14.

Knudsen, for example, writes of the significance of carefully crafted "stories" told to the relief workers: "Vietnamese in Norway often stress that the brutality of the wars has engendered suspicion, individuality, and distrust rather than forthrightness, cooperation, and trust. Hence even daily communications is described as more indirect than direct."[12] The camps provide little opportunity for building trust. The refugee quickly learns which kinds of stories will result in early departure and which stories (however "true" they may be) will result in camp arrest. Eftihia Voutira and Barbara Harrell-Bond are a bit more forthright: "As one refugee summed it up, 'To be a refugee means to learn to lie.' Although this situation of mistrust may be taken as characteristic of the different ways in which the 'us' and 'them' relate, the actual situation is far more complicated as regards the relevant interests of the two groups that are at stake."[13]

What would happen if we attempt to read wisdom literature as a genre that is related to the genre of biblical trickster and diaspora tales, and thus also a product of the social circumstances of exilic subordination? Can we speak of Proverbial wisdom as consisting of "subcultural ethics"? I contend that some of the problematics of wisdom ethics become more intelligible under such a reading strategy.

Wisdom as Diaspora Ethics
In his classic commentary on Proverbs, Crawford H. Toy first argued that the opening advice of Proverbs (1:10-19) may well refer to "organized banditry"[14] in the Hellenistic urban context, and thus the "sinners" who try to "entice" the young man are actually calling on him to join in social banditry. According to Toy, "the organized robbery here referred to suggests city life of the later time, the periods when, under Persian and Greek rule, Jerusalem and Alexandria sheltered a miscellaneous population, and a distinct criminal class became more prominent."[15] Toy related this to other biblical texts that sounded to him like allusions to urban violence, such as Hos 4:2; 6:8-9; and 7:1; as well as Ps 10:8. While not frequently taken up in contemporary commentaries, Toy's suggestion deserves a second look and can commend a different context in which to read wisdom literature and also to relate wisdom literature back again to the tales of

12. John C. Knudsen, "When Trust Is on Trial: Negotiating Refugee Narratives," in *Mistrusting Refugees*, ed. E. V. Daniel and J. C. Knudsen (Berkeley: Univ. of California Press, 1995) 18.

13. Eftihia Voutira and Barbara E. Harrell-Bond, "In Search of the Locus of Trust: The Social World of the Refugee Camp," in ibid., 216.

14. Crawford H. Toy, *A Critical and Exegetical Commentary on the Book of Proverbs*, ICC (Edinburgh: T. & T. Clark, 1899) 14–16.

15. Toy, *Proverbs*, 14.

Daniel (and Joseph), as originally suggested by Eichrodt, but along different lines.

I suggest in this chapter that the literature of wisdom, especially Proverbs and Ecclesiastes, is literature that makes the most "sense" when read in the context of the Diaspora. To state it another way, this literature is the "wisdom" of the minority group that particularly focuses on lessons in "how to survive." Such lessons, whether explicitly called "lessons" or not, are familiar to every member of a minority group who sat around a dinner table listening to parents explain how to "get ahead by not making trouble." Here is also the connection with the tales of Daniel. Daniel lived, and indeed "got ahead," but "watched his back" as a member of a minority people in a diaspora situation. That we previously have not read Daniel or Proverbs in this light is due in no small measure to the context from which we *have* read this material—usually not as subordinates in an imperial regime, much less like minorities in a dominant culture. Let us begin with an analogy from Egyptian wisdom literature, a literature often cited as important precedent (if not, sometimes, actual sources) for Israelite wisdom literature.

Analogies to Wisdom and Quietism in Egyptian Wisdom Literature
Can one speak of an implied "ideal person" in Egyptian wisdom literature?[16] In an important study of Egyptian wisdom values, Nili Shupak notes that a certain "quietism" is typical of the Egyptian ideal: "the ideals of quietness and self-control hold pride of place in the *Weltanschauung* of the Egyptian sage and of his Hebrew counterpart. Words in praise of restraint—evinced principally in silence and in the avoidance of dispute and quarrel—are a consistent theme in Egyptian and Biblical wisdom."[17] This ideal can be further enumerated: "The 'silent man' is he who is thoughtful in manner and modest in conduct; he eschews strife and garrulousness; he is kind and gives of his possessions to others; he is honest and obedient towards his superiors. The 'silent man' is the devoted pious man, and his lips and heart are one."[18] While Shupak maintains that the exact equivalent is not present in biblical literature, he recognizes that one who is "slow to anger" is certainly present in proverbial wisdom:[19]

---

16. It is a large question that I can only briefly discuss here and defer to more qualified Egyptologists for more extensive comments.

17. Nili Shupak, *Where Can Wisdom Be Found? The Sage's Language in the Bible and in Ancient Egyptian Literature*, OBO 130 (Göttingen: Vandenhoeck & Ruprecht, 1993) 150.

18. Ibid., 165.

19. Ibid., 170.

"one of the most important virtues in Biblical wisdom, as in the Egyptian wisdom, is moderation and restraint. The ideal man is tolerant, cooltempered, balanced in his conduct, sparing of speech, keeps secrets and eschews quarrels. . . . 'Silence,' as part of the proper behavior of the believer who submits to the god, expressed in the later Egyptian literature beginning with the New Kingdom period (especially in the hymns of personal piety), is present in the Bible only in non-wisdom books."[20]

This contrast between the Egyptian "silent man" and Hebrew ideals of restraint can be exaggerated, however, especially when one reads Prov 17:27-28: "One who spares words is knowledgeable; one who is cool in spirit has understanding. Even fools who keep silent are considered wise; when they close their lips, they are deemed intelligent." Furthermore, there is an interesting change in the wisdom literature that we have available to us from Egyptian sources, particularly in those texts written by Egyptians under foreign domination. Consider a series of ethical maxims of restraint over a period of time from the Sixth Dynasty (before 2000 BCE) work, the *Wisdom of Ptahhotep,* to the Persian period *Instruction of Ankhsheshonq.* As is widely noted, Ankhsheshonq is written on the premise that it is the collected sayings of an Egyptian priest in prison (for participating in a palace revolt?[21]) who is writing to a general populace of Egypt, not to an elite.[22] First, from the older writing of Ptahhotep:

> Don't be proud of your knowledge
> Consult the ignorant and the wise
> The limits of art are not reached
> No artist's skills are perfect

> If you meet a disputant—a powerful man superior to you
> Fold your arms, bend your back,
> To flout him will not make him agree with you
> Make little of the evil speech. . . .

> If you meet a disputant . . . who is your equal
> You will make your worth exceed his by silence
> While he is speaking evilly
> There will be much talk by the hearers
> Your name will be good in the mind of the magistrates
> If you meet a disputant . . . a poor man, not your equal

20. Ibid., 182.
21. Crenshaw, *Old Testament Wisdom,* 215
22. "The aura of the court, which could be detected in the older instructions, is absent; Ankhsheshonq is writing for ordinary people, not for officials" (*Tree of Life,* 167).

> Do not attack him because he is weak
> Let him alone, he will confute himself.
> Do not answer him to relieve your heart
> Wretched he is who injures a poor man.[23]

This kind of advice, which clearly presumes that one has superiors in addition to inferiors, can be read either as advice for succeeding in the civil service, or as advice or self-serving ideas about staying clear of trouble. The *Wisdom of Ptahhotep* has most often been read in the former manner, as an ethics for civil service. But consider the growth of what some have called "cynicism," or perhaps greater self-interest, that is typical of the *Instruction of Ankhsheshonq*. After an introduction that enumerates all people to be served, the later advice with regard to superiors is interesting. There is the expected calls to respect station in life:

> Do not insult your superior (7:13)
>
> Do not neglect to serve your master (7:15)
>
> Do not neglect to serve him who can serve you (7:16)

But there is also a clear level of advice that admonishes self-interest and local loyalties:

> Do not go to court against your superior when you do not have protection against him (8:11)
>
> Do not be a neighbor to your master (9:13)
>
> You may trip over your foot in the house of a great man; you should not trip over your tongue (10:7)
>
> Do not deliver a servant into the hand of his master (16:6)
>
> Do not conceal yourself from a stranger who comes from the outside (16:19)
>
> He who battles together with the people of his town will rejoice with them (18:10)
>
> If you come to say something to your master count on your fingers till ten (22:18)
>
> A slip of the tongue in the royal palace is a slip of the helm at sea (23:10)
>
> Learn how to sit in the presence of Pharaoh (25:11).[24]

---

23. Miriam Lichtheim, "Ptahhotep," in M. Lichtheim, *Ancient Egyptian Literature: A Book of Readings*, vol. 1 (Berkeley: Univ. of California Press, 1973) 63–64.
24. Ibid.

In his survey of Egyptian wisdom literature as a prologue to the study of Proverbs, William McKane evaluates the Instruction of Ankhsheshonq in rather negative terms: "The earthiness of Onchsheshonqy is unmistakable. It harks back to the soil and addresses itself to those who engage in the back-breaking tasks of cultivation and are resigned to the unpredictability of agriculture."[25] McKane contrasts this work with the rather high-mindedness of older wisdom works, such as the Wisdom of Ptahhotep: "It does not give advice to a clientele of high calibre, who have expectations of eminence and power. It has to do with less distinguished individuals who have adjusted themselves to life at lower levels and whose claims to self-fulfillment are modest."[26] McKane, however, did not make note of the introduction of a certain cynicism in Ankhsheshonq that is reminiscent of Ecclesiastes:

(26:3) [There is a] [missing text] for throwing a man out
(26:4) There is a stick for bringing him in
(26:5) There is imprisonment for giving life
(26:6) There is release for killing
(26:7) There is he who saves and does not profit[27]

I propose that it is not "earthiness" that is evident in these teachings; rather it is the growing awareness of "watching your back" that seems to have disturbed McKane. But it is precisely this change that is interesting, given the political occupation of Egypt in the Persian period. Is there a similar shift in self-interested loyalties in biblical wisdom literature as life under empire settles into the realities of diaspora existence?

Ecclesiastes: Dark Humor in Occupied Palestine?

It is often noted that Ecclesiastes exhibits far less confidence in the established ways of the world. It is precisely in the somewhat cynical observation that "things do not always work out the way they are supposed to" that introduces an interesting level of self-interest. One could argue that these admonitions seem to call into question the "myths" of general social well-being and perhaps an admonition to be wary of what I am calling, after Scott, the "official transcript." It is perhaps in this context that we should read the "subcultural observations" of Eccl 9:11-12: "Again I saw that under the sun the race is not to the swift, nor the battle to the strong,

25. McKane, *Proverbs*, OTL (Philadelphia: Westminster, 1970) 118.
26. Ibid., 122.
27. Miriam Lichtheim, "Ankhsheshonq," in *Ancient Egyptian Literature*, vol. 3, 161–84.

nor bread to the wise, nor riches to the intelligent, nor favor to the skill-
ful; but time and chance happen to them all. For no one can anticipate the
time of disaster. Like fish taken in a cruel net, and like birds caught in a
snare, so mortals are snared at a time of calamity, when it suddenly falls
upon them." What then is this sage's advice to minority existence in Persian
or Ptolemaic imperial Palestine? "I have also seen this example of wisdom
under the sun, and it seemed great to me. There was a little city with few
people in it. A great king came against it and besieged it, building great
siegeworks against it. Now there was found in it a poor wise man, and he by
his wisdom delivered the city. Yet no one remembered that poor man. So I
said, 'Wisdom is better than might; yet the poor man's wisdom is despised,
and his words are not heeded.' The quiet words of the wise are more to be
heeded than the shouting of a ruler among fools. Wisdom is better than
weapons of war, but one bungler destroys much good" (9:13-18).

This call to seeking counsel instead of brute strength is not necessarily
a "principled nonviolence" in the sense of a universal ethical wisdom;
rather, it appeals to a profound sense of diasporic practicality: Why die for
this state? Why pretend that what exists is according to some myth of
dominant ability on their part? This cool attitude can perhaps help us to
understand other sober assessments of Ecclesiastes:

> The wise have eyes in their head, but fools walk in darkness. Yet I
> perceived that the same fate befalls all of them. (2:14)

> What do mortals get from all the toil and strain with which they toil
> under the sun? For all their days are full of pain, and their work is a
> vexation; even at night their minds do not rest. This also is vanity.
> (2:22-23)

> So I saw that there is nothing better than that all should enjoy their
> work, for that is their lot; who can bring them to see what will be
> after them? (3:22)

> With many dreams come vanities and a multitude of words; but fear
> God. If you see in a province the oppression of the poor and the vio-
> lation of justice and right, do not be amazed at the matter; for the
> high official is watched by a higher, and there are yet higher ones
> over them. But all things considered, this is an advantage for a land:
> a king for a plowed field. (5:7)

Ecclesiastes is dated by Crenshaw to 250–225 BCE.[28] Ecclesiastes is clearly
more critical than Proverbs, and there are already signs of self-interested,
rather than official, ethics for getting ahead and attaining advantage even

---

28. Crenshaw, *Old Testament Wisdom*, 132.

in terms of being subservient. Ecclesiastes reads far more subversively if the famous "cynicism" is directed not toward a Jewish state, or even toward traditional Jewish values of social existence, but rather toward the gentile state—the *goyim naches*[29]—absurd preoccupations of the non-Jews under whom Jews are forced to live. Do some of the Proverbs already show signs of this ironic teaching about "watching your back," and learning cleverness as strength or, in other words, the survival tactics of the tricksters? I would suggest that Ecclesiastes sounds like the musings of a Jacob-like trickster. Ecclesiastes is upsetting for the same reason trickster ethics are offensive to dominant cultures: they represent a lack of trust and faith in "the system," a cynical disbelief that the political realities under which the people are living are either inevitable or good. In such a case, one cannot trust the system to have one's best interests at heart—one must fend for oneself. With regard to Ecclesiastes, then, I tend to agree with the sentiment expressed recently by Elsa Tamez: "Qoheleth's day was not the time for liberation, as was the case in the past when Israel was formed as a people. The Jews would soon come into struggle with the Seleucids. But Qoheleth does not announce, much less promote, the Maccabean revolt. For him, the time of revolution is not propitious. His advice takes another route: resist wisely in the face of absurdity. This is the most important message of his discourse: how to survive with dignity in a dehumanizing and annihilating reality."[30]

Rereading Proverbs from Below

Contemporary refugee studies have noted that among the realities of the dispossessed and the forcibly resettled there is a certain temptation to break ranks, to perpetuate rivalries in the competition for resources that only eventually come to the foreigners. As Patrick Matlou observes: "The deprivation and uncertainty that refugees often suffer sometimes lead them into conflict with each other over scarce rewards. In this regard, exile often serves as an arena for the continuation of conflicts begun at home and leads to the intensification of discriminatory practices that were already in

---

29. I confess that I find this a delightful "in-house" term, although it is used rather disparagingly by some Jews about the incomprehensible (and usually thought to be silly) "preoccupations" of the non-Jewish world, and is often considered to be quite a rude expression. But it was introduced to me (rather bluntly, in reference to something I was enthused about, as I recall) by my teacher Dr. Steven Schwarzschild, and I have been fond of the term ever since.

30. "Ecclesiastes: A Reading from the Periphery," *Interpretation* 55 (2001) 256.

place."³¹ Similarly, Voutira and Harrell-Bond note: "Despite the apparent commonality of their experience vis-à-vis their country of origin, one seldom finds a sense of political solidarity among refugee populations. More often than not, refugee populations are highly factionalized in relation to their different strategies for resolving the causes that led to their flight."³²

In this light, consider the advice of Prov 3:28-30: "Do not say to your neighbor, 'Go, and come again, tomorrow I will give it'—when you have it with you. Do not plan harm against your neighbor who lives trustingly beside you. Do not quarrel with anyone without cause, when no harm has been done to you."

Does Proverbs council against breaking ranks with your fellow minority-group member? Along similar lines, it has often been noted that some pieces of advice in wisdom literature seem contrary to the spirit, if not also the letter, of the Mosaic legislative texts. For example, loans are not prohibited in Deuteronomic law, including loans to foreigners. The difference is only in the matter of interest charged, according to 23:20-21 (Eng. 19-20): "You shall not charge interest on loans to another Israelite, interest on money, interest on provisions, interest on anything that is lent. On loans to a foreigner you may charge interest, but on loans to another Israelite you may not charge interest, so that the LORD your God may bless you in all your undertakings in the land that you are about to enter and possess." Prov 11:15 famously counsels against loans to strangers, though stopping short of contradicting the law: "To guarantee loans for a stranger brings trouble, but there is safety in refusing to do so." Is the difference in attitude noted in Proverbs simply a sage disagreement with Mosaic law, or has the social circumstance changed so dramatically that circumspection is now valued more highly than the proverbial generosity of Deuteronomic law? It is not difficult to argue that the Proverbial spirit differs significantly from a sentiment like Deut 5:11: "Since there will never cease to be some in need on the earth, I therefore command you, 'Open your hand to the poor and needy neighbor in your land.'" Is it an error to suspect that a certain self-interest among exiles or occupied peoples is at work here?

Again, despite the spirit of Exod 22:26, a spirit even further elaborated in Deut 24:12, 17, where garments must not be kept overnight, Prov 20:16 seems to be written in the opposite spirit, being concerned more with the safety of the loan than the comfort of the person: "Take the garment of one who has given surety for a stranger; seize the pledge given as surety

---

31. Patrick Matlou, "Upsetting the Cart: Forced Migration and Gender Issues, the African Experience," in *Engendering Forced Migration: Theory and Practice*, ed. D. Indra (New York: Berghahn, 1999) 136.
32. Voutira and Harrell-Bond, "In Search of the Locus of Trust," 218.

for foreigners."[33] While we may argue that different social classes are being addressed here, wouldn't another way of accounting for this difference be that circumstances have changed?

Many passages suggest that Proverbs is speaking to those outside the sphere of political power and influence. The following series of images in Prov 30:24-28, often noted for their "zoological observations," are united by one interesting element—they advise unsupervised responsibility: "Four things on earth are small, yet they are exceedingly wise: the ants are a people without strength, yet they provide their food in the summer; the badgers are a people without power, yet they make their homes in the rocks; the locusts have no king, yet all of them march in rank; the lizard can be grasped in the hand, yet it is found in kings' palaces."

It seems apparent that the following pieces of advice fit with the circumstances of Hebrew folklore in the Daniel stories:

> The dread anger of a king is like the growling of a lion; anyone who provokes him to anger forfeits life itself. (Prov 20:2)
>
> Do not desire the ruler's delicacies, for they are deceptive food. (23:3)
>
> Take away the wicked from the presence of the king, and his throne will be established in righteousness. Do not put yourself forward in the king's presence or stand in the place of the great; for it is better to be told, "Come up here," than to be put lower in the presence of a noble. (25:5-7)

As mentioned, the Daniel tales more than once can be read to illustrate some of the same self-guarding wisdom advocated in the book of Proverbs. I am not arguing for a strong relationship between the two; I am simply noting that when one is encouraged to read Proverbs under the context of a potential threat, as an exiled or occupied and colonized citizen of imperial Persian or Ptolemaic Palestine, the possibility becomes even stronger. Let us now return to the idea that Daniel exhibits a Proverbial ideal of clever (e.g., trickster) wisdom.

The Wisdom Warrior: Diasporic Cleverness over Imperial Brute Strength

Daniel exemplified a diasporic ethic of wise, clever survival—the ethic of a minority. The Persian period of the Hebrew people (597–333 BCE), of

---

33. McKane, *Proverbs*, 543, suggests that it should be read as concern to secure debts: "If you are to have dealings with a person who is a bad risk and is liable for dubious debts, secure yourself immediately!" Either way, this spirit is clearly not the same as that of Deuteronomy.

course, began a process of unprecedented contact with international peoples and ideas of the ancient Near East that was accelerated dramatically with the conquests of Alexander the Great. The great studies of Judaism in the Hellenistic period emphasize the enormity, not to mention the complexity, of this exposure to varieties of ideas and cultures and its impact in the later development of Judaism and early Christianity.[34] However, did the very fact of imperial existence, with its concomitant realities of coexistence by different religions, attitudes, peoples, and cultures under an overarching military and administrative presence, bring about the need to rethink previous attitudes? Did cleverness come to replace older military and "civic" virtues of the monarchical period?

John J. Collins first proposed that the book of Daniel represented a "pacifistic" religious document from a group known as the "wise ones."[35] Collins's reading of Dan 11:34 (as a critique of the violent resistance as "little help") has been challenged by Gordon Zerbe.[36] Zerbe maintains that, based on a review of extensive apocalyptic literature, there is very little evidence to support the idea of "pacifistic strains" in apocalyptic writing, and thus it seems difficult to accept Collins's view with regard to the authors of Daniel 7–12. As I have argued here, however, the apocalyptic literary tradition is not the only religious and ethical tradition on which the book of Daniel builds. Although Daniel does represent an alternative to violent Hebrew ethics of self-preservation, this does not arise from the apocalyptic tradition, but rather from the wisdom tradition of clever, strategic "quietism."

A further hint of a "wisdom peace ethic" comes from Paul's use of Proverbs. In Rom 12:20 Paul famously quotes the advice of Prov 25:21-22 to feed and give water to one's enemies: "By doing this, you will heap burning coals on their heads." The passage from Proverbs is quoted virtually word for word, except for the final clause: "and the LORD will reward you."[37]

---

34. Including the studies of E. Bickermann, *From Ezra to the Last of the Maccabees: Foundations of Post-Biblical Judaism* (New York: Schocken, 1962); M. Hengel, *Judaism and Hellenism: Studies in Their Encounter in Palestine During the Early Hellenistic Period*, trans. J. Bowden (Philadelphia: Fortress Press, 1974); and V. Tcherikover, *Hellenistic Civilization and the Jews*, trans. S. Applebaum (Philadelphia: Jewish Publication Society of America, 1959).

35. See John J. Collins, *The Apocalptic Visions of the Book of Daniel*, HSM 16 (Missoula, Mont.: Scholars, 1977) 212–18.

36. See Gordon Zerbe, "'Pacificism' and 'Passive Resistance' in Apocalyptic Writings: A Critical Evaluation," in *The Pseudepigrapha and Early Biblical Interpretation*, ed. J. H. Charlesworth and C. A. Evans, JSPSup 14 (Sheffield: JSOT Press, 1993) 65–95.

37. J. Piper, *Love Your Enemies* (1979; repr. Grand Rapids: Baker, 1981) 30, argues that Paul intentionally left off the final phrase so that one would not think that the motive for this action was purely a reward from God.

The commentary literature surrounding Paul's use of this passage either repeats Augustine's famous suggestion that these are the "fires of remorse"[38]or attempts to understand how Paul himself may or may not have understood the Proverbs reference.[39] The latter discussion then tends to focus on key essays by Sigfried Morenz, Krister Stendahl, and William Klassen,[40] all dealing with the images of "coals of fire." Stendahl has argued that Paul's admonition, when read in comparison with 1QS, actually seeks the punishment of the enemy by God instead of the faithful Christian. Note, however, that Ernst Käsemann protested that Stendahl is in error in his reading of the Dead Sea material, since it was written to advise behavior toward errant members of the Qumran community, not in reference to outsiders.[41]

What is missing in the discussion of Paul's use of the passage, however, is whether a "trickster" meaning of "coals of fire" is the force of the original Proverbs setting. For example, in an important monograph, Klassen included a wide-ranging survey of irenic attitudes toward enemies in the Old Testament and specifically noted that biblical wisdom literature— which contains a number of such references—draws on similarly irenic attitudes, even toward enemies, in both Egyptian and Mesopotamian wisdom literature.[42] But neither here nor in his important essay, "Coals of Fire," does Klassen go further to develop the possibility of a wisdom "peace ethic."

Elmer Martens, however, has suggested precisely such a line of analysis: "Living skillfully entails living in ways that de-escalate conflictual relationships, by speaking and acting in ways that result in peace."[43] I want to go further, however, and suggest that what Martens

---

38. So C. K. Barrett, *The Epistle to the Romans*, Harper's New Testament Commentaries (New York: Harper & Row, 1957) 242–43.

39. In Brendan Byrne's *Romans* (ed. D. Harrington, Sacra Pagina 6 [Collegeville, Minn.: Liturgical, 1996]), the author divides Proverbs from Paul's understanding, suggesting that Proverbs was more violent.

40. The studies are Sigfried Morenz, "Feurige Kohlen auf dem Haupt," *Theologische Literaturzeitung* 78 (1953) 187–92; W. Klassen, "Coals of Fire: Symbol or Revenge?" *New Testament Studies* 9 (1963) 337–50; K. Stendahl, "Hate, Non-Retaliation and Love: 1QS 10:17-20 and Rom 12:19-21," *Harvard Theological Review* 55 (1962) 343–55. See also L. Ramaroson, "Charbons ardents: 'sur la tête ou 'pour le feu' (Pr 25:22a—Rm 12:20b)," *Bibl* 51 (1970) 230–34.

41. E. Käsemann, *Commentary on Romans*, trans. G. Bromiley (Grand Rapids: Eerdmans, 1980), 349, who otherwise refers back to the original Morenz argument further supported, with some amendment, by Klassen.

42. *Love of Enemies: The Way to Peace*, OBT (Philadelphia: Fortress Press, 1984) 34–37.

43. Elmer Martens, "The Way of Wisdom: Conflict Resolution in Biblical Narrative," in *The Way of Wisdom*, FS Bruce Waltke, ed. J. I. Packer and S. K. Soderlund (Grand Rapids: Zondervan, 2000) 75–90.

has identified may well be rooted in the exilic context of wisdom and diaspora tales. Along what lines might we begin to construct a sociologically significant "peace ethic" in Israelite wisdom literature that amounts to a practical quietism of the minority?

The Wisdom Warrior: An Ideal Type in Wisdom Literature

Wisdom literature employs a number of well-known images in teaching about wisdom, preeminently "Lady Wisdom/Sophia," but also the fool, the wicked, the father, the mother, and the young. Among the less prominent images used are those borrowed from warfare. Social conflict, therefore, is obviously an aspect of life from which wisdom is certainly not removed as an operant series of principles to attend to. Therefore, one can argue that in Proverbs and Ecclesiastes there emerges an image of what I call the "wisdom warrior." I have intentionally avoided "wise warrior," because that is precisely part of my point—we are not speaking simply of a warrior who has added wisdom to his arsenal. Rather, we are intended to contrast the wisdom warrior with standard warriors. The wisdom warrior is calm and self-restrained: "One who spares words is knowledgeable; one who is cool in spirit has understanding" (Prov 17:27).

Of course, many scholars have compared this image to cool-headed ideal of Egyptian wisdom, and the connection seems possible, as I have indicated. The wisdom warrior seeks to end conflict before it begins, as Prov 17:9 enjoins: "One who forgives an affront fosters friendship, but one who dwells on disputes will alienate a friend"; and note also 17:14: "The beginning of strife is like letting out water, so stop before the quarrel breaks out" (cf. 25:8-10, which advises that one settle matters out of court, which sounds like Matt 5:25).

The wisdom warrior will not return evil for evil but seek the welfare even of his enemies. According to Prov 17:13, "Evil will not depart from the house of one who returns evil for good," and 24:29 repeats the thought more directly by demanding that the wise one must not say, "I will do to others as they have done to me; I will pay them back for what they have done."

Particularly when contrasted with militant Hellenistic virtues of the gallant hero-warrior, the wisdom warrior appears in the eyes of the dominant to be weak and ineffectual. Even in his apparent weakness, however, the wisdom warrior is protected by God: 2:7: "He stores up wisdom for the upright; he is a shield to those who walk blamelessly"; 16:7: "When the ways of people please the LORD, he causes even their enemies to be at peace with them"; 18:10-11: "The name of the LORD is a strong tower; the righteous run into it and are safe. The wealth of the rich is their strong city; in their imagination it is like a high wall."

To argue that such random comparison of texts constitutes a theme seems haphazard methodologically, but it is important to point out that scholarship in wisdom literature is still enmeshed in the debates about how relevant, if at all, discussions of context are in a study of individual proverbs in the books of Proverbs and Ecclesiastes. While there is widespread agreement about the longer instructional poetry of Proverbs 1–9, the sections beginning with ch. 10 appear to McKane, for example, to reveal no discernible principle of theme or arrangement.[44]

Raymond Van Leeuwen's objections and his attempts to show a discernible contextual pattern to chs. 25–27, however, involve such meticulous comparison of specific word forms that a generally recognizable implication for the clear meaning of the individual proverbs is not really advanced beyond the assumptions one can make on a cursory reading of the section. There seems no serious objection, therefore, to comparing individual proverbial thoughts, with attention given only to the larger units of division indicated by the text itself and supported by contemporary redactional research.

Wisdom against Weapons

It is particularly interesting how often the wisdom of the wise is contrasted with the fortifications of a town, such as Prov 16:32: "One who is slow to anger is better than the mighty, and one whose temper is controlled than one who captures a city."[45] The key here is the contrast between the ways of the strong warrior (who is successful, after all, in this proverb), and the self-control, restraint, and indeed peacefulness, of the wise. This is particularly evident in 21:22: "One wise person went up against a city of warriors and brought down the stronghold in which they trusted." On reflection, it seems clear that we are not intended to imagine a Samson-like conquest of an entire city by brute strength, since it is precisely apparent strength that is being contrasted with wisdom (perhaps we are to think of the power of wisdom, as noted in 25:15: "With patience a ruler may be persuaded and a soft tongue can break bones"). Compare this sentiment with 25:28: "Like a city breached, without walls, is one who lacks self-control," which in a similar fashion contrasts apparent strength with the strength of wisdom.

---

44. Much of the debate is summarized in Raymond C. Van Leeuwen, *Context and Meaning in Proverbs 25–27*, SBLDS 96 (Atlanta: Scholars Press, 1988) 5–58.

45. Toy, *Proverbs*, 333. Toy compares this with the Greek virtue of *soproysyne*, but notably, Helen North's impressively sweeping survey of this virtue in Greek literature includes no examples of this virtue as a contrast to warfare or the spirit of the warrior. See North, *Sophrosyne* (Ithaca, N.Y.: Cornell Univ. Press, 1966).

180 A BIBLICAL THEOLOGY OF EXILE

Furthermore, this theme of the "one wise person" against military strength is also reflected elsewhere in wisdom literature. In his commentary, McKane suggests that this tradition of the single wise person refers to military strategists, whose counsel can turn defeat into victory through their superior tactics.[46] Similar is the suggestion of Michael Fox regarding Ecclesiastes: "Ingenuity provides power. It enables one to devise clever stratagems capable even of delivering a city from siege (9:13-15). Hence it is more powerful than a warrior's might (9:16) and weapons of war (9:18)." Fox presumes that "ingenuity at warfare" is the central point here. Much more consistent, however, would be wisdom in *avoiding* conflict.[47] This point can be further advanced on the basis of the famous passage in Eccl 9:13-18a.

How can these images of the single person against warriors and weapons make any sense? Some commentators have pointed to the Yahweh war/divine war tradition to explain this, citing Joshua as an example ("One among you puts flight to a thousand," Josh 23:10). Certainly we have the comparison of one versus many. But we do not have wisdom contrasted with military strength in this older tradition—indeed in the Joshua passage, greater strength is the issue.

A more helpful comparison, however, would be an examination of the tradition of the "wise women" in 2 Samuel. Jacob Hoftijzer and Claudia Camp have made important contributions to our understanding of the two famous cases of "wise women" who intervene in military circumstances.[48] Camp's study establishes how women could be in positions of family and tribal leadership by recognizing their importance as advisers and local leaders. Although her study does not go in the same direction as the present one, she has made many observations relevant to my argument. First, it is clear that the wise woman of Abel practices a form of proverbial wisdom in her dealings with Joab and exercises considerable diplomatic skills. Camp then compares this with a number of other occasions for "discussions at the city wall" in narrative literature. Although alluding to the possibility, Camp does not suggest that what she has identified is a peacemaking role, rather than a military role, for the wise woman of Abel or the men who talk with siege armies before battle. The wise woman of Abel is wise, especially when compared to wisdom literature dealing with "wisdom more important than walls" sentiments, pre-

46. McKane, *Proverbs*, 551.

47. "Wisdom in Qoheleth," in *In Search of Wisdom*, 117–18.

48. See Claudia Camp, "The Wise Women of 2 Samuel: A Role Model for Women in Early Israel?" *CBQ* 43 (1981) 14–29; and Jacob Hoftijzer, "David and the Tekoite Woman," *VT* 20 (1970) 419–44.

cisely because she *avoids* warfare. Her Solomonic decision is hardly Gand-
hian (she cuts off the head of the fugitive who has threatened the city),
but commentators have missed the connection between her single act and
the "single act of the wise" against warriors in wisdom literature. Indeed,
except for the gender of the terms, the Ecclesiastes passage is a striking
parallel to the story of the woman of Abel. I am not suggesting an actual
connection between the story and the Ecclesiastes passage, but rather that
both illustrate the ideal of practical peacefulness against military solu-
tions—negotiation rather than indignation.

In 2 Samuel 14 and 20, women again act as peacemakers in situations
that clearly bode ill for military violence. This raises interesting questions
about the interpretation of Prov 24:5-6: "Wise warriors are mightier than
strong ones, and those who have knowledge than those who have strength;
for by wise guidance you can wage your war, and in abundance of counselors there is victory." The abundance of counselors is contrasted with an
abundance of soldiers. We may well be in the realm of Yahweh war theology, where the number soldiers is irrelevant when faith is the controlling
issue (this would be supported by a proverb such as 21:31: "The horse is
made ready for the day of battle, but the victory belongs to the LORD").
But in wisdom literature, we may also be dealing with a decidedly non-
military ideal of wisdom, which would also be consistent with the tendency in Proverbs to contrast wisdom with military strength. It is not
that the wise are pacifists (yet!), but there is a clear preference in wisdom literature for settling matters peaceably rather than with force. Are
we dealing with a practical minority commitment to clever strategies of
survival?

Wisdom of Solomon
Finally, we can cite one of the most interesting features of the late diaspora text known as the Wisdom of Solomon. Great pains were taken by
the hellenized Jewish author to explain two of the most violent episodes
in the history of the Jewish people. As David Winston points out, it seems
clear that the author feels constrained by Greek sensibilities to explain the
behavior of God in reference to the killing of the Egyptians at the exodus
and the annihilation of the Canaanites at the time of the conquest.[49] What
is particularly interesting about Wisdom of Solomon on this matter is the

---

49. See David Winston, "Wisdom in the Wisdom of Solomon," in *In Search of Wisdom*,
ed. Perdue, Scott, and Wiseman, 149–64. Note esp. p. 163, where Winston argues that the
author has no "scruples" about idealizing the accounts of the exodus and the conquest in
order to suit his purposes. But such a tendency only serves to make the point.

strikingly modern sound of the author's attempt to "justify God." It is a measure of the impact of Greek rationalism on modern thought that the Wisdom of Solomon attempts to portray God as a compassionate and merciful God who tried peacefully and nonviolently to persuade the Egyptians and Canaanites again and again, but to no avail. Only when that tack was unsuccessful did God carry out what is suggested as the lone remaining alternative, and thus the responsibility for the violence is transferred to the enemy. Here, even God is taking the roll of the wisdom warrior, seeking positive ways to cleverly avoid conflict.

What is often not pointed out in research on Wisdom of Solomon, however, is the "guilty conscience" that stands behind these attempts to rationalize these more violent aspects of Israelite history. The values that the writer applies to his explanations are clearly foreign to the original texts—namely, a strong preference for mercifulness and the preference by God for persuasion rather than violence. In short, some kind of ethic of "justice in warfare," if not a distaste for warfare itself, is operating on the conscience of the writer. But it is also true that the Wisdom of Solomon sets forth a line consistent with the wisdom tradition of Israel that is well established by the time of Wisdom of Solomon. Thus the very historical discussion exhibited in Wisdom of Solomon illustrates how deeply ingrained into Jewish wisdom thinking the ethic of peaceful restraint has become. Now, the writer must write an "apology," and the result is a text that has all the trappings of an ancient apologia in the classic sense but also elements of the modern use of "remorseful request for forgiveness."

That Daniel embodies precisely this ethic of the wisdom warrior is clear from an examination of some features of chs. 1–6.

Daniel as the Wise Warrior

The tales of Daniel 1–6 represent Jews in the position of being in the service of Neo-Babylonian and Persian rulers.[50] Given their nature as folklore rather than historical report, it is important to be careful about the subtleties (such as the presumed level of compliance and the presumed attitude to the foreign rulers), which modern scholars have often overstated.

Whatever date scholars assign to the tales of Daniel 1–6, whether as early as the late Persian period (my own view of their oral origins) or as late as second century BCE (still the majority view), one thing is undeni-

---

50. For a full discussion of Daniel, I refer readers to my commentary, "Daniel and Additions to Daniel," in *NIB* 7:17–194.

able: the stories of Daniel arise from cross-cultural encounter. This encounter, like all cross-cultural encounters, was both fascinating and threatening—it was exotic and at the same time dangerous. The setting is in the most sumptuous circumstances imaginable for Jews in late Persian or Ptolemaic or Seleucid Hellenistic cultures—the very court of the Babylonian or Persian emperors. In all six stories, the exotic enticements include political influence and wealth. But the encounter is also dangerous. There are no less than four threats of death in six stories—threats often spectacular in their calculated frightfulness (e.g., burning in overheated furnaces or mauling by starved wild animals). Thus, we find the ambiguities of minority existence illustrated in the folklore of Daniel.

Furthermore, the stories of Daniel clearly arise as part of the social mythology of self-conscious Jewish people in circumstances of (1) diaspora existence, (2) cross-cultural contact, and (3) uneven distribution of power. The Daniel stories presume each of these realities (1:1-2), and any reading of these stories must remain alive to these realities of the compositional community of these tales. Take the theme of dream interpretation in Daniel 2 (and by extension, the dream interpretation themes in other Hebrew texts such as the Joseph story, and the clearly related interpretive abilities noted in Daniel 5). That Daniel interprets the dreams of the conqueror of Jerusalem, and that dreams are seen as messages from God, make clear that in Daniel dreams represent a power greater than the worldly power of the conquerors. To assert the power of God over Nebuchadnezzar is an inherently political act. Dreams represent a power that even Nebuchadnezzar cannot resist, and it is *the Jewish interpreter* who becomes the mediator of that power. In the context of the political subordination of the Jews under Babylon, Persia, and the Hellenistic heirs of Alexander's conquests, dream interpretation is an act of spiritual warfare or "wisdom warfare."

Consider a most interesting comparative case. In the Yuan period (1200–1300) the Mongol peoples conquered Han China. During the reigns of the notable Mongol emperors Genghis and Khublai Khan, both men employed Confucian scholars from among the occupied Chinese. Interest in these advisers to the Mongol conquerors has given rise to a literature that raises similar questions to the Daniel tales: How "loyal" were these advisers? Did they, in fact, share a positive view of the conquerors, or did their willingness to advise the conquerors help to mitigate the negative aspects of Mongol rule?[51] What is interesting is precisely the role of

---

51. See *In the Service of the Khan: Eminent Personalities of the Early Mongol Yuan Period (1200–1300)*, ed. I. de Rachewiltz et al. (Wiesbaden: Harrassowitz, 1992). I am indebted to

dream and portent interpretation. Later legend frequently ascribed to the Chinese advisers negative interpretations of omens and dreams of the Mongol conquerors, including even an end to their rule.[52] These tales became orthodoxy during the Ming restoration that followed the Mongol period. So also Daniel 2, for all its imagery of the loyal servants of Nebuchadnezzar, concludes with Daniel "advising" Nebuchadnezzar that his regime will come to an end, if not perhaps in his lifetime. Despite this, and the spectacular threats of death noted in virtually all of these stories, many Daniel scholars maintain a more optimistic view of Daniel's attitude toward rulers. In his impressive opus on the book of Daniel, John J. Collins acknowledges the importance of an essay by W. Lee Humphreys about a "lifestyle" for the Diaspora represented in Daniel and Esther.[53] Humphreys's article, based on a dissertation at Union Theological Seminary (1970), inaugurated what may be described as a paradigm for viewing the *social* significance of the Daniel stories in chs. 1–6 and, one might also argue, the additional stories in the Septuagint.

Although the social setting was not a central part of Humphreys's argument (which was rather more concerned with literary forms), his assumptions about the social setting are clearly stated when he surmises that the stories presume that "in certain circles at least the possibility of a creative and rewarding interaction with the foreign environment was present and could work for the good of the Jew."[54] He concluded by similarly suggesting: "One could, as a Jew, overcome adversity and find a life both rewarding and creative within the pagan setting and as a part of this foreign world."[55]

Prof. Hok-lam Chan for his advice on these matters. See also John D. Langlois Jr., ed., *China under Mongol Rule* (Princeton: Princeton Univ. Press, 1981), esp. Hok-lam Chan, "Chinese Official Historiography at the Yuan Court," 56–106; on omens that seem to portend the fall of the Mongols, see Albert Chan, *The Glory and Fall of the Ming Dynasty* (Norman: Univ. of Oklahoma Press, 1982) 1; and Henry Serruys, "The Mongols in China During the Hung Wu Period (1368–1398)," in *Mélanges chinois et bouddhiques*, vol. 11: 1956–1959 (Brussels: Juillet, 1959) 29; and esp. John D. Langlois Jr., "Chinese Culturalism and the Yuan Analogy: Seventeenth-Century Perspectives," *Harvard Journal of Asiatic Studies* 40, no. 2 (1980) 355–98; and Patrick Hanan, "Judge Bao's Hundred Cases Reconstructed," *Harvard Journal of Asiatic Studies* 40, no. 2 (1980) 301–23.

52. See Hok-Lam Chan, "A Mongolian Legend of the Building of Peking," in *Asia Major*, 3d series, vol. 4, part 2, (1990) 63–93; idem, "Chang Chung and His Prophecy: The Transmission of the Legend of an Early Ming Taoist," *Oriens Extremus, Zeitschrift für Sprache, Kunst, Cultur der Lander des Fernen Ostens*, ed. O. Benl, W. Franke, and W. Fuchs (Hamburg: Harrassowitz, 1973) 65–102.

53. Collins, *Daniel*, 45–47; W. Lee Humphreys, "A Life-Style for Diaspora: A Study of the Tales of Esther and Daniel," *JBL* 92 (1973) 211–23.

54. Ibid., 213.

55. Ibid., 223.

It is easy not only to trace the persistence of this view of the "attitude" of the stories of Daniel but also to note that it had precedents in the literature surrounding the book of Daniel. Let a few examples suffice. James Montgomery's classic commentary on Daniel contains relatively few comments giving away the social assumptions behind his analysis of chs. 1–6. But he writes as an aside that "we see the Jews of the Golah, no longer hanging their harps on the willows, but bravely taking their place in the world and proving themselves the equals and superiors of their Pagan associates, not by reason of their race or human excellences, but through their constancy of character founded on faith and trust in God."[56] Along similar lines, Louis Hartman and Alexander Di Lella suggest: "The fact that Daniel and his companions are said in chs. 1–5 to have achieved high position in the Babylonian court may perhaps suggest that life for the Israelites in exile was not all hardship and distress."[57]

Noting that previous scholars often suggested that the positive attitude to foreigners in chs. 1–6 differs from the more negative portrayal in chs. 7–12, Norman Porteous cautions that there is a "double attitude," that is, both positive and negative, throughout the book as a whole.[58] André Lacocque, however, repeats the standard view that the "atmosphere" of chs. 7–12 and that of chs. 1–6 are quite different. Chapters 7–12 are more negative precisely because "it is no longer a question of the apparently tranquil existence of the Jews in the midst of pagans, but of religious persecution and martyrdom."[59]

Finally, Lawrence Wills concludes his impressive study about the genre of Hebrew court tales: "It is a popular genre, but it probably does not extend to the lower classes. It reflects the orientation of the administrative and entrepreneurial class. The scribal ideals inherent in the stories might restrict this circle somewhat to the extended court circles."[60]

Certainly there are contemporary scholars who have suggested alternative ideas. In his analysis of Daniel stories, Philip Davies also notes how these stories contain a "symbolic denial of the king's implicit claim to be sole provider."[61] Danna Fewell's study of the Daniel legends also takes a more critical view:

56. James Montgomery, *A Critical and Exegetical Commentary on the Book of Daniel*, ICC (Edinburgh: T. & T. Clark, 1927) 101.

57. Louis Hartman and Alexander Di Lella, *The Book of Daniel*, AB (Garden City, N.Y.: Doubleday, 1978) 34.

58. Norman Porteous, *Daniel*, OTL (Philadelphia: Westminster, 1965) 19.

59. André Lacocque, *The Book of Daniel* (Atlanta: John Knox, 1979) 9.

60. Lawrence M. Wills, *The Jew in the Court of the Foreign King*, Harvard Dissertations in Religion (Minneapolis: Fortress Press, 1990) 197.

61. Philip R. Davies, *Daniel*, Old Testament Guides 4 (Sheffield: Sheffield Academic, 1985) 91.

> In every story in Daniel 1–6, the sage is called upon to hold to values that somehow oppose the existent political authority. The story of deception in ch. 1 lays the groundwork for the remaining stories. In this first story, the young Judeans, by refusing to eat the food from the king's table, affirm that, though they are willing to serve the king, the source of their wisdom and the subject of their ultimate fidelity is their god, not their king. In this story and the ones that follow, the sages show that they are ready to oppose political power for higher values—whether this challenge entails speaking the truth about an unpleasant dream or vision (chs. 4, 5) or disobeying the command to pay ultimate allegiance to some king who thinks his sovereignty to be supreme (chs. 1, 3, 6).[62]

Indeed, as Luigi Lombardi-Satriani writes, "Folk culture . . . marks the outer limit of the hegemonic culture, whose ideological tricks it reveals, contesting at times only with its own presence, the universality, which is only superficial, of the official culture's concepts of the world and of life."[63]

In Daniel 2 Daniel and his friends pray to God for the wisdom needed to interpret Nebuchadnezzar's dream. In other words, Daniel escapes death by talking his way out of the dilemma, only to turn to God with the request to bail him out with the requisite information. The tactic is worthy of a Jacob. Then, when the "answer" is delivered, it surprisingly and cleverly announces a coming end to the regime of the emperor, who only moments before threatened them all with horrendous execution. "Wisdom" in this case was a tactic of resistance. In virtually all the stories, cleverness and "wisdom" are contrasted with the brute power of the empire, or the worthlessness of its proud information (e.g., from the rival advisers). In short, Daniel defeats his enemies by means of wisdom—he is the quintessential wisdom warrior (as noted by Gandhi in South Africa, who occasionally cited the biblical Daniel as a historical example of satyagraha—the movement of social resistance that Gandhi himself pioneered[64]).

---

62. Danna N. Fewell, *Circle of Sovereignty: A Story of Stories in Daniel 1–6*, JSOTSup 7 (Sheffield: Almond, 1988) 154–55.

63. Luigi Lambardi-Satriani, "Folklore as Culture of Contestation," *Journal of the Folklore Institute* 11 (1974) 99–121.

64. I have analyzed Gandhi's interest in Daniel at some length in "Gandhi on Daniel 6: Some Thoughts on a 'Cultural Exegesis' of the Bible," *Biblical Interpretation* 1 (1993) 321–38.

"And Daniel Laughed. . . ."—Diasporic Nonviolence: Laughing at the State

I suggest that there is most certainly a direct connection between the clever wisdom advised by Proverbs, which is often contrasted with brute strength, and Daniel, for example, who clearly embodies a wise figure (as von Rad surmised) but only because he is, at the same time, the figure of a wise trickster in the court of the conqueror. This becomes particularly clear in the level of satire and irony in the Bel and the Dragon stories in the Septuagint tradition, where Daniel actually laughs at the gullibility of the emperor for believing that an idol actually eats (Daniel's laughter forms an *inclusio* of the solution to the "mystery" of the eating idol, Bel 7, 19). The point is made even stronger with the realization that "laughter" in the Bible is almost always associated with mockery (Gen 18:15; Job 5:22; Pss 52:6; 59:8; Hab 1:10; etc.). Wisdom ethics are subcultural ethics in Proverbs, Ecclesiastes, and Daniel. Whatever nonviolent witness there may be, I would argue, is also subcultural.

Where is the nonviolent witness of the Hebrew Bible? If we look for a Hebrew Gandhi, we will not find him/her. Principled nonviolence as a tactic of national politics is not a diasporic virtue and thus arguably not the Hebraic form of nonviolence. Hebrew nonviolence is found in the same place it is found in the New Testament—as a value of diaspora existence living under imperial regimes (cf. Epistle of James, 1 Peter).

The teaching "love your enemies" can never be separated from Jesus' statements standing before the ruling authorities—like Daniel before Nebuchadnezzar, or Hananiah, Mishael, and Azariah (= Shadrach, Meshach, and Abednego) before the fiery furnace. Jesus stands before Pilate (John 19:11) and states that Pilate has no power apart from that which is given by God. When a certain group of Pharisees (clearly in this case sympathetic to Jesus) warned Jesus that he was being threatened by Herod with death, Jesus replied that there were more important things happening: "He said to them, 'Go and tell that fox for me, "Listen, I am casting out demons and performing cures today and tomorrow, and on the third day I finish my work"'" (Luke 13:32).

The nonviolence of the Hebrew diasporic ethics is a nonviolence of radical doubt and irreverence to the self-proclaimed state power and piety, a nonviolence based on the fact that God's plans are centered on the people of God primarily, and the nation-state is not the center of the universe. In other words, for the wisdom warrior, the nonviolence of the Hebrew Diaspora is a nonviolence based on the wise awareness that the empire, despite all its attempts to convince itself otherwise, is not of ultimate significance.

It is not worth losing sleep over (it is the emperor's sleep that is disturbed!) much less a reason for killing others. It is the clever and wise insight of the diaspora community that their life as the people of God is far more important than the success or failure of the empire, which is, after all, merely a statue whose dust will be blown with the wind (Dan 2:35). Indeed, one may well serve the emperor, but only as long as that service does not conflict with the *real* world—the world of seeing through God's intentions in the world: "casting out demons and performing cures."

Am I suggesting that diaspora trickery and self-interested cleverness are positive virtues of the exilic experience? It is a complex question, of course. The irreverence toward the state and the advice to keep one's wits in relation to the state are quite simply the practical wisdom of the Diaspora. Such wisdom does not believe in the myths of the state. It is, however, the embodiment of Jesus' classic advice to his minority, subcultural followers: "See, I am sending you out like sheep into the midst of wolves; so be wise as serpents and innocent as doves" (Matt 10:16). To develop this further takes us into the final chapter.

8.

TOWARD A DIASPORIC CHRISTIAN THEOLOGY:

The Theology of Tobit and Daniel Revisited

W̶E NOW RETURN TO THE TASK OF TRYING TO THINK AGAIN ABOUT A modern "biblical theology of exile." I have had occasion to refer in this work to the book of Tobit, a collection of tales set in the Assyrian capital of Nineveh dealing with the lives of a family of northern exiles, and to Daniel 1–6, a collection of resistance stories about maintaining witness and identity in Babylon. The modern theological task will include the raising of new heroes, new stories that become exemplary for the new situation. The corpus of "resistance stories" known as Daniel 1–6, as well as the Esther tradition, are certainly about maintaining identity and witness under the pressures of surrounding cultural values and contrary ethical behavioral norms. Daniel's resistance, Esther's courage, and Tobit's faithfulness become the new virtues, and they are the new stories with which to raise the young.

The setting of the tale of Tobit in the diaspora and the frequently noted use of many Near Eastern folklore motifs (Ahiqar, The Grateful Dead, etc.) makes the specific dating of this work difficult, but Carey Moore suggests 225–175, or before the Maccabean period in any case.[1] As a diaspora tale, however, it deserves a more important place in (particularly Protestant) analysis of the diaspora literature that includes Daniel, Esther, and the Joseph narratives.

---

1. The motifs are helpfully summarized by Carey Moore, "The Book of Tobit," in *ABD* 6:585–94; on the date, see 591.

The fourth chapter, particularly, contains an important body of "teaching." The setting is the sage advice given by the old man Tobit to his son, thinking that he is soon to die and must therefore pass advice to him. It amounts to advice about living in diaspora as a righteous Jew. There are many elements of this advice from the diaspora that make this passage a particularly noteworthy collection of "commandments." First, there is the general emphasis on remembering commandments—the ethical expectations that make a Hebrew who he/she is in the context of mixed populations. This dramatically parallels the Hebrew penitential prayers with their emphasis on the Mosaic law as the characteristic element of Hebrew identity, if not also the Sermon on the Mount for modern Christians.

Second, there are particular pieces of advice that seem significant. The first "commandments" all share the elements of social solidarity—giving alms and caring for the poor (vv. 7-11). The advice returns to social solidarity and the poor in vv. 16-17.

Then there is the expected message of internal solidarity in marriage (vv. 12-13). I have already noted the significance of identity and marriage as issues of purity and survival.

Finally, there are the interesting comments related to relationships with "the nations." The advice is guarded: "None of the nations has understanding" (v. 19), but there is a possibility that God has further plans for their use and may give them "good counsel." On the other hand, it may be that God will punish—but this remains the business of God. The general tone of the advice seems quite compatible with my suggestion that wisdom literature and the Diaspora tales feature a "stay out of trouble" element in combination with an emphasis on socially just behavior, both of which seem characteristic of its exilic social ethic.

Tobit, like Daniel and Mordecai, and Zerubbabel (in the tales of 1 Esdras 3–4), all can at times find themselves in the service of the emperor. All of them, however, face questions of remaining true to their identity in difficult times. Compromise is a constant temptation, assimilation a constant threat, but justice and exemplary behavior are the consistent advice of these works. At the end of a survey of ideas read from biblical texts in the context of exile, is there any possibility of building a normative theology from these suggestions? What does it mean to listen to Tobit and Daniel?

An exilic theology for modern Christianity is certainly a theological move that involves a radical rethinking of previous assumptions of power, involvement, and ministry in wider society. Are these "exilic theologies" surveyed in the chapters above simply the values of a particular social circumstance? A Nietschean "slave morality"?

The twentieth-century American ethicist Reinhold Niebuhr is most often associated with a reformist call for Christians to admit that their involvement in social change in society is inevitably a sinful involvement in an immoral society. All we can hope for is to make immoral society a bit less immoral. But this guilty involvement in fallen systems was defined by Niebuhr as the only viable Christian way to remain committed to positive change. To work on alternative social formations is often written off as "withdrawal from the world"—defined negatively as utopian, and by his brother Richard Niebuhr as "sectarian," but altogether morally unacceptable.[2] Is such theological cynicism an inevitable reading of diaspora ethics and values? Is a call to a normative ethic of exilic existence merely an attempt to put a pleasant face on defeat and self-proclaimed irrelevance? I contend that this would be so only under the assumption that violent power is the sole viable context that is characteristic of Christian morality. I would further argue that an ecclesiology built on "exile" as a biblical paradigm represents a revolutionary regrouping, rethinking, and restrategizing option for contemporary Christian existence.

The easy identification of church, society, and nation that has served Western Christians for centuries is becoming increasingly difficult in the modern secular society. Much of the present identity crisis boils down to a loss of power and influence—a loss of moral power because of a history of compromise, and thus a loss of authority behind most attempts at persuasion.

In other words, exile is not merely a suggested paradigm, but a radically sobering diagnosis for the present reality of Christian existence in the world. It would be a fascinating historical exercise to debate whether Christians should ever have wielded the kind of secular and military power that they once had, but the debate would not matter with regard to present realities. The present reality is an exile even if there is not much awareness of this exilic circumstance.

The question is, How ought modern Christians cope with this loss of power? One response is to convince ourselves that this recently clear marginality is not our proper place in society, and so we ought to try to reassert some kind of moral authority by raising our voice rather than sharpening our analysis. There has been a resurgence of religious references in the wake of the crusading mentality that gripped the United States after the tragic events of September 11, 2001. Much of this, however, is not a careful consideration of the role of Christians as voices of both compassion and moderation, but rather an exercise in doing theology by

---

2. See Stanley Hauerwas, "On Being a Church Capable of Addressing a World at War: A Pacifist Response to the United Methodist Bishops' Pastoral *In Defense of Creation*," in *The Hauerwas Reader*, ed. J. Berkman and M. Cartwright (Durham, N.C.: Duke Univ. Press, 2001) 447–48.

megaphone. Once again, "just-war" language is quickly dusted off and twisted into a rationale for bombing—only the latest in a long history of the uses of just-war language to "include" or "account for" the latest military innovations.[3]

Along with this attempted reassertion of political and social authority, there is an exegesis of power that uses the monarchy of ancient Israel (the right) or the exodus (the left) to justify contemporary power tactics in national political systems. Either way, we have abandoned the moral authority that comes with *living and offering* a true social alternative. In either case, our preexistent convictions about the role of power in Christian life have effectively preselected those parts of the Bible that we highlight as somehow theologically exemplary and those we simply ignore. Inevitably, either the monarchy or the exodus becomes the focus of attention. Postexilic Hebrew history and literature are left as representing the period of sad decline and loss, a once robust national existence that had slowly descended into petty religiosity. Simon Dubnow's interesting insights about diaspora Jewish existence, however, have more relevance for Christian denials of exilic theologies of diaspora than his own context of questioning forms of Jewish existence in the modern world:

> The effective educational worth of the biblical part of Jewish history is disputed by none. It is called "sacred" history, and he who acquires a knowledge of it is thought to advance the salvation of his soul. Only a very few, however, recognize the profound, moral content of the second half of Jewish history, the history of the diaspora. Yet, by reason of its exceptional qualities and intensely tragic circumstances, it is beyond all others calculated to yield edification to a notable degree . . . if Israel bestowed upon mankind a religious theory of life, Judah gave it a thrilling example of tenacious vitality and power of resistance for the sake of conviction.[4]

I have argued that there is another way of reading postexilic Hebrew literature as reflecting the difficult birth pangs of dramatically new conceptions of religious life—vibrant, active, and self-consciously strategic formations of community existence that are designed to respond to the realities of empire. Whether one decides that exile is only the regrettable fate of the Hebrews, or is also the creative period of phoenix-like transformation, largely depends on one's presumptions about political viability outside the nation-state model. To use the language of many dominant

---

3. On this problem see John Howard Yoder, *When War Is Unjust: Being Honest in Just-War Thinking* (Minneapolis: Augsburg, 1984).
4. Simon Dubnow, *Nationalism and History* (Cleveland: Meridian, 1958) 269.

Christian social ethics and "theologies of social action," Christians who are "engaged with the world," "living up to their responsibilities," and "working for the common good" are almost always—by definition—participating in (even if no longer in actual control of) the power of the state. Concomitant to this is the notion that, if one challenges this definition of "Christian responsibility," one is "withdrawing from the world," and by implication withdrawing from any authentic political involvement and thus any real concern for "the common good." But as Stanley Hauerwas warns, modern Christian attempts to "relate" to the realities of the world have led to shocking extremes: "The project, begun at the time of Constantine, to enable Christians to share power without being a problem for the powerful, had reached its most impressive fruition. If Caesar can get Christians there to swallow the 'ultimate solution,' and Christians here to embrace the bomb, there is no limit to what we will not do for the modern world. Alas, in leaning over to speak to the modern world, we have fallen in. We had lost the theological resources to resist, lost the resources even to see that there was something worth resisting."[5]

Yet there is a clear hope that one source of a critique of this compromise is a new reflection on the biblical witness. John H. Yoder's critique of "Constantinianism" was decidedly based on his Anabaptist-informed reading of the biblical message: "If, as the New Testament indicates, extending certain phases of the Old, God calls his people to prophetically critical relationship to the structures of power and oppression, then the alliance between Rome-as-Empire and Church-as-Hierarchy, which the fourth and fifth centuries gradually consolidated, is not merely a possible tactical error but a structured denial of the gospel."[6]

An exilic biblical theology that can provide the building blocks for a modern Christian ecclesiology of exile arises from precisely these concerns. Attention to the transformations of community represented in the late Hebrew experience of exile presents modern Christians with an ecclesiastical strategy that is particularly relevant to the modern circumstances of transnational commodification and nationalist destruction of the human experience.

But a viable biblical model is, paradoxically, not a biblical model! What I mean is that the viability of a radical Christian community in the modern world is not a return to some pristine past—which was not often so pristine if we are honest readers of church history. We look back for moral guidance, not blueprints or cast-iron molds. By reflecting on the biblical

5. Stanley Hauerwas and William H. Willimon, *Resident Aliens* (Nashville: Abingdon, 1989).

6. John Howard Yoder, "The Disavowal of Constantine: An Alternative Perspective on Interfaith Dialogue," in *The Royal Priesthood: Essays Ecclesiological and Ecumenical*, ed. M. Cartwright (Grand Rapids: Eerdmans, 1994) 245.

witness of exile, we learn that we are in Babylon, not Jerusalem. Jerusalem has too often served as the capital of our imagined powerful "Christian" state from which we may impose our will on others. That was Constantine's, and our, mistake. But the biblical text ultimately leaves it to us to strategize what the radical gospel of Christian community means in this particular neighborhood of Babylon (Nineveh, Rome, Antioch, London, Los Angeles . . .), and in this particular year of its reign over humanity. Our "new David," having disarmed the model of the "old David," leaves us to creatively apply our strategies in the world—strategies of faith and wisdom. Christian strategies seek, like Daniel and Tobit, to assert nonviolently alternative strategies for human existence in the world that are lived out in conscious nonconformity to the world and its various value systems.

The precise terms of a diasporic Christianity must be revisited in each different geographical location. For Indian Christians, the witness will include an embracing of the witness of "low-caste" Dalit peoples. For Japanese Christians, the witness will challenge nationalist bravado and embrace the rejected Barakumin, the Ainu, and non-Japanese Asian workers (a witness understood profoundly in the writings of the Christian Shusaku Endo). For American Christians, the task will be the painful process of disengaging from the myths of the dominant "Christian nation" that has so deeply corrupted a radical Christian witness in the world. Note that the prayers of penance examined above, being a largely negative exercise, rarely asserted a positive program apart from lamenting the abandonment of the Mosaic values of the Law. For the Christian, one could argue that this translates into the centrality of the "new law" of Christ as the most defining element of Christian faith and practice.

However, one of the problems of articulating a detailed positive model of "Christian life" rather than the negative model of "the exilic Christian movement" is the difficulty of advocating any static model that represents *the* exilic model for Christian communal life in all contexts. The problem is precisely one of context. Yoder, and later Walter Brueggemann, noted this difficulty in using exilic models for Christian life: "By the nature of the case it is not possible to establish, either speculatively or from historical samples, a consistent anti-Constantinian model. The prophetic denunciation of paganization must always be missionary and ad hoc; it will be in language as local and as timely as the abuses it critiques."[7] As Brueggemann stated, the life of a theological exile involves "an endlessly cunning, risky process of negotiation."[8] Under a vision of the exilic para-

7. Ibid., 250.
8. See Walter Brueggemann, *Cadences of Home: Preaching among Exiles* (Louisville: Westminster John Knox, 1997) 11.

digm of the church, Christian theology would be in a process of constant negotiation with the realities thrown against it in a secular context.

Christian exiles, Christian diasporas and minorities, and Christian subcultures have the biblical resources to live an alternative existence that affirms justice and peace, seeking to move forward God's holy experiment of creating an authentic humanity that is consciously gathered in non-conformity to the structures around them. But in a related move, I also suggest that a theology of abandoning Constantine, and Constantinian exegetical models of doing biblical theology, is to assert a postcolonialist, as well as exilic, biblical theology.

The Postcolonialist Mandate of the Church in Exile

The violent appropriation of humanity, resources, and territory in the nineteenth and twentieth centuries (with roots much earlier) still lives on in the legacies of colonialism. Colonialism was, and is, an expression of nationalist existence, and counternationalism is often seen as the only relevant countermeasure to colonialism. In other words, becoming a national entity—no matter how small or economically unviable—is posited as the only true existence of an authentic "people." But this dominance of national power models is a clear denial of the viability of what Lisa Lowe and David Lloyd[9] have called "subnarratives"—and also obviously related to denials of what I call "the exilic paradigm of Christian existence." One of the great ironies in the development of an exilic biblical consciousness for "Christian community" is that a primary source of advice, models of existence, and strategies of resistance, come from the life of cultural minorities in wider societies, or what Nelson Graburn has called "the Fourth World."[10] My discussion of exile as a source of theological reflection is not intended to be a false romanticization of the often tragic injustices suffered by exiles throughout the world. In an important remark in the context of his extolling the Jewish virtues of diaspora existence, Dubnow powerfully challenges Christians to consistency: "The Jewish people is deserving of attention not only in the time when it displayed its power and enjoyed its independence, but as well in the period of its weakness and oppression during which it was compelled to purchase spiritual development by constant sacrifice of self. A thinker crowned

---

9. Lisa Lowe and David Lloyd, "Introduction," in *The Politics of Culture in the Shadow of Capital,* ed. L. Lowe and D. Lloyd (Durham, N.C.: Duke Univ. Press, 1997) 1–32.

10. Nelson H. Graburn, "Introduction," in *Ethnic and Tourist Arts: Cultural Expressions from the Fourth World,* ed. N. H. Graburn (Berkeley: Univ. of California Press, 1976) i–xv.

with thorns demands no less veneration than a thinker with the laurel wreath upon his brow."[11]

Along these lines, it is worth pausing a moment to consider the warning of Sze-Kar Wan. The values of diaspora existence may seem like cold comfort for those who have worked to end "diasporas" of exclusion. Wan reacts to Daniel Boyarin's call for affirming diaspora existence: "Now that we have learned to speak and write like our white teachers, we are told we should develop and construct our own narratives, or, in Boyarin's terms, divest ourselves of power and the basis for that power, neither of which we have, even now. Well, not so fast. Give us a chance to consolidate our community, to create a place for ourselves in the academy, to have some power, if you will. Once that is established, then and only then can we fully embrace Boyarin's suggestion that a diasporized identity can in fact be the key to communication with all other diasporized groups."[12] Wan is quite right that diaspora identities require great strength of will and organization: "Our ambivalence towards diaspora theory may paradoxically well be a result of our present state of diaspora existence."[13] But the further challenge is how one can gain the strength to redefine a diaspora existence as creative and empowering without participating in a power system that tempts its participants, and its aspirants, with a power that is measured in terms of one's ability to protect privilege—most often violently—or the ability to assert one's will over others.

Still, I take Wan's warning against advising for others what we have not fully embodied in ourselves (not particularly a valid critique of Boyarin himself, however, I might add). Further, I wish to take seriously Caren Kaplan's critique of contemporary literary discussions about marginal identities that use terms such as *borderlands* and *hybridity*. Kaplan issues an interesting warning to those (like myself) who would borrow some of this language for theology: be on guard lest a genuine exilic theology decompose into a temporarily faddish "tourist" theology.[14] To put it in another set of terms, a diasporic Christian theology does not consist in creating ever more exotic multicultural rituals to perform in the cathedral—it is to abandon the cathedral and all it represents as an icon of

---

11. Dubnow, *Nationalism*, 269.

12. Sze-Kar Wan, "Does Diaspora Identity Imply Some Sort of Universality? An Asian-American Reading of Galatians," in *Interpreting Beyond Borders*, ed. F. F. Segovia, Bible and Postcolonialism 3 (Sheffield: Sheffield Academic, 2000) 119.

13. Ibid., 120.

14. See Caren Kaplan, *Questions of Travel: Postmodern Discourses of Displacement* (Durham, N.C.: Duke Univ. Press, 1998) 63.

power or a chaplaincy to the state. To offer the prophet Amos a comfortable room in the palace, perhaps as the new director of the Institute for Faith and Society, may not represent the most notable success of his prophecy.

The alternative, I insist, is not to reinvest in power by statecraft. Lest we also react by further romanticizing the nation-state, exiles are after all not merely sufferers, nor are they inevitably incomplete, nor are they always handicapped without the trappings of statehood. This is not to deny the often negative conditions under which many exiled peoples must function; it is rather to recognize fully the creativity and resourcefulness with which these peoples remain firmly engaged in the world despite their inability to assert themselves violently—among other privileges of a state! Exiles cannot be reduced to mere sufferers of statelessness. Exiles can be creative master strategists and often dedicated students of the realities of the world. Thus, to turn to cultural or theological minorities in the churches is not a matter of "doing good" or simply attempting to correct historical injustices. To turn to the minorities within the Christian churches and movements is a matter of survival, because their minority existence is the model of the exilic church.

A biblical theology of the Christian diaspora needs to focus on the resources of existing diasporic movements and peoples. But this would include not only the important resources of Asian, Hispanic, and African American Christian movements, as well as Pacific Islander and Native Peoples Christian movements in the United States, Canada, Australia, and New Zealand (among others), but also studies of the rarely recognized Armenian and Greek diasporic experiences. In addition, it would include theological minority movements such as the Hutterian and other Anabaptist communities, the Tolstoyan Christian subcultures in Russia and Europe that responded to Tolstoy's vision of a peasant-driven Christianity, the worker-priests of postwar Europe who attempted to identify with class-driven "diasporas" of economic power and privilege, and a rediscovery of the theories of such Yiddish social visionaries as Chaim Zhitlovsky or the territorialist theories of Dubnow. In short, it is to focus on what has been written off (under the mandate of statehood) as marginal in order to mine the creative resources of diasporic existence. These (and many other minority and subcultural) experiences can "become for us, the body and blood" of theological and ecclesiological wisdom.

Furthermore, postcolonialist social thinkers who express a modern fascination with "borderlands," "nomads," and "hybrid identities" can become highly suggestive for the more flexible definitions for a diasporic biblical theology for modern Christians. My conviction is that Christian study of subcultural experiences are critical to the task of being the church—these diasporas and their exilic members can become our teachers of the diasporic, minority strategies that the church must learn if it is to survive in exile. It is time, in short, to end the colonization of Christian biblical theology by the Davidic state with its nostalgia for power and see a future of "critical localism" or "creative diasporic existence" in Babylon. Tobit, not David, is our saint for the third millennium.

Social Elements of a Christian Diasporic Theology

What I have learned in my studies of the exilic events of the Bible is that there are a number of important religious and sociological responses to these events that provide some bases for a theology of exile. Here I outline only a few, in hopes of generating further critical discussion and dialogue on the task that confronts us. I make no particular claim to comprehensive coverage here, only suggestions of how our textual study can lead to pastoral reflection.

Honoring Ezra: Purity and Nonconformity

A commitment to identity requires a commitment to the internal maintenance of identity. I have often commented in classrooms and lectures that even though I share the general disgust with the episode of Ezra's breakup of foreign marriages and consider that action to be extreme, there are other perspectives to consider. If one speaks, for example, to Native Americans in the United States about the adoption of Native children by non-Native families, one quickly finds oneself in the presence of Ezra-like concerns[15] that allow us to appreciate what it means to worry about the very existence and viability of cultural survival. Identity, whether cultural or religious, is a matter of discipline. This is a lesson well learned by minority peoples. But what must be developed is the insight that this discipline need not be draconian, cruel, or insidiously closed-minded. It is true that only a self-consciously exilic Christian community can function with the ability to constantly monitor the social realities of the age—the many changing moods and faces of Caesar—and respond with building institutions based on a life-affirming nonconformity that offers an alternative reality for human existence.

But with Ezra, there is a constant danger that is also noted in the cultural studies approaches to "localism." As Arif Dirlik warns: "The affirma-

---

15. For example, *Children of the Dragonfly: Native American Voices on Child Custody and Education*, ed. R. Bensen (Tucson: Univ. of Arizona Press, 2001).

tion of the local, and of diversity thus defined, is not without its own problems. . . . One such problem is the celebration of premodern pasts which, in the name of resistance to the modern and the rationalist homogenization of the world, results in a localism or a 'third-Worldism' that is willing to overlook past oppressions out of a preoccupation with capitalist or Eurocentric oppression and that in the name of the recovery of spirituality affirms past religiosities that were themselves excuses for class and patriarchal inequalities . . . insistence on local 'purity' may well serve as excuses for a reactionary revival of older forms of oppression"[16]

Modern Christians need not embrace an Ezra-like exclusivity, or a bigoted notion about "appropriate marriage partners," or the repression of women in the name of a regressive ideal about "restoring the family" to recognize that Christian identity does involve appropriate attention to issues of maintaining a viable, gospel-informed social witness. To take an example from my own tradition, the Society of Friends (Quakers): The Quakers have never been "withdrawn from the world" in any Niebuhrian sense of that term. But they have arguably been the most effective agents for social change in the wider world (abolitionism, women's equality, establishment of fixed pricing, entrepreneurial innovations in the early Rowntree and Cadbury companies, experiments with alternative models of criminal justice, peace work) precisely when they were stronger and clearer about their unique identities as "strangers in a strange land." That is, they saw themselves as exilic Christians, deeply aware of how their values differed from the surrounding society, and built their unique institutions accordingly. I would further contend that Quakers enter into periods of notable ineffectiveness precisely when moving toward more liberal "engaged with the world" strategies (lobbying or the bland and often meaningless rhetoric of "advocating" for "systemic change") that would keep the Niebuhrians happy. Misery, it seems, wants company. But I argue that in a diasporic model of Christian action, social change is better modeled than merely "advocated for."

As Jesus trenchantly warned using images of Christians as "salt" or "light" in modern society, if the church does not pay attention to maintaining its differences from the surrounding society toward which both its mission and prophetic judgment must be directed, it clearly will have lost its way. The priests of the exile, including Ezra, were not wrong in emphasizing the need for identity and maintaining borders between the

16. Arif Dirlik, "The Global in the Local," in *Global/Local: Cultural Production and the Transnational Imaginary*, ed. R. Wilson and W. Dissanayake (Durham, N.C.: Duke Univ. Press, 1996) 37.

community of faith and the surrounding society. They erred only in their failure to apply such concerns with an equal concern to maintain an ethic of radical "missionary responsibility." In short, Ezra fails where the biblical canon itself does not, because the witness of Ezra is supplemented by Deutero-Isaiah and Jonah. Ezra teaches us to remain committed to unique identities, with all the appropriate discipline that this requires.

Diaspora Existence and Critical Analysis as Theology

In chapter four above, examining the tradition of the penitential prayers in the postexilic texts, I noted an interest in history; thus a significant strategy of creativity in exile is to do critical historiography. We are in this circumstance as modern Christians for very good historical reasons, and as I have argued, in Western history particularly the Christian experiment with power has had devastating results for the modern world. Like the Deuteronomistic editors and authors after the exile, it is a part of our task as modern Christians to rethink our history and thus to engage in the critical historiography that will condemn the "sins of the ancestors" (and relegate their advocates to lesser roles in courses in Christian history).

When we read biblical exilic texts as well as Christian history, as modern Christians, it is not so easy to identify with the diaspora Jew named Daniel and his fellow exiles in Babylon. On the contrary, as First-World Christians we are much closer to Ashpenaz (Dan 1), the king's guard, who learned from his minority charges. In Roman Palestine we are much closer in social and political status to the jailors, not to Paul and Silas, the two subcultural Jewish Christian prophets. Do we find ourselves in the modern church, on our knees with the jailor, asking: "What must I do to be saved?" (Acts 16). That is precisely the task of the constant analysis that is exemplified in the penitential prayers. As in the context of the Armenian, Jewish, and many other diaspora peoples, the inability (if not refusal) to exercise blunt power forces a drawing on critical thought. Wisdom becomes the "sword of the word." The doing of "critical history" is a part of this constant revisionism—a constant openness to the always new possibilities for "remembering these commandments" (Tob 4:18-19). In short, among other results, worldly power makes Christian analysis lazy. Why be convincing when we can simply draw a sword?

Jonah: Ecclesiology as Missiology

To be a diaspora people is to be a people of mission. Redefining ourselves as a people of social, but not violent worldly, power is to redefine the very meaning of power, but it is also to redefine the meaning of mission. Our gospel is not based on the influence of our "get out the vote" campaigns, but rather on the integrity of our faith and practice. Those who advocate "engagement with the world," and accuse the already more "diasporic"-oriented Christian traditions of "withdrawal" or "isolation" (frequently directed at Anabaptist theological formulations) typically undervalue, or are not even aware of, the worldwide involvement of these supposedly "withdrawn" Christian activists in direct service projects that are not mediated by any state authorities.[17] The very effectiveness of these hundreds of outposts of diasporic Christian action can usually be measured by the authenticity of their theological self-identity.

I maintain that the New Testament's deeply held sense of social marginality has been radically misread in popular Christian piety. For Jesus to say that his kingdom is "not of this world" (John 18:36); for Paul to say that our struggle is not with enemies of flesh and blood (Eph 6:12); for Peter to refer to living in Babylon (1 Pet 5:13); and for the seer of Revelation to refer to Babylon (Rev 14:8; 16:19; 17:5; 18:2, 10, 21) has altogether too often fed the mistake that all these images point to spiritual and nonmaterial realities accessible only in thought, prayer, and charismatic emotion. But this is not the language of spiritualized, Neoplatonic, or escapist inwardness and retreat; this is the language of alternative corporeal, material, and social realities that refuse to accept the dominant mythologies and ideologies all around them.

There were, apparently, frequent accusations made by Roman writers against the early Christians to the effect that they were "atheists" because of their refusal to honor the state gods.[18] I contend that this "political atheism" was fueled by an even more profound radical faith in an alternative social existence that was now in the world.

But the reality is that modern Christians rarely exemplify such political atheism in relation to the gods of the state. Like Jonah, who was disappointed at the failure of God to exercise impressive (and destructive) power on the Ninevites (and thus act precisely like Assur, the warrior god

17. I once sat in a lecture presented by a mainline Protestant "expert" on world missions, delivered to a largely Mennonite audience. Her patronizing tone, expressed in constant references to "places in the world I doubt you folks have even heard of," was quite properly met (even among usually tolerant Anabaptists) with a barrage of names, projects, and dates of Mennonite Central Committee workers who for years had been in precisely the countries she mentioned. One must keep in mind that this did not even include projects administrated by Quakers, Church of the Brethren, and other supposedly "withdrawn" or "isolated" Christian movements.

18. I used the metaphor of "political atheism" first in my essay, "Political Atheism and Radical Faith: The Challenge of Christian Nonviolence in the Third Millennium," in Subverting Hatred: The Challenge of Nonviolence in Religious Traditions, ed. D. L. Smith-Christopher, Faith Meets Faith (Maryknoll, N.Y.: Orbis, 2000) 141–66.

of the Neo-Assyrian Empire[19]), American Christians too often find themselves in deep regret at the loss of the privileges of being the chaplains to power. The Religious Right in the United States grasps desperately for nostalgic signs of "influence" and occasionally works up enough political influence to warrant the passing notice of partisan machines. But their accomplishments are heralded by the world not because of their unique Christian witness, but precisely because of their ability to express support for the gods of the state and engage in banal "politics as usual." As Stanley Hauerwas and William Willimon keenly note, what passes for a "responsible" Christian mission in the world sounds much like a religious flavoring put on the party platforms of the major political parties: "People often complain that the political agenda of conservative Christians looks suspiciously like the political agenda of conservative secularists—the Republican party on its knees. And it seems inconceivable that an agency of any mainline, Protestant denomination should espouse some social position unlike that of the most liberal Democrats. The church is the dull exponent of conventional secular political ideas with a vaguely religious tint. Political theologies, whether of the left or the right, want to maintain Christendom, wherein the church justifies itself as a helpful, if sometimes complaining, prop for the state."[20]

A critical obsession with peace and justice and a devotion to careful analysis replace the enticements of the laziness of worldly power that does not need to "understand" because it needs only to force its way. Such power was among the privileges of being the chaplaincy to the colonial powers. Like diasporic peoples throughout history, the church needs to replace the enticements of power with sharp wit and the cultivation of education and analytical skill. Building Christian schools ought to be a revolutionary activity in Babylon, like the building of hospitals once was.

It may come at some cost to our pride or even our sense of how the universe is supposed to work to sit on the hillside with Jonah and be amazed at God's larger plan for the world; but to be a diaspora church means that there is no longer any discernible difference between missiology and ecclesiology. Our task is Jonah's sense of mission to the world, informed by Ezra's attentive eye to nonconformity, and embodying Tobit's compassion and wise practicality. These are models that buttress the radical reading of the exemplary life and central teaching of Jesus already anticipated in Yoder's central text, *The Politics of Jesus* (1972).

---

19. Sa-Moon Kang, *Divine War in the Old Testament and in the Ancient Near East*, BZAW 177 (Berlin: de Gruyter, 1989) 40.
20. Hauerwas and Willimon, *Resident Aliens*, 38.

Finally, however, I do not think that an exilic biblical theology for modern Christians depends on the cogency of my attempt to analyze biblical texts historically and theologically. I have no ambition to write definitive statements—only to provoke dialogue and try to clarify my own thoughts on the matter. As I have gratefully acknowledged throughout this work, many others (more capable than I) are working on the same issues. In this I take great comfort and further invite critical dialogue and response to an unfinished project.

Praise the LORD!
Praise the LORD, O my soul!
I will praise the LORD as long as I live;
    I will sing praises to my God all my life long.

Do not put your trust in prices,
    in mortals, in whom there is no help.
When their breath departs, they return to the earth;
    on that very day their plans perish.

Happy are those whose help is the God of Jacob,
    whose hope is in the LORD their God,
who made heaven and earth,
    the sea, and all that is in them;
who keeps faith forever;
    who executes justice for the oppressed;
    who gives food to the hungry.

The LORD sets the prisoners free;
    the LORD opens the eyes of the blind.
The LORD lifts up those who are bowed down;
    the LORD loves the righteous.
The LORD watches over the strangers;
    he upholds the orphan and the widow,
    but the way of the wicked he brings to ruin.

The LORD will reign forever,
    your God, O Zion, for all generations.
Praise the LORD!
                                        —Psalm 146

Index of Biblical Passages